ECHOES OF A SAVAGE LAND

'An enthralling book . . . The writing is poetically descriptive, flowing along enthusiastically from the laptop of a talented researcher and chronicler about a life unchanged for centuries and then suddenly gone . . . a valuable addition to a genre whose formidable icons have been Kevin Danaher and Robin Flower.'

JOE KENNEDY, THE IRISH INDEPENDENT

'Sligo native Joe McGowan has written a fascinating account of country customs . . . Through scrupulous research and many interviews, he's recreated an almost vanished world of superstition and magic.'

ANNA CAREY, THE SUNDAY TRIBUNE

'Linking the ways of Ireland with Ancient Greece, the Aztecs of South America and with the Dyaks of Borneo and illustrating his points with quotations from Chaucer and Shakespeare as well as Yeats and Manley Hopkins, McGowan has produced a book that is more than the usual chronicle of country life. In *Echoes of a Savage Land*, he has produced a work of depth which presents a picture of Ireland in the twentieth century with both affection and a gifted use of language.'

BOOKVIEW IRELAND

First published in 2001 by
Mercier Press
5 French Church Street Cork
E-mail: books@mercier.ie

16 Hume Street Dublin 2
Tel: (01) 661 5299; Fax: (01) 661 8583
E-mail: books@marino.ie

Trade enquiries to CMD Distribution
55A Spruce Avenue
Stillorgan Industrial Park
Blackrock County Dublin
Tel: (01) 294 2560; Fax: (01) 294 2564
E.mail: cmd@columba.ie

© Joe McGowan 2001

ISBN 1 85635 363 X

10 9 8 7 6 5 4 3 2 1

A CIP record for this title is available
from the British Library

Cover design by SPACE
Printed in Ireland by ColourBooks
Baldoyle Industrial Estate Dublin 13

ECHOES OF A SAVAGE LAND

JOE MCGOWAN

MERCIER PRESS

Folk-art is, indeed, the oldest of the aristocracies of thought, and because it refuses what is passing and trivial, the merely clever and pretty, as certainly as the vulgar and insincere, and because it has gathered into itself the simplest and most unforgettable thoughts of the generations, it is the soil where all great art is rooted.

W. B. Yeats
Mythologies

ACKNOWLEDGEMENTS

The publishers wish to make acknowledgement to the following for granting permission to use copyright material: the Blackstaff Press for 'A Holy Place' and an extract from 'The Swathe Uncut' by John Hewitt; Faber & Faber Ltd for an extract from 'Little Gidding' from *Four Quartets* by T. S. Eliot; Nuala Ní Dhomhnaill for an extract from 'An Chaor Aduaidh'; Michael Yeats for extracts from 'Parnell's Funeral', 'The Wanderings of Oisín' and *Mythologies*, all by W. B. Yeats; Oxford University Press for extracts from *The Western Isle* by Robin Flower; D. F. McCarthy for an extract from 'The Paschal Fire'; Biddy White-Lennon for 'Will-o-the-Wisp' by Nora Murray; Random House UK Ltd for an extract from *Reading in the Dark* by Seamus Deane; extracts from 'Temptation in Harvest', 'Requiem for a Mill', 'October 1943', 'A Christmas Childhood', 'Lough Derg' and 'The Old Time Christmas Story 1960' by Patrick Kavanagh are reprinted from *Selected Poems*, edited by Antoinette Quinn (Penguin Books, 1996), with the permission of the Trustees of the late Katherine B. Kavanagh, through the Jonathan Williams Literary Agency; extracts from *The Green Fool* by Patrick Kavanagh are reprinted from *Selected Poems*, (Penguin Books, 1975), with the permission of the Trustees of the late Katherine B. Kavanagh, through the Jonathan Williams Literary Agency.

The author also wishes to thank the head of the Department of Irish Folklore, UCD, for permission to reproduce material from the department's archive.

To the builders of the great stone ditches: nation-builders;
to Hugh Gilmartin and Ann Gillen,
to Petie and Mary Kate

Contents

1

—

Blood Sacrifice

We shall not cease from exploration
And the end of all our exploring
Will be to arrive where we started
And know the place for the first time . . .

T. S. Eliot
from 'Little Gidding', *Four Quartets*

Blood was spattered everywhere. Bright red droplets smeared the whitewashed wall, dripped from the feathered head and formed small puddles in the muddy street. A struggling bird hung upside down, incongruously, its feet fastened with parcel twine to a rusted spike embedded in the lime-encrusted wall. Claws extended, it jerked desperately, clawing at air. Convulsed in dying spasms, it twisted and grew weaker, its lifeblood seeping into the earth.

Like the sombre shadow of the grim reaper, an old woman watched the death struggles of the cock. Sharp, steady eyes looked out dispassionately from bony, dark-circled sockets. A black woollen shawl wrapped the wrinkled parchment of an ancient wind-weathered face. The burnished steel of the bloodstained knife in her hand reflected the glow of a blood-red harvest sun dropping serenely into the turbulent Atlantic beyond Inishmurray Island. Its crimson path blazed a mystical highway westward to Tír na nÓg, enchanted land of youth and immortality, of faerie and ancient warriors, from which few return. Long, cold shadows slanted across the cobbled street from the neatly thatched row of byres and outhouses that squared the farmyard. Forming western bulwarks, they provided vital shelter to the street and dwelling house against the ferocity of the frequent Atlantic gales.

A small, short-trousered boy, blond curls flamed by the setting sun, swung around the gable of the house. Confronted with the strange sight, he clutched the tin can tighter in his hand and, startled, half turned to flee. Gaping, traumatised, his eyes widened in shock as they took in the unexpected, bloody scene before him. He was afraid – this hideous spectacle was outside any experience of his limited young world. His mind scrambled as he tried to cope with the barbaric scene. Kate was a gentle person well known to all her neighbours. Had he discovered a dark side that lay concealed, a secret kept from all who knew her? He had heard the older people tell stories around the fire at night of banshees that screamed their anguish on the night air, of hares that turned into witches. Was this Kate's demonic other self? Was she a witch engaged in some satanic ritual?

A ghost-wind ruffled the rooster's iridescent feathers. Its futile thrashing grew weaker and the blood dripped, slower now, the last drops gathered into an old jam jar placed beneath the dying bird. The boy tensed. Dare he ask this black-clad, stern-faced woman to explain what she was doing? It was the Ireland of the fifties. Rod rule was golden rule: 'Spare the rod and spoil the child' was dogma. I was that small boy and can see him now, standing there, transfixed. The image is printed forever on my mind.

To be 'seen and not heard' was a virtue then, an oft-repeated rule. When broken, it brought swift censure. With trembling lip, I ventured a timorous, 'Wh-what are you doing, Kate?'

Startled out of her reverie, she turned, looked at me and hunched her bony frame against the cold November breeze that whipped and skirmished in fitful gusts around the house and byres. Her face softened, a hint of amusement lit her stern features.

'Aah, bleeding for St Martin, *agradh*,' she said. 'Bleeding for St Martin,' she repeated gently, in a voice that bespoke an ancient wisdom.

'Did ye come for the milk,' she asked, noticing the can as she gathered the shawl tightly around her thin shoulders. She turned to the now-lifeless bird; a deft slash of the razor-sharp blade dropped it crumpling to the ground. She shivered as capricious cat's paws of wind plucked at her shawl. Hurrying past, they lifted wisps of hay and withered leaves, tripping and whirling, into sheltered corners.

Did the sky darken then or was it my imagination playing tricks? The whine and moan of the breeze that soughed in off the grey Atlantic chased skeins of mare's tails across the trembling sky; a sigh of infinite sorrow, a breath of departed souls. Was it the wind that whispered around the bushes and through the chinks of the old stone ditches there on that November day or was it the ghosts of our Celtic ancestors breathing their approval of the blood sacrifice? A sacrifice as old as God's instruction to Abraham, 'Take your son, your only child, Isaac, whom you love, and go to the land of Moriah. There you shall offer him as a burnt offering, on a mountain I will point out to you.'

In later years, my thoughts often strayed back to this extraordinary childhood experience. It held a strange fascination for me. It still does. This evidence of a continuum of sacrifice from biblical times through the development of civilisation to the present day is striking. How much has changed! How little has changed! Our Lord on the cross – a human sacrifice. 'This is my blood – *hic est enim calix sanguinis mei,*' the priest recites as he renews Christ's Atonement at the consecration. Ritual practices are the stigmata of human history. Our mortal condition still demands a sacrificial offering – although, thankfully, bloodless now. Kate, without being conscious of it, was carrying on a custom of human and animal sacrifice passed on to her through countless generations – customs whose origins recede into the dim and distant past, a patrimony of the birth and development of civilisation itself. Reincarnated earth mother, she had stood there a thousand years before and five thousand before that.

We Irish, who held on to our pagan ceremonies long after St Patrick brought Christianity, are not alone in practising the ancient rituals. Even yet on Rosh Hashanah, the Jewish New Year, Hasidic Jews swing a live chicken around their heads like a lariat. The observance, known as *Shlogn kapores,* is a vicarious atonement accompanied by a prayer that says, 'This chicken shall meet death but I shall find a long life of peace.' The bird is then slaughtered and eaten or given to the poor. Each year, in New York City, stalls selling chickens for the sacrifice jostle for space with shops such as 'Kosher Komputer', selling the latest in modern technology.

I will never forget my gory introduction on that memorable November day to 'Bleeding for St Martin', a custom that has now all but disappeared. Allowing for the Gregorian calendar conversion of 1582, St Martin's feast day, or Oul' Halloweve, as it is also known, coincides exactly with the ancient festival of Samhain, the Celtic New Year, which begins on 1 November. There is nothing strange about this, as it was common practice for the early Church to substitute a saint's festival for an earlier pagan one. 'Bleeding for St Martin' was commonly practised in most parts of western Europe up to the middle of this century. It was an essential part of the old way of life: a symbolic purging in rural agricultural societies that were acutely aware of cyclical regeneration.

Does the slaying of a chicken or farm animal today have its origins in human sacrifice? Did the ancient Celts indulge in ritual human and animal sacrifice? Perhaps the only thing that should surprise us – the practice being universal – would be if they did not! Evidence of human and animal offerings has been found at Celtic sites in Bavaria, at Vendée in central France and at many other locations in Europe. On our neighbouring island, evidence of ritual oblation has been found at Ewell in Surrey and at Ashill in Norfolk. In Scotland, the skeleton of a man in a vertical position was found three metres underground with his spear close by. Offerings such as harness pieces, tools, weapons, statues and bracelets often accompany these burials. An old legend relates that Vortigern, the fifth-century British warlord, taking the advice of the Druids, sought out a human victim to sacrifice at the foundation of his castle. Vortigern bears the same opprobrium in England that Dermott McMurrough (Diarmuid na nGall) carries in Ireland: historians blame Vortigern for bringing the Saxons to Britain in 449 to help him defeat the Picts. McMurrough brought the Normans to Ireland in the twelfth century following his appeal to the English King Henry II for help to defeat his Irish rivals.

Old customs die hard. Human sacrifice did not cease with the introduction of Christianity: when Colmcille was banished from Ireland, his attempts to build a monastery on Iona were frustrated by an evil spirit who knocked the walls down as fast as the saint and his men could erect them. During the night, he had a revelation that the walls would not stand until a human victim was buried alive beneath the foundation. Depending on which account you believe, Oran, one of the saint's followers, was chosen or volunteered for this fate and was accordingly buried beneath the structure.[1]

After three days, Colmcille, wishing to take a farewell look at his old friend, ordered the removal of the earth: 'Oran therefore raised his swimming eyes and, addressing Colmcille, said, "There is no wonder in death, and hell is not as it is reported".' The saint, aghast at the news and fearful of its implications for his preaching – and for the church coffers – immediately ordered the clay to be flung in again on Oran, uttering the imprecation: 'Earth, earth, in the mouth of Oran, that he may blab no more'. Poor Oran! Martyr or victim, his end was the same. His sacrifice was not in vain, though, as his death had the desired effect of allowing the building to proceed without disturbance.

That blood-bonds or covenants existed in Ireland in olden times there is no doubt. Such a pact was made in 598 AD between Branduff, King of Leinster, and the King of Ulidia (East Ulster) prior to a battle with the King of Ireland. Similar rituals were practised as recently as the seventeenth century in the western islands of Scotland, where 'ancient leagues of friendship were ratified by drinking a drop of each other's blood, commonly drawn out of the little finger'. This pledge was as strictly observed as a religious bond; whoever violated it was utterly discredited, 'so that all people avoided him'.[2]

Absolute statements about rituals and practices in prehistoric times are difficult to make but the fact that the Celtic religions practised human sacrifice can be verified. In Gaul, according to contemporary reports, the Druids took part in sacrifices, and even ordered the ceremony, acting as ministers when human beings were offered up.[3] Commenting on this, Julius Caesar wrote: 'They judge that the only way to save a man's life is to placate the anger of the gods by rendering another life in its place, and they have regularly instituted sacrifices of the same kind. Some tribes have colossal images made of wickerwork, the extremities of which they fill with live men; they are then set on fire, and the men burnt to death.'

Another observer of the time, Strabo, stated that when the Druids offered their sacrifices, they 'used to shoot men down with arrows, and impale them in the temples or, making a large statue of straw and wood, throw into it cattle and all sorts of wild animals and human beings, and thus make a burnt offering.'

Some scholars claim that such accounts are not in themselves evidence that similar practices occurred among the Celtic tribes in Ireland. The weight of evidence, however, suggests that ritual human sacrifice did occur among these tribes, although not on such a grand scale as elsewhere. Human remains from the Iron Age recovered from Neolithic tombs at Carrowmore, County Sligo, indicate human sacrifice.[4] An Iron Age body discovered buried in a bog at Castleblakeney in County Galway in 1821 offers strong evidence that the victim was garrotted and ritually buried. It is indeed possible that those sacrificed were not victims at all but willing participants who believed it a great honour to give their lives for the good of the community. They may even have been prominent members of that society. Why should we be surprised at this? Was it not God's Son who died to redeem the world?

In recent times – 1994, to be precise – a burial ground discovered while building a new road at Knoxspark, County Sligo, suggested ritual burials related to the Celtic cult of the severed head.[5] Some burials were in groups; one of the corpses was a woman whose head had been removed. Alongside her were the remains of three children, of whom only two had heads.

In another part of the cemetery, two mature males were buried together with linked arms. A spearhead was found close to one of these men; the other man's head had been cut off and placed nearby.

According to some accounts, condemned criminals were kept to be sacrificed to the gods at a great festival which took place once every five years. The greater the number of victims, the greater was believed to be the effect on the fertility of the land. If the number of criminals available to be sacrificed in the flames was found to be insufficient, then captives taken in battle were added to the number. It is likely that bonfires that take place at Epiphany and on St John's night, in various towns and villages, are a continuance of these early practices.

Reinforcing the importance of the severed head to early societies, Eugene O'Curry in his *Lectures* series of 1861 wrote of an Iron Age battle which took place at Beann Eadair (Howth) between the men of Leinster and the men of Ulster. Following the battle, in which the Leinstermen were routed, Conall Cearnach of the Royal Branch killed Mesgedhra, King of Leinster, in single combat and beheaded him. This was in revenge for the killing during the battle of Conall's two brothers.

When Conall presented the head to Mesgedhra's wife, she 'shrieked aloud her grief and sorrow with such intensity that her heart burst and she fell dead from her chariot'. Conall and his servant made a grave on the spot, in which they buried her, together with her husband's head. Before burying the head, they extracted the brain, according to custom.

Extracting the brain in this manner was normal practice in Conall's time. It is a custom that has continued in many parts of the world until relatively recent times. Whenever one champion killed another in single combat, the victor cut off his adversary's head, split it open, took out the brain and, mixing the tissue with lime, rolled it up into a ball. This was then dried and placed in the conquering warrior's armoury as a trophy of the nation. Conall placed the preserved brain of Mesgedhra in the great house of the Royal Branch at Emania in Ulster, in the care of Conor Mac Nessa, King of Ulster, during the period of the Incarnation of Our Lord. It was held in great respect and awe by the men of the northern province.

Mesgedhra's brain was eventually stolen by Cet Mac Magadh, champion of Connacht, who returned immediately with his prize. As there was a prophesy that Mesgedhra would avenge himself on the Ulstermen, Cet never went out on any border excursion without carrying the king's brain in his girdle, in the hope that he would fulfil the prophecy. Shortly after this, in a skirmish with the Ulstermen, Cet 'cast from his sling the ball made from the fatal brain and succeeded in striking Conor with it on the head, lodging the ball in his skull.'

The blow did not kill Conor. His physicians, on deciding it was too dangerous to remove the ball, brought him home and nursed him back to good health. Although he had to be careful to avoid all violent exercise, horseback riding, excitement or anger, he enjoyed good health for years afterwards.

On the day of Our Lord's Crucifixion, observing the eclipse of the sun, Conor called for his chief Druid, Bachrach, to explain it. The Druid consulted his oracles and informed the king that Jesus Christ was at that moment suffering at the hands of the Jews.

'What crime has he committed?' asked Conor.

'None,' said the Druid.

'Then are they slaying him innocently?' said Conor.

'They are,' said the Druid.

At this, Conor became enraged and drew his sword. Rushing

out to the wood, he began to hew down the trees there in a violent temper, shouting, 'Oh, if I were present, this is how I would cut down the enemies of this innocent man!'

His rage continued to increase until at last the fatal ball, which was lodged in his skull, fell from its place and damaged his brain. Conor Mac Nessa fell dead to the ground. In this way the prophecy was fulfilled: Mesgedhra had avenged himself on the Ulstermen. The incident happened in the fortieth year of Conor's reign. Because of it, he is counted ever since as the first man who died for the sake of Christ in Ireland!

Before we judge the practices of previous times as the conventions of primitive, uncivilised barbarians, we should think of what 'civilised' human beings have done to each other in relatively recent times. The penalty of hanging, drawing and quartering remained on the English statute books until 1870. The sentence carried out on the Irish insurgent Silken Thomas and his five uncles in London in 1537 read as follows: 'That you be led to the place from whence you came, and from thence be drawn upon a hurdle to the place of execution, and then you shall be hanged by the neck and, being alive, shall be cut down, and your privy members to be cut off, and your entrails taken out of your body and, you living, the same to be burnt before your eyes, and your head cut off, your body to be divided into four quarters, and head and quarters to be disposed of at the pleasure of the King's majesty, and the Lord have mercy on your soul.' The head and quarters of those executed in this way were parboiled in heavily salted water and impaled on spikes on the city walls and gates.[6]

Later in the same century, Humphrey Gilbert, charged with suppressing the Desmond rebellion, 'demonstrated an unprecedented ruthlessness, lining the pathway to his tent with the severed heads of his Irish enemies, with the deliberate intention of terrorising the natives.'

It was not only in Ireland that heads rolled. Yagan, an Australian warrior and Nyoongar tribesman, was a resistance fighter against British colonisation in 1833. When he was captured, his head was smoked, taken to England and exhibited as a curio until it was buried in a pauper's grave thirty years ago. The head was exhumed in 1998 after repeated pleas by the Aboriginals for its return.

Did Yagan reach out from the grave to avenge his death? A recent newspaper article created a furore when it reported that a member of the party which came to England to reclaim the head asserted that the car-accident death of Diana, Princess of Wales, 'was spiritually linked to Yagan's decapitation.'

In a recent BBC television documentary, it emerged that a public exhibition of enemy dead was used as recently as the 1950s to intimidate rebellious natives. At the height of the British campaign in Kenya, captured Mau Mau were hung and their bodies displayed at crossroads and market places.

Such vindictive barbarity has never been a part of the origins or custom of bleeding for St Martin. Here are the last vestiges of ancient rituals that have survived to modern times in many parts of rural Ireland and further afield. Even now the ceremony is still carried on by a few believers – mostly older people – here and there. In north Sligo, a woman told me she continued the tradition by sprinkling blood that had gathered on the plate from her portion of butcher's meat. Because of changes in farming practices, she could no longer find a cock or chicken. When St Martin's Day came again, we celebrated the feast with a cock I had acquired: her husband held it while she cut its throat, allowing the sanctifying blood to flow again.

There are several St Martins in the church calendar. The man we honour is the great fourth-century saint, St Martin of

Tours, born in 316, a convert to Christianity and the son of an officer in the Roman army. A pioneer of Western monasticism, he came to Ireland with the advent of Christianity. He is said to have conferred the monk's tonsure on St Patrick. This was the event that inspired our patron saint to Christianise this Celtic festival and initiate the custom of presenting a pig for sacrifice to every monk and nun on the eve of Martin's feast. St Martin, whose grave was discovered at Tours by Colmcille, is believed to have been Patrick's maternal uncle. His feast day in November is the anniversary of his burial in 402.[7] Another day in the calendar of the Church, 4 July, commemorates his ordination and appointment to the See of Tours.

Formerly, St Martin's Day was one of the great feast days of the Church, decreed so by Pope Martin I in the seventh century. In most parts of Ireland it was usual to kill any animal, from a bullock to a cock, for this special day; the type of animal chosen depended on the wealth of the individual or the size of the family. Strangely enough, no trace of the custom now remains in Cork, north Leinster, most of Ulster or parts of Kerry, even though it was 'more important than Christmas' at one time in both west Kerry and Connacht.

Where observed, it was the custom to kill a fowl on Oul' Halloweve night, prior to St Martin's feast day on the 11 November.[8] There was strict adherence to the principle that the bleeding must be done between 1 November and the eve of the feast. As it was said, '*Glacfaidh Mairtín roimhe ach ní ghlacfaidh sé ina dhiaidh.*' ('Martin will accept before his feast but not after it.')[9]

When I witnessed my neighbour Kate slaying the rooster, she commenced the sacrifice by slitting the skin along the comb on the bird's head. Others performed the ceremony by cutting the neck and then hanging the bird, to allow the blood to fall on the ground or be gathered into a jar. Sometimes the blood was sprinkled on the four corners of the house by carrying the bleeding fowl there. The bird was then hung on the wall prior to preparation for the pot.

When the blood was not sprinkled by carrying the bleeding bird, it was daubed in the shape of a cross on the front and back doors while the following was said: 'I shed this blood in honour of God and St Martin to bring us safe from all illnesses and disease during the year.' On Inisheer in the Aran Islands, the blood was used to make the sign of the cross on the forehead. The flesh of the animal or bird was cooked and eaten soon after the killing. It was said that the person who ate the meat would be free from disease during the coming year.

In his visits to the houses of the Sligo people, W. B. Yeats observed a related custom: sprinkling the doorstep with the blood of a chicken on the death of a very young child. This, it was believed, drew the malevolent influences from the immature soul. 'Blood is a great gatherer of evil spirits,' he wrote.[10]

The custom of applying blood to the entrance doors is suggestive of the Old Testament instruction of God to the Israelites to take a lamb's blood and 'apply it to the two doorposts and the lintel of every house', so that He would know the houses of the Israelites and pass on while he 'struck down the Egyptians'. This event is still celebrated by the Jews each year at the festival of Passover.

The very life is in the blood. It is the richest gift. On Mount Tabor, God established a covenant with man: 'I will be your God if you will be my people'. The sign of the covenant was sacrifice, an offering of blood – no longer a human victim but cattle. Two things were done to seal the covenant: half of the blood had to be spilled on the altar, representing Divinity; the other half

Moses was told to sprinkle on the people. There followed a feast: a great celebration and rejoicing in the pact, at which the meat was roasted and eaten.

In Sligo and Leitrim, the blood was sometimes kept in a 'ponjer' (tin cup) on the dresser and left there until it solidified. In Roscommon, the blood was put on a piece of cloth which was placed on an egg-stand on the dresser or kept in some vessel where it would be safe. The cloth or congealed blood was then said to have a cure. If anyone in the house got sick or had a sore throat, the blood-soaked cloth was applied to the affected part.

The blood, when it was retained, was often kept in a jam pot and stored in a spring well or other cool place. When applied during the year, it was reputed to contain a cure for toothache and colds. It also relieved rheumatism and was effective in the treatment of cattle. Where collecting the blood was not part of the ceremony, it was drained into the ground and kept pure: no dogs or farmyard animals were allowed to touch it.

In Ballina, County Mayo, a special market was held in former times called 'St Martin's Market', where various fowl (mainly geese) were sold for the feast. Amhlaoibh Ó Súilleabháin recorded such a fair he had witnessed in Kilkenny in 1830: 'It is usual to shed blood, on Martinmas eve; this is to say, blood of goose or gander, hen or cock, pullet or chicken, duck or drake, fat porker or great and good beef, big wether or bleating kid; blood of sprightly lamb or bleating sheep or ragged goat or of some other good meat. It is a good old custom, which ought to be kept up, wherever no butcher's meat is to be had. Every strong farmer and every country gentleman ought to kill a beef or a sheep or a porker, and share it with the hovel-dwellers of the neighbourhood, and with God's poor. Today, the poor wandering labourer has his back to the bush, perhaps without breaking his fast.'

If a beast fell ill during the year, it could be cured by bleeding the ear and dedicating the sick animal to St Martin. There was a catch, however: the person doing this had to promise to sacrifice the creature to the saint if it recovered. There are many accounts of misfortune that befell the person who failed to honour this promise. St Martin was one of the most unforgiving saints in the Church calendar. One person, having made the commitment, decided not to honour it when the calf recovered, and sold it at a fair. The stranger who bought it there turned out to be St Martin in disguise. He disappeared without paying for it and in this way claimed his due right.

But the saint could be generous too, and rewarded those who struggled to honour him in the traditional way. The story is told of a poor man who killed his only cow at Martinmas. Following the butchering, he threw the skin away. In the morning, when he got up, the cow was there as usual in place of the discarded hide.

In north Sligo, there was a man who had no cow, hen, duck, calf or anything else to kill for St Martin. Anxious to honour the saint, he bled his own shin. Next morning, a cow came to the house, and the man milked it. Following the milking, he drove it away but it kept coming back. After some weeks of this, he sought the advice of the local priest, who told him to keep the cow. He did so, and prospered from that day on.

An anecdote revealing a more humorous side to the goodness of Martin illustrates the maxim that God helps those who help themselves. In the days of hiring fairs, a farm labourer fell on hard times when he took up employment in a house where he was badly fed. Coming up to Martinmas, he was hopeful that, when the sacrifice was made, he would come in for a good meal or two. When the woman of the house proved too mean to sacrifice an animal, the servant was in a bad way. The following night, in desperation, he disguised himself and hid outside the window. Facing the house, he intoned a ghostly warning:

Nancy Farrell, are you within?
I am St Martin outside your house;
Unless you kill the black wether
I'll be at your wake a week from tonight!

The frightened woman killed the sheep the next day and the enterprising *spailpín* enjoyed his share of a hearty meal soon after.

In addition to bleeding, it was also a tradition that no wheel should be turned on Martin's feast day. This prohibition was firmly held in Ireland and Scotland, in the belief that the saint was killed by a wheel.

Dominick Harte, a farmer and fisherman living on Inish-murray Island off the Sligo coast, related in 1940 that no work was allowed on the island on Martin's feast day. Neither was it permitted to turn a wheel because, he explained, 'Caitheadh Mairtín isteach i sruth muilinn agus maraíodh é ag an roth agus dá bhrí sin ní ceart roth d'aon saghas a casadh an lá sin' ('Martin was thrown into a millstream and he was killed by the wheel and because of that it was not right to turn any kind of wheel on that day').

Typical of the legends explaining why no wheel should turn is that Martin was employed in a mill. When the owner ordered the unwilling workmen to labour as usual on 11 November, Martin refused, saying that no wheel should turn on that day. The miller threw him under the wheel and he was ground to death.[11]

In the middle of the nineteenth century, the flour mill at Ballisodare, County Sligo, owned by Robert Culbertson, was one of the most profitable of its kind in Ireland. Workmen there, wishing to honour the prohibition, declined to work on 11 November. Management insisted that the mill operate as usual. On the afternoon of St Martin's Day, 1856, the mill caught fire in mysterious circumstances. Nine workmen were burned to death or died jumping from the building; major damage was done to the fabric of the mill and the contents were destroyed. Following the disaster, the owner fell into bad health and died some years later. In the succeeding years, the mill was closed on each feast of St Martin until the outbreak of war in 1939. Shortly after the burning, at least two ballads were written to commemorate the event; the following is an excerpt from one of them:

> Come all you loyal heroes wherever you may be,
> Come and pay attention and listen unto me,
> Concerning this sad accident, a burning now beware,
> And pray for nine who lost their lives
> In the mill at Ballisodare . . .
> There was one man on the top loft;
> The fire it did pursue.
> Being suffocated with fire and smoke,
> Not knowing what to do,
> He struggled to the window,
> For mercy he did cry;
> He was mangled on the river rocks
> After leaping three storeys high . . .

In today's high-powered existence, the custom of not turning wheels seems quaint: it would stop the world. St Martin's condemnation would fall on the entire race. But not so long ago in Ireland, when hands provided energy and faith ruled the land, no wheel, whether millwheel, cartwheel, spinning wheel or ship's wheel, turned on his feast day. Maybe St Martin was God's labour representative, declaring a day of rest, a period of recovery!

Fishermen too observed the festival. Good weather or bad, boats would not put to sea on Oul' Halloweve, in the belief that this brought bad luck. A Wexford legend relates that, centuries ago, boats at Rosslare which had set out on the saint's day were startled 'by an apparition of Martin pacing among the waves', warning them to return to harbour. Seventy fishermen who refused to take the advice were lost in a storm that sprang up shortly afterwards. It was not until 1945 that the centuries-old curse was broken, when the fishermen of the area defied the ban by putting to sea on Martinmas. No harm came to the fleet this time but some of the older men, not wishing to take any chances, refused to go out. The report of the event in a newspaper at the time recorded that the catch was poor.[12]

A group of fishermen from Castlegal in County Sligo, ignoring the prohibition, went to sea on Oul' Halloweve. Tempted by a spell of fine weather, they went out after herring. During the night, a change came and they were caught in a sudden storm that threatened to swamp the boat. The small craft was driven relentlessly out to sea. It heaved and tossed as if in the clutch of a mighty hand. Water swept in sheets across the gunwale and filled the boat faster than they could bale it out. In the pitch black, they soon had no idea of where they were. Drenched and cold, death seemed certain. An old man, acknowledging that they were beyond human help, tried one last desperate measure. 'There's only one thing left,' he said, taking off his scapulars and throwing them on the heaving water. 'I always bled for St Martin, and if I get home this night it'll be the first thing I'll do.'

Soon afterwards, the winds calmed and the storm cleared. By starlight, they steered the boat to a safe landing at the mouth of the Duff river. Barton, the local landlord – and a Protestant – was one of those on board. As they pulled the boat ashore, he spoke to the skipper. 'Look here,' he said, pointing to the water, 'what you threw out on the sea is still here floating alongside!' Mary Kate McGloin, who heard the story from the old people of the neighbourhood, recalled that the old man kept his promise. Shortly after he got home, he killed a bullock in thanksgiving for his safe delivery.

A group of fishermen from Rosses Point in County Sligo went out on the saint's feast. They caught so many fish the boat was in danger of sinking. On reaching the harbour, they tied up for the night, satisfied with their catch and convinced the prohibition was nothing more than *piseogs*. Elated with the prospects of a handsome reward at market next day, they laughed and joked all the way home. St Martin had the last word. To the consternation of the boat's crew, when they came back in the morning to box their catch all that was left were fish-heads.

In many rural areas – and certainly in north Sligo – it is firmly held by many that whichever direction the wind blows at midnight on Oul' Halloweve Night it will blow for the winter. Tommy Fowley always filled his pipe before twelve to have it ready for the experiment. Going outdoors, he lit up at the appropriate time, took a few puffs and observed carefully which direction the smoke went. Northerly airs indicated the wind would prevail from that direction for the rest of the winter, bringing cold weather, frost and snow; if it blew from a southerly or westerly direction, then a wet winter with rain and wind would follow.

There are some believers who continue the practice to this

day. It is not at all unusual to hear any discussion on the prospects of good or bad weather punctuated with a query as to whether anyone had noticed the wind direction at twelve o'clock on St Martin's Eve. Curious to test the old belief, I have gone out to see for myself. Now, at the end of December, the wind is from the north-east – the same direction as on Oul' Halloweve night!

Spells of fine weather which often occurred at this time of year were known as 'St Martin's Summer' or 'Goose Summer', a prelude to the onset of winter. The story goes that on a raw, frosty morning in early November, Martin tore his cloak in two and gave half to an old beggar clad only in rags and shivering with cold. It seems that God was so pleased with this act of generosity on Martin's behalf that he let the sun shine for several days until such time as he could repair his cloak. To commemorate this event, God has sent a few days of unseasonable and sunny weather each November since then. This unexpected respite has always been a welcome bonus to farmer and fisherman – a last chance to complete the harvest before the harsh winds blow.

The name 'Goose Summer' is said to have originated with an incident that happened some time prior to Martin's ordination as Bishop of Tours. Martin was a modest man. On his nomination, he was so overawed at the prospect of this elevation that he hid in a barn to avoid the Church authorities. However, a noisy goose complaining about sharing his quarters with anyone, even a man of Martin's importance, gave the game away. The Church officials, attracted to the noise, discovered his hiding place. Martin may have been a saint but he had a human side. After he was ordained, he avenged himself on the disagreeable goose by having it for dinner, thus establishing the tradition of having goose for dinner on St Martin's Day.

Goose Summer also found its way into the English language: there are species of spider that propagate and disperse their populations by allowing themselves to be carried some distance on the breezes at this time of year. They climb as high as they can on a tree, house or bush and weave a thread that may be several yards long. When this is completed, they crawl out along its length until it breaks off. Spider and web are then transported by the breeze for some distance before coming to ground. The silken thread, relieved of its weight, continues on its way, and dozens of these are often seen shimmering and reflecting the Goose Summer sunlight. Thus was originated the term 'goose summer', or gossamer thread.

Michaelmas, the old English name for the feast day of Saint Michael and All Angels, occurring on 29 September, also had connections with the goose. The date is said to have been selected originally because it is the anniversary of the dedication of the Church of Saint Michael and All Angels on the Salarian Way in Rome in the sixth century. This day was of considerable importance in the Anglo-Norman calendar, being a quarter day for the fulfilment of contracts, grants, payments of rent, wages and so on. The other quarter days were Lady Day (25 March), Midsummer Day (24 June) and Christmas Day.

The custom of eating a goose on Michaelmas Day was primarily associated with Munster but was honoured in Sligo too. One version attributes the choice of fowl to Elizabeth I of England. She was feasting on goose on 29 September 1588 when news came to her of the destruction of some of the ships of the Spanish Armada in bad weather off the Blasket Sound in County Kerry. In order to celebrate her good fortune, she proclaimed that goose should be eaten on the anniversary of the event from that day forward to commemorate her great victory.

Elizabeth might have predicted the weather too, had she known that the breastbone of the Michaelmas goose was considered a harbinger of the elements. If the bone appears dark on being held up to the light, a hard winter is in the offing, if it is speckled, the weather ahead will be variable, and if the bone is almost transparent, then the winter months ahead are sure to be mild.

The oldest reference to the bestowing of food as a gift at Michaelmas dates from the fifth century, when St Patrick, through the intercession of St Michael, brought Lewy, son of Laoire, King of Ireland, back to life. 'The young prince's mother, Aongus, was so overjoyed at having him restored to her alive that she placed herself under a solemn vow to bestow annually on the poor on Michaelmas Day one sheep out of every flock she possessed, in honour of the archangel.'[13]

Although St Martin is a popular saint in Ireland, it is remarkable that there are very few churches named in his honour. Perhaps his name has been too closely associated with rituals that have their origins in paganism to make him a popular choice for church leaders! One of the churches dedicated to him is the ruined Teampall Liath within the enclosure of an earthen *lios*, located near the railway line at Lispole station in County Kerry. A 'pattern' (patron day or day of pilgrimage) was held there at one time, and another at St Martin's Well on the road to Dingle. Visits to these sites were believed to be very effective in the curing of diseases concerning cattle, with the odd proviso that any animal so cured must be slaughtered on the following St Martin's Eve. Other wells dedicated to the saint are found at Shillelagh, County Wicklow, in Cloghane parish, County Kerry, and in Noughaval parish, County Clare.

Exploration of old beliefs provides a window into the past. Such windows are fast closing as we rush to open promising new portals, swept into the future on a tide of electronic marvels: computers, cell phones, the Internet – virtual offspring of virtual reality! Technology replaces mythology! All Saints, All Souls, Oul' Halloweve, once fervently observed feasts, pass with little notice now. Does St Martin's retribution not cover non-stop production lines and super-trawling, record-breaking fishing fleets, in deference to a disbelieving society whose miracles are all scientific? Did he lose his power – or could it be that he has grown weary of a world that is too self-assured for faith?

2

AMORAL AUTUMN

Whatever befalls the earth befalls the sons of the earth.
If men spit upon the ground, they spit upon themselves.
This we know. The earth does not belong to man; man
    belongs
To the earth. This we know. All things are connected like
the blood which unites one family. All things are
    connected.
Whatever befalls the earth befalls the sons of the earth.
Man did not weave the web of life; he is merely a
    strand in it.
Whatever he does to the web he does to himself.

Chief Seathl's Testament[14]

Like the sweet hope and gentle touch of new love, the flirtations of giddy summer are often a false seduction. They herald a season of back-breaking work, resulting more in frustration than delight. The long-awaited sunny days do not appear. Rain, rain, rain, rather than the desired warm, drying breezes essential for saving hay and hardening turf. Once arrived, the blazing sun is a harsh taskmaster, demanding much during its all-too-brief visits. It has no kindness. For me it meant long, hot, wearisome days footing turf or shaking hay under the watchful eye of a sinewy-armed father whose work-driven ethic, oft repeated, was 'Never put off till tomorrow what you can do today.'

'Anything that's worth doin' at all is worth doin' right' was his dictum as he led by example, moulding perfect cocks of hay and handsome turf clamps or elegant stooks of rye and oats. Less would do me as I followed in his wake and, to his despair, I justified my careless creations with the rationale that these were temporary things: trampcocks of hay that the cows would shortly devour or turf clamps that would soon meet a blazing demise in our winter's fire.

Passing years mellow callow youth, however, and I'm sure, had he lived long enough, he would be pleased to know that the wisdom in his homespun expressions eventually penetrated closed ears. Motivation comes with responsibility. Counsel that sat lightly on young shoulders took root eventually. Now far removed from the soil, mired in paperwork and hi-tech, the new generation can benefit from age-old maxims rooted in experience.

All I craved on the long, sultry days was for the interminable jobs to be over. I longed for the lazy days of Hallowe'en, when the aching hard work of July and August became nothing more than a painful memory. An Indian summer was my delight: 'a second youth in which to sing and dance and love'. Time to relax now. Minds swimming with a sense of fulfilment as well as accomplishment, we looked out over pastures softly lit by mellow tones of slanting light. Observing the New England countryside in autumn, the American writer Nathaniel Hawthorne expressed similar sentiments. Nature was spilling over in 'a blessed superfluity of love', he enthused. 'She has leisure to caress her childen now. It is good to be alive at such times.'

The amber rays of a harvest sun tint the landscape in soft pastels. The ground is a patchwork quilt of golden-stubbled corn squares; the freshly dug potato fields are earth-darkened and

decorated with ravelled threads of bone-bleached potato stalks.
The emerald green of the after-grass meadow is polka-dotted
with perfect white rings where the stately, sculptured trampcocks
recently stood.

> *And the azurous hung hills are his world-wielding*
> *   shoulder Majestic – as a stallion stalwart, very-*
> *   violet-sweet! –*
> *These things, these things were here and but the*
> *   beholder*
> *Wanting; which two when they once meet,*
> *The heart rears wings bold and bolder*
> *And hurls for him, O half-hurls earth for him off under*
> *   his feet.*

> Gerard Manley Hopkins
> from 'Hurrahing in Harvest'

The limits of these masterful autumn landscapes, conspired by
God and man, are bounded by great moss-covered stone walls
that square the countryside. Laborious in their construction,
they bear the handprint and the heartbeat of resourceful,
beleaguered men who valued every inch of soil they cleared. As
carefully laid as the finest mosaic, these stark walls are monuments
to our forefathers – rugged chains of stones that dignify the land.
Undiminished by time or season, they stand witness to survival.
Was it the legendary Óisín, the fabled Fianna or our own
ancestors who carefully laid the ancient rock, protective barriers
around precious acres, once the cherished territory of Irish
chiefs and their clans?

But 'the gods a long time are dead'! My young, prying fingers
found the broken clay pipes of these forgotten builders hidden

in the dark and secret crevices of lichened walls. Holding the baked-clay bowls that sometimes read 'Home Rule' or 'Erin go Brágh', I thought of the strong, work-roughened hands that had drawn comfort from them – hands permeated with the juices of the crops they tended, pigmented by the soil they tilled. What kind of lives did these silent, remote ancestors live? My mind reached through space and time to meet theirs as I gripped the broken shank. Eyes tightly shut, I sought the link of soul and mind to make me one with these nameless, faceless forebears – the key to enable me to share their secrets. But the spirits remain silent, the great stone ditches their monuments, the broken pipes their mute and cryptic message.

A distracted race of modern men now desecrate these memorials, built by giants. We wait for a modern Oisín to ride back from Tír na nÓg on a white steed to chide or wonder.

> In what far kingdom do you go,
> Ah, Fenians, with the shield and bow?
> Or are you phantoms white as snow,
> Whose lips had life's most prosperous glow?

W. B. Yeats
from 'The Wanderings of Oisín'

I found the brass rifle cartridges hidden in the stone walls by my father and his comrades of the Irish Volunteers. White-knuckled, I clenched them tightly in my fist. Eyes closed, I watched them walk in the sheltering darkness, these modest men, who touched their foreheads to the enemy by day but drilled and trained in secret by night. Training their rifles on the lights of English trawlers fishing close to 'their' shores, they practised their marksmanship. 'Yer father was a great shot,' the old men have told me with a knowing shake of the head.

I found too the secret rifle nest, an oblong wooden box sloped into the moss-covered ditch, its entrance cleverly concealed. When desolation gripped the land, our masters looked contemptuously from castle windows on to peasant fields below. They thought they 'had purchased half of us and intimidated the other half.' The fools! They looked with eyes that could not see, for the seeds of their destruction lay unseen in these walls, placed by men they scorned. Proud Classiebawn, where now your vanity?

> . . . Beware,
> Beware of the thing that is coming, beware of the risen
> people,
> Who shall take what ye would not give. Did ye think
> to conquer the people,
> Or that Law is stronger than life and than men's desire
> to be free?
> We will try it out with you, ye that have harried and
> held,
> Ye that have bullied and bribed. Tyrants, hypocrites,
> liars!'

P. H. Pearse
from 'The Rebel'

But that was long ago. Will we honour the land? The imposing stone walls with their mouldering secrets are crumbling now, prey to the modern Joshua. The new imperialism, that great monolith, the European Union has, by our own choice, decreed the failure of smallholdings. These ancient stone walls, the walls of our temple surrounding the fields from which sprung life itself, decay. Soil that nurtured countless generations, land that our ancestors clung to and fought for; earth fertilised by their sweat, their tears, their blood – like the walls of Jericho, there shall not remain a stone upon a stone; the old ways fade from the landscape like old writing on parchment.

> *I should not have wished, should not have seen how white*
> *The wings of thistle seeds are, and how gay*
> *Amoral Autumn gives her soul away*
> *And every maidenhead without a fight.*

Patrick Kavanagh
from 'Temptation in Harvest'

Farmers liked to have the grain crops cut and stored in the garden by 1 October. On small farms a hook or scythe was used. As rye straw was needed for thatching only hand-cutting or shearing, fistful by fistful, with a hook would keep the straw neat enough and the ends suitably uniform. The oat crop was often cut with a scythe or horse machine as this straw was used only for animal foodstuff, a favourite with horses or asses. It was not durable enough for the dwelling house but was sometimes used for the byres.

Scythes were in common use on small farms as recently as the latter part of the nineteenth century. Developed originally as a grass-cutting implement, over fifty of these blades have been discovered in excavations from Roman Britain. When the instrument made its way to Ireland in post-Norman times it was called a speal. The absence of any evidence, either archaeological or documentary, of scythes in early Christian Ireland supports the view that little or no hay was cut at that time.

The hook as a reaping instrument dates back to the Bronze

Age. It was the main implement used for cutting grain until medieval times. From that time forward the sickle with its toothed edge became dominant and was used on small farms until the middle of the twentieth century. Early hooks were made by the local blacksmith until eventually replaced by improved foundry versions commonly used everywhere by the late nineteenth century. Sickles had a serrated blade whereas the hook blade was smooth. The advantage of the sickle's toothed blade was that it did not need sharpening. The hook had a sharp toothless edge that became dull with use. It was faster, though, and had a smoother cut.

In north Sligo it was called a Scotch hook. Judged to be dangerous in use it was not highly regarded for shearing rye straw. Lacking the grip of the toothed blade it rebounded off pebbles and stones hidden in the stubble. Users recalled it would 'take the finger off ye if ye weren't careful.' It had its advantages, however, as it was a favourite with some for cutting 'famluc' or black wrack along the shore. Others felt it had the same shortcomings here as with cutting grain.

With either instrument there was a constant danger of slashing the fingers that held the fistful of grain about to be cut. The little finger being closer to the blade was most vulnerable. It tingled in anticipation of that moment when concentration lapsed and the jagged edge sliced through tender flesh. The tearing sound of the steel teeth cutting through the straw held a deadly menace. When engaged in the work the 'wee' finger was an alert sentinel indeed!

The teeth on the sickle, through time, wore smooth. When this happened some may have thrown it aside, but we sharpened it with a stone and continued to use it as a hook. The instrument was never handed to another person by its blade for the same reason that a knife is never offered by its pointed end. George

Siggins of Cloghboley, County Sligo reminded me that when a hook changed hands, the person offering it either left it on the ground to be picked up or stuck the point into the sod. With its curved shape, a hand-to-hand exchange had the potential to inflict injury on one party or the other.

As the straw was being cut with the right hand it was gathered with the left. A handful was called a *doirnín*. A sheaf comprised three *doirníní*, which were bound by a 'strap'. The knot used to join two slim lengths of corn together to make a strap was nothing more than a simple twist. Yet there was a knack to its simplicity that took some time for a beginner to master. It wasn't found in books; it wasn't a clove hitch, a half hitch, a granny knot or a bowline; it was a conjurer's trick, a flick of the wrist. I worked my way through several ragged permutations of this deceptively simple-looking bond while trying to emulate the effortless skill with which my father made his. When I came up with a reasonable facsimile it made a mockery of my efforts by jumping up from the ground like a coiled spring and unravelling as soon as I left it down on the stubble. More complicated secure knots that would damage the straw were not allowed as the strap too was used for thatching.

In present times there is little or no possibility of ever being called upon for a demonstration so I can safely claim to have eventually added strap-making to a list of skills learned long ago, as boy and man, which have absolutely no use in this modern world!

The sheaves were tied up as the day's shearing progressed and left like so many fallen soldiers on the ground. When the straw was wet it was left loose and tied in the evening after having the benefit of a day's sun. Weeds were cleaned from each handful, as it was cut, by running the fingers through the straw before placing it on the strap for tying. Stooped from the waist, cutting rye or oats with a hook was hard labour comparable only to footing turf for the agony it brought to spines bent double all day. 'Down with the head and up with the tail' was an apt expression. Some small amount of relief, even if it was only psychological, was brought if the ground was sloping and the worker facing uphill.

It was arduous labour in those well-tended fields of long ago but it had its rewards. Most of the present generation of young people will never know the wild freedom of those open, busy acres or the taste of a carrot pulled from a drill, washed in a running stream and eaten on a grassy bank. The terms 'organic gardening' or 'environmentally friendly' had not been thought of yet. But we had it then. And long before it became fashionable too!

The Industrial Revolution began in Britain at the end of the eighteenth century. It had some beneficial effect on farming as efforts were made then to develop reaping machines. It wasn't until the latter half of the nineteenth century that such horse-drawn implements manufactured by McCormick, Hussey and Pierce of Wexford became available on the Irish market. Reapers and binders continued in use well into the twentieth century until they too were replaced by the combine harvester.

The advantages of such machinery were experienced only by larger farms. These changes had no impact on the smaller farmer working twenty acres or so. Sickles, hooks and scythes continued to be used on these smaller holdings.

At the end of a day's cutting or shearing, the sheaves were set on end, grain side up, and built into 'stooks'. Single stooks had eight upright sheaves for a base, four on each side, leaning against each other in such a way that created a tunnel underneath allowing the drying breezes to pass through. Two 'head-sheaves' were tied over this base, grain-side down, to run the water off and give a measure of protection from opportunistic birds.

Summer ends now;
now, barbarous in beauty,
the stooks arise

Gerard Manley Hopkins
from 'Summer Ends Now'

Single stooks were made only if the grain was not fully ripe or if it was damp. If the grain was sufficiently dry double stooks were constucted. This meant duplicating the process and elongating the single stook by adding a further six or eight sheaves underneath and two more head-sheaves. These golden stooks of rye or oats were a typical feature of the Irish harvest-time countryside. They stood to attention in dignified ranks across the stubbled cornfields, statuesque, like some mighty army ready to march. When carted in from the fields and stacked in the garden[15] prior to scutching the same method of building was used. Sheaves were added continuously until this storage stook was twelve, fourteen or twenty feet long.

E. Estyn Evans in his book *Irish Folk Ways* records that 'shearing songs, music and magic to ease the labour was part of the harvesting scene'.[16] Well, I must have been born in either the wrong place or at the wrong time and missed all that because we had neither music nor magic to help us. What we did have was a loud and unmelodious yodelling from an irate father if the work was not going fast enough. As far as I was concerned the only time I felt like singing was when the day's work was done and we left the field in the evening! Even then it was difficult to raise even a chirp as it took a long time to encourage an aching back to a fully upright position in time to milk cows, feed calves and take care of the waiting evening chores.

In many places throughout Ireland, 'cutting the *cailleach*' or 'hunting the hare' was a time of celebration. The *cailleach* was the last sheaf of corn left standing in the grain field. The origin of the rituals attached to cutting the last sheaf is lost in antiquity but seems to have been a residual remnant of primitive man's belief in a corn-spirit.

> *And so of old the country folk declared*
> *the last swathe holds a wayward fugitive,*
> *uncaught, moth-gentle, tremulously scared,*
> *that must be, by the nature of all grain,*
> *the spirit of the corn that should be slain*
> *if the saved seed will have the strength to live.*

John Hewitt
from 'The Swathe Uncut'

The custom of cutting the cailleach and the associated harvest-knot tradition were widespread in England and Scotland in former times. The harvest knot is thought to have been introduced to Ireland by the Normans on their arrival in the twelfth century. This tradition, like so many others, has now all but died away. Many of the older generation still remember the custom and speak of it as a time of great celebration at the end of the harvest – and celebrate they might, as their very survival depended on the bounty of a good crop.

In many places the last sheaf was plaited, knotted and then brought home and hung in the farm kitchen until the next harvest. In Derry and Antrim straw from the sheaf was given to the milking cows on New Year's morning and grain from it mixed with the seed corn at the spring sowing.[17]

In Ireland no one wanted to be the last to finish harvesting as the imaginary spirit hare was hunted across the fields to the tardy reaper bringing bad luck with her. In the Hebrides there was once an actual dread of being the last to finish harvesting as it was believed that the man who did so would become the host of a bogey known as 'the famine of the farm'.

Sean Furey of Skreen in County Sligo related in 1940 that the hook was thrown or fired at the last patch and the reaper shouted *'Imithe leat!'* or at other times, 'Be off with you!' On other farms, as they were cutting the last bit, the reapers shouted, 'There she is; there she is,' and kept chasing an imaginary hare until she escaped over the next fence. They would then shout to the neighbour that she was gone over to him.

The last person to reap in an area was required to keep the phantom hare and feed her for the winter. Because of this everyone worked very hard to avoid keeping an unwanted guest for the year. It was bad enough to have to feed her for any period of time but no one was prepared to run the gauntlet of misfortune that was also believed to come with this ill-starred creature. The very least the last reaper suffered was injured pride as his status in the community took a fall.

Regarding the cutting of the last sheaf it appears that luck was a fickle companion being good or bad depending on the tradition of the area. In some places the youngest person present was chosen to fell it. In others lots were drawn. Reluctant were the hands that held the hook where it was believed that whoever cut it would die unmarried. In Carlow, by contrast, all the eligible girls were asked to have a slash at it; the girl who knocked it with a single swipe was to be the one married within the year. Frequently skill was more important than luck. In many places throughout Ireland the workers tested their ability by standing back some distance and throwing their hooks at the last bit standing. As this required a great deal of accuracy, the man who succeeded in cutting the last of the corn in this way got a great cheer from those present.

Pat Whyte was the last man to practice the tradition of the harvest sheaf in north Sligo. Here it was slightly different in that it was not actually cut at all but remained standing. A small piece was left untouched in the corner of the field for the fairies or 'good people'. The same applied to potatoes as a small piece, a yard or two, at the end of a drill was set aside and left untouched until the following spring.

The practice died out in most areas in the first half of the twentieth century. A Ballintrillick, County Sligo man heard the old people talking about it. 'Aye, sure, cutting the cailleach, there'd be a dance the night the corn'd be all cut, 'twas the same the night the rick would be made. There'd be *poitín* and all kinds of food but no tay because the tay was scarce then. There was dances, fiddle players and melojins in every house and townland then; everyone'd gather at a neighbour's house and have good innocent fun. When ye put the hook in for the last bit, that was cutting the *cailleach*, I only heard of it – putting the hare over to you. There was truth in that, ye had to let young hares or corncrakes out of the last bit. I often did it. Pheasants the same.'

Bernie Barry from Bunduff, County Sligo told me of a neighbour who saw a hare leap from the last piece of corn and run past. Startled, he threw the hook at the fleeing animal. It struck the hare, wounding it, but the creature made good its escape with the blade embedded in its side. The man was forced to get another hook to finish his day's reaping.

Some time after, on returning from market in Sligo, he took shelter from a downpour of rain in a house by the side of the road. The house was full of smoke caused by a temperamental chimney. Through the gloom he saw an old man sitting in the corner and his wife lying in the kitchen bed. As his vision became accustomed to the scene about him he spotted his hook stuck in the rafters. This gave him pause for thought so, after a while, he ventured to ask the man where he got the instrument. The question seemed to make him uncomfortable. His reply was evasive. The old woman in the bed who had been quiet till then piped up. 'Arrah, why don't ye tell him,' she said throwing back the bedclothes. Pointing to her backside she said, 'That's where he got it, stuck in my arse, and it was you that put it there!'

In olden times the end of the harvest was a time for celebration called the 'harvest home'. This might be the night the rick was made or the night the potatoes were dug or when all the harvest had been gathered. In most country houses a dance was held in the kitchen with drinks and food but on the larger farms of the midlands and in the south it could be a much bigger affair held in the barn.

A description of one of these celebrations held in 1815 is interesting. 'Mrs Greene and her daughters and her servant maids, and a few helpers, had been engaged from breakfast time in getting the mighty dinner ready – kitchen and parlour fires, and one or two in an outhouse being fully occupied. The barn had been cleared out the day before, and in the course of the present morning was made as spruce as brushes and besoms could make it, and enlivened by two rows of tables, covered with clean table cloths, and furnished with dishes and well arranged rows of plates, knives, forks, etc. Several fine bunches of full-eared wheat were suspended from the collar beams, chairs were set at the ends of the tables and the sides furnished with forms and stools. Those who were only used to see the place in its litter of straw, grain and sheaves, were delighted with its now neat and orderly appearance.'

The narrative goes on to describe the food, 'mighty slices of bacon or roast beef reposing on beds of white cabbage,' good 'cup' potatoes, sides of bacon, rounds and ribs of beef, mugs of home-brewed beer. At the end of the meal all the guests went outside for a while and on their return the barn was cleared and ready for the dance. Punch was freely available and music provided for the festivities that went on into the early hours of the morning.[18]

Sometimes ornate harvest knots were plaited out of straws from the last sheaf and worn at the harvest home, or fashioned earlier and worn at the 'cutting of the cailleach'. This custom was more prevalent in Ulster, primarily in Armagh and Donegal and also in Cork, Offaly, Laois and parts of Dublin. It is believed to have been introduced by planters from England and Scotland where this tradition was widespread.

In Roscommon, if the wife, sons or daughter were present when the last sheaf was cut, they were blindfolded. It was held that if they saw the witch hare they would die. When the men had cut the last piece of corn they said: 'Thanks be to God we have the witch hare defeated,' to which the women answered, 'Amen'.

In parts of Sligo, the last sheaf was brought home unbound, to be fed to the ass or hens. Some of it was retained until a cow was calving. It was then pushed up the chimney and given to the beast to help her to 'clean' – to purge the afterbirth. A few straws of the sheaf hung by the fire assisted in finding lost articles. A stem of the sheaf made to smoulder and put on a hen's nest when she was hatching brought good luck to the brood.

A sheaf could be put to a more sinister use too. Plaited into a human shape, given the name of an enemy and buried in the ground, it had hurtful powers. This custom was primarily associated with the midlands and north Antrim. The belief was that as the grain rotted so too the person whose name was given to the sheaf declined and died. The only way of averting the curse was to find the sheaf and dry or burn it.

Any sheaf of corn is said to have the power to find a drowned person. The last sheaf is said to be especially effective in this regard and in some places is thought to be the only one that can do this. In order to find the body the sheaf, with a lighted candle attached, is put in the water at the place where the victim is believed to have entered. It is then set adrift with the tide or current and will come to rest at the place where the victim's body will be found. A variation of this method of divining was used as recently as 1996 at a drowning in Mullaghmore, County Sligo.

Belief in a corn spirit was widespread in various forms throughout all European countries. It is also recorded in places as far apart as Peru, where it was practised by the native Indians, and in Borneo by the native Dyaks.

It is probable that the stately figures of Greek mythology, Demeter and Persephone, gods of the crops, grew out of such beliefs and practices in Greece. In ancient times the man who cut the last sheaf was sacrificed so that his blood would soak into the soil to appease the Gods or spirits of the earth and ensure good harvests in future. In ancient Egypt it was believed that 'the slain corn-spirit – the dead Osiris – was represented by a human victim, whom the reapers slew on the harvest-field, mourning his death in a dirge'.[19] This terrible practice fell into disuse with the arrival of Christianity. It has survived, however, until recent years, but in a different form, in the ceremony and mystery surrounding the cailleach.

It is recorded that among the American Indian tribes in 1838 a fourteen-year-old Sioux girl was captured by the Pawnees. At the end of six months, during which she had been well treated, she was taken out and 'attached to a sort of gibbet and roasted for some time over a slow fire, then shot to death with arrows. While her flesh was still warm it was cut in small pieces from the bone, put in little baskets, and taken to a neighbouring cornfield. There the head chief took a piece of flesh from a basket and squeezed a drop of blood on the newly deposited corn. His example was followed by the rest till all the seed had been sprinkled by the blood; it was then covered up with earth.'[20]

Aztec culture was deeply embedded in the world of nature. They too attempted to manipulate the elements through appeasement of the controlling deities. Some ceremonies were of an appalling nature, such as the rituals of Tlaloc, god of the mountains, rain and spring, which required the sacrifice and eating of children and infants, some still at the breast. Equally grisly was the sacrifice to Tezcatlipoca, the sun god and most feared of the Aztec pantheon. To him went the still-beating human heart cut out of the victim's chest with a special knife.

Sacrificial offerings were not motivated by sadistic cruelty but by an overwhelming belief that the controlling deities of nature had to be appeased or else the life cycle, as the Aztecs knew it, would come to an end. They could not take the risk that Tezcatlipoca might wreak revenge on them or disappear altogether if he was not rendered his proper due.

These examples serve to illustrate the measure of importance placating the gods had in diverse civilisations. It shows clearly that the customs described above are the surviving remnants of what we now consider to be barbaric rituals in which human beings were commonly killed to promote the fertility of the field. Similar sacrifices were made in most parts of the world by which the sacrificers hoped to obtain good crops.

The ceremony of the last sheaf, like so much else, is largely a thing of the past, although I have heard the older men talk jokingly about putting the hare over to a neighbour when they had finished cutting a field of rye or oats. Hugh Gallagher's mention of the reaper's consideration for the corncrake reminds me of seeing the mother bird with its legs almost sheared off by the blade of a horse machine. Dragging its mangled body, it still struggled to hide and protect its young. The small black chicks instinctively scuttled for cover under the swathes of freshly cut green meadow and quickly disappeared from sight. Seeming too small to fend for themselves, the little things probably didn't survive the devastation of their world. I never saw them again. Perhaps they did survive, against the odds, to grow up and make their way back to Africa. More than likely, the downy orphans fell victim to a foraging cat.

The corncrake is heard no more in most parts of Ireland, partly because of its incautious habit of lying still when disturbed. They moved ahead of the rattling machinery when it was too late. Sometimes they made it to the cover of the remaining diamond of grass, dying there, a victim to the sharp blades. Their only chance of survival was a thoughtful 'mowyer' like Hugh who left the last bit standing as a refuge or herded them on to freedom.

With the demise of the corncrake went many of my generation's memories of growing up in the Irish countryside. Its clamorous love call disturbed many an early morning slumber. As we walked or pushed a bike home from a dance along country roads in the early morning, the first pink blush of a summer dawn tinting the eastern sky, their harsh 'kraak-kraak' was heard from every field. It was an unwelcome reminder that we had overstayed our time at dance or céilí; it elicited fervent prayers that the bird's harsh call wouldn't waken watchful parents. The bike was carried past the baleful eye of their watching window for fear a rattling mudguard, like the sentinel geese of ancient

Rome, would arouse the sleeping garrison.

We chased no hare out of the corner of our cornfield and the tradition of the last sheaf had disappeared before my time. But we chased rats! The big circular stack of corn built in the shape of a trampcock was a natural home for them. It provided warmth, lots of material for a nest and an endless supply of food. In other words: Rat Heaven! These stacks were always of oaten straw. Rye straw needed for thatch was handled more carefully and brought straight from the stooks in the field into the barn.

The round oaten stacks, known in some areas as 'barts', were expertly built and sometimes raised off the ground on timber legs to deter invasion by rats. Sloping outwards to run the water off, the sheaves were placed layer by layer around in a circle with the head facing out and the grain end in the heart of the stack. To overcome the difficulty of bringing the straw to a weatherproof point the sheaves were brought to a rounded cone shape. This was then topped with hay, thatched with rushes and tied with hay ropes.

In country fields, rats were always with us. They were just as much a part of the wild landscape as the hare, the fox, or the rabbit. In a rat hierarchy, however, they seemed a cut above the slithering rodents that haunt sewer and garbage can. You might say that to be a field rat then had some status! They had as much a right to make a bid for the bounty of the fields as we did and they had gathered their food there as long and possibly longer than man. That said, we hated and feared them and could only hope, at best, to control their numbers. Despite constant war being waged on them they could not be eradicated. There was just too much food everywhere in field and barn.

Although regarded as pests some had great respect for their intelligence. Believing they could understand human speech farmers would not speak out loud of what they planned when putting down traps in case the rats might hear. It was held by some that if you wanted to rid an area of the rodents all that was needed was to stand near the entrance to their holes and tell them where they could find other accommodation. But it had to be much better! A wise man might make sure the new home was across running water as rats, like witches, detested this and would be unlikely to return even if they didn't like the new place. In County Tyrone and in Antrim it was judged prudent to find the head rat and address any advice to him.

The practice of talking to rats was not confined to Ireland. In France a special formula was used: 'Male rats and female rats, I conjure you by the great God to go out of my house, out of my habitations and to betake yourself to [Cliffoney] there to end your days.' In 1943 in the USA the magazine *Colliers* published an account of similar practices by farmers in Maine.

Sir James Frazer in *The Golden Bough* (1890–1915) quotes an ancient Greek tract on farming which advises anyone wishing to rid their lands of mice to take a piece of paper and write on it: 'I adjure you, ye mice here present, that ye neither injure me or suffer another mouse to do so. I give you yonder field [specify the field] but if ever I catch you here again, by the Mother of Gods I will rend you in seven pieces.' Enough to intimidate a strong man, never mind a humble mouse! The procedure was to stick the paper on an unhewn stone in the field before sunrise with the written side up.

The last such recorded banishment in Ireland happened in the parish of Riverstown, County Sligo, at the end of the nineteenth century. A woman who lived near Kilross graveyard, concerned with an infestation of rats there, went to a local priest for help. She was afraid they might colonise the thatched roof of her house and so place her in great danger. The priest wrote something out in Latin on a piece of white paper for the worried woman with the instruction to say certain prayers for a given number of days. She was then to attach the paper to the gate leading into the graveyard.

Following all instructions carefully she waited and watched. Some time later, to her astonishment, she saw the leader of the rat colony take the paper in his mouth. Gathering behind him, the rest of the rodents, 'swarmed through the bars of the old gate, crossed the road and plunged through into the townland of Knockatubber and were never seen afterwards.'[21]

In an incident recorded in an American magazine in the 1920s a farmer there took a much more diplomatic approach. Appealing to the rodents' sense of fair play he wrote a civil letter to them and pinned it up in the barn. The note advised them that the farmer's 'crops were short, that he could not afford to keep them through the winter, that he had been very kind to them, and that for their own good he thought they had better leave him and go to his neighbours who had much more grain than he.'

Tom Healy, a fiddle player from Ballymote, County Sligo, was reputed to have powers akin to those of the Pied Piper. A pleasant man who travelled far to play for dances and parties, he had a darker side for people who aroused his anger: he could billet rats with those who offended him. Anyone doubting his abilities was directed by John Kearns of Drumfin to two houses in the townland where a plague of rats visited the occupants at the fiddler's command. Following this demonstration of his mastery only the very brave crossed Tom Healy.

When the last few sheaves of our straw stack were moved indoors for scutching, the rat-families' homes, nests and tunnels were exposed to the bright sunlight. Evicted from their hidden havens and left with no place to hide, they were forced to make a run for it.

The race was on – big rats, small rats, little huddles of blind, pink, hairless baby rats still in their nest of chopped straw; rats that scurried through the long grass darting here and there in search of a place to hide; smarter ones that went straight for the cover of the stone ditch. Like the rats of Hamelin made famous in Robert Browning's poem:

> They fought the dogs and killed the cats,
> And bit the babies in the cradles,
> And ate the cheeses out of the vats,
> And licked the soups out of the cook's own ladles,
> Split open the kegs of salted sprats,
> Made nests inside men's Sunday hats,
> And even spoiled the women's chats
> By drowning their speaking
> With shrieking and squeaking
> In fifty different sharps and flats.

Some rats in blind panic went straight for the opening at the bottom of the nearest trouser leg. Unfortunate neighbours who didn't have the foresight to tie the bottom of their trousers had the terrifying experience of having the rat climb up inside. There was nothing for it then but to try and hold the twisting, clawing, biting beast through the cloth until the trousers were removed and the by now mangled rat with them.

We had never heard of the more genteel methods of persuasion mentioned above and we had no Pied Piper to help us but the family dog was in his element. He darted here and pounced there barking madly; snatching the escaping rats with bared teeth, he tossed them high in the air. Grabbing them by the back of the neck he bit through the spinal cord and left them chewed and lifeless on the grass.

The children whooped as the grown-ups chased the rats with

pitchforks, following their rapid movements as they twisted through the grass. Impaled on the sharp prongs the rats twisted in agony, squealed horribly and died.

The rat is not native to Ireland. Although reputed to have been introduced, as was the rabbit, by the Normans in medieval times, recent research has identified their presence in Ireland in the early Christian period. The Irish version of their name used in some parts, *luch francach*, 'French mouse' is thought to be an indication of a dramatic increase in their numbers following the Norman invasion. Their potential for harm was immediately recognised: their numbers multiplied rapidly, their bite was poisonous, they ate and spoiled grain as well as potatoes and so were a great pest. It was believed at one time that they came and drank from the breasts of sleeping women. And it would not be surprising if they did.

Fleas carried by rats were responsible for the bubonic plague which devastated Europe in the Middle Ages. They still pose a formidable hazard to health. Pathogen 4 or P4 is the highest classification of deadly diseases known to man. There are only four specially equipped laboratories in the world capable of providing the security necessary to study these killer viruses. Salmonella and legionnaires' disease are categorised P2 and the HIV virus that causes Aids as P3. A recent newspaper article reported two new P4 viruses which have appeared in this decade: Ebola, which leads to massive internal haemorrhaging and a speedy and almost certain death and the equally deadly Lassa fever, transmitted by rodents. At last count Lassa had already killed 15,000 people. Another deadly infection is Weil's disease, transmitted to humans by water or food contaminated by rat urine.

Because of the dearth of any redeeming features, man, not only in Ireland but all over the world, has for ages tried, without success, to exterminate rats. Even today, despite the best efforts of professional exterminators, the experts claim that we are never more than a hundred yards from a rat! As recently as June 2000 a report in the *Irish Times* stated that two operating theatres at St Mary's Orthopaedic Hospital in Cork were forced to cancel all scheduled surgery and close because of 'rodent activity' in the vicinity. If only the unfortunate corncrake or cricket was nearly so adaptable to change or resistant to extermination!

Legend has it that rats formed a part of the arsenal of Ghoibhneann, magical smith of the Tuatha dé Danann. The story goes that a giant who lived on the Beara peninsula in County Cork once demanded that Ghoibhneann make a perfect razor for him. This he did, using the blood of rats to temper the steel. So effective was the blood and so sharp the razor that with one stroke it shaved off both beard and epidermis from the giant without in any way causing pain!

In ancient Ireland it was commonly held that rats could be killed through rhyming verses. This power, held by the poet classes, was recognised outside Ireland and recorded by the playwright Ben Jonson who wrote, 'Rhyme them to death as they do Irish rats.' Even Shakespeare was aware of this humane and uniquely Irish method of pest control. In *As You Like It*, Rosalind notes the charming practice of lulling rats to death through poetry. 'I was never so be-rhymed since Pythagoras' time that I was an Irish rat,' she says. Yeats was familiar with this power, too, and mentions it in his poem 'Parnell's Funeral':

> *All that was sung,*
> *All that was said in Ireland is a lie*
> *Bred out of the contagion of the throng,*
> *Saving the rhyme rats hear before they die.*

The poets exercised their power to kill lower animals through a spell called an *aer*. The distinction of being the first person on record to apply this unique power is held by Senchan Torpeist, a seventh-century chief poet of Ireland. Once, in anger, when his dinner was eaten by rats he uttered an *aer* on them which began, 'Rats though sharp their snouts, are not powerful in battle . . . ' It is recorded that, following this contemptuous slur, ten of the hairy mischief-makers dropped dead on the spot. Noble rats, no doubt, who were so humiliated at such an insult to their valour that they just fell over and died! A time of honour, warriors and heroes indeed – even in the rat world.[22]

The year wore on. Daylight hours receded. Longer nights gave respite from the hard grind of field and meadow. Precious time was not wasted though and indoor work now commenced. 'Scutching' or 'lashing' was done by the light of a candle or lamp.

In preparation for this we laid a flat stone on an upturned creel or old creamery can in a corner of the barn. Sheaves were untied, gripped by the fistful at the stubble end, swung over the shoulders, and brought down hard on the slab which was worn smooth by the work of many generations. The grain, thus beaten from the heads, was caught on a canvas laid on the ground. Any final residue of grass or weed was cleaned from the sheaf. Fistful by fistful, sheaf by sheaf, the crop was tediously and laboriously lashed and cleaned. Straw prepared in this way was ideal for thatching as it was straight, firm and undamaged in any way.

Threshing with a flail was another method used by many farmers to remove grain from oaten straw. Originating in Gaul in the third or fourth century AD this procedure spread from there throughout most parts of Europe (including Ireland) and

Asia. Mention of rules governing the flail in the Brehon laws is evidence of its use in Ireland as far back as the fifth century.[23]

The flail consisted of two straight sticks, one a 'hand-piece' of ash, pine or oak attached by a flexible tie to another shorter 'beater' known as a 'cat' or 'souple' made from hazel, holly or blackthorn. In Mullaghmore, County Sligo, branches of the whin bush were sought for both handle and souple.[24] The skin of a goat or eel was favoured for joining the two sticks, but straw rope, willow withies and sheepskin were used as well. The method of binding the two sticks to each other varied from one area to another. In Connacht the 'double loop' was favoured, the 'double hole' in parts of Ulster, the 'eye' in Donegal and so on.

Some farmers threshed on a wooden platform raised a few inches off the ground. In other places barn floors, often of clay, were especially laid with threshing in mind, having a horse's skull buried underneath to give bounce to the floor and a special resonance. This gave a pleasant sound and rhythm when the straw was struck with the flail. Other countries, such as Sweden, also used this method. Sometimes a steel wire was stretched underneath a wooden floor to increase the resonance!

Threshing with a flail required a great deal of expertise and practice to get the desired rhythm and control of the spinning souple. Bystanders, and indeed the thresher himself, needed to be alert. If you didn't get it right it would, 'cut the face o' ye' if ye weren't careful', an expert in the use of the instrument told me. Two rows of five sheaves each were laid on the floor, grain heads together and overlapping. Sometimes two men threshed together, one standing on each side, striking alternate blows in perfect coordination.

Bertie Monds of Drumcliffe, County Sligo, described the rhythm: 'After beating, on the draw back, the cat (souple) was given an extra flourish or twirl so as to keep time and allow the other thresher to strike and draw back.' Onlookers needed to keep well clear of the flailing sticks. Any foolish person coming too close risked a serious injury. The ancient Brehon laws, comprehensive in their scope, covered everything. One clause stipulated that any person struck by a flail at threshing time could not claim compensation unless he could prove good cause for being in the working area!

As the threshing proceeded, the grain fell onto a canvas or, in some cases, linen sheets which were spread on the floor. When the two rows of sheaves had been thoroughly beaten on one side they were turned over with a flick of the foot and threshed on the other side as well. They were then put aside and two fresh rows of sheaves put down. With expert workmen a good stack of one hundred sheaves, or even two stacks, could be dispensed in a night.

When oaten straw was fed to cattle the sheaves were not untied for threshing. Some grain was purposely left as extra nourishment. When needed for thatching they were opened, cleaned of weeds and grass and every two sheaves joined together. It was particularly important that no grain be left on the head then as it would germinate and grow on the roof shortly after being laid. It was a dead give-away and very public evidence of the incompetence of the thresher. You might say it was shouted from the rooftops!

Threshing could be performed in the open air during good weather. Early in the nineteenth century it was sometimes done in the middle of the public road. A researcher for the Ordnance Survey in 1835 reported that 'Threshing machines are unknown: the flail and the centre of the road in fine weather supply the convenience of barns and threshing machines, and indeed the scanty stackyards are speedily disposed of when submitted to the influence of a couple of active flails; and it is worthy of record, and almost incredible, how gigantic are the labours of two resolute Hibernians when engaged by the bulk on this duty.'

This was considerable praise for native Irish workers all too often labelled idle and shiftless by overlords who ground their tenants down and then despised them for being poor and ragged. Energy abounds when the rewards are your own!

A barn was used when it was available but even into the early 1900s threshing was often done in a spare room in the house or kitchen. 'Ramblers' who came in to pass the time often gave a helping hand. This may have been a very sociable way to get the work done but it was not a popular choice with the woman of the house. The dresser was covered to keep the dust out. Even though linen sheets were draped around the room and on the floor to gather grain, chaff and dust, there was still a lot of cleaning up when the men were finished. Scollops for thatching were pointed and prepared in the kitchen too by the light of a 'Paddy lamp' in the hob-hole by the fire.

There were other hazards when the roof beams were low. Joe Kane, veteran thresher of Ederney, County Fermanagh, lived in his own 300-year-old house. 'A young fella used to thrash here with the flail in the kitchen an' it used to upset the whole house,' he told me in August 1995. 'The stack of corn was carried in an' built up in the room an' then he thrashed away at night till the whole thing was done. Then ye had to clane it up an' put the corn in bags. The couples used to be very awkward if they weren't high enough – ye'd have to be very careful ye wouldn't hit the couple with the souple or that ye wouldn't hit the dresser.' The 'couple' was the horizontal roof beam and the 'souple' the swinging part of the flail.

The story is told of a man who threshed year after year at a certain corner of his barn even though the lack of clearance on the overhead roof beam made the work difficult for him. A neighbour came in one day and, observing the man's difficulty, remarked that if he stood in a different spot the flail would clear the beam. 'I know that,' said the man resignedly, 'but you've got to understand that this is the spot where my father stood and his father before that again, and if it was good enough for them all those years, well then, it's good enough for me!'

When the threshing was completed, the grain had to be cleaned. This meant it had to be run through a sort of sieve called a 'riddle'. The first run was done in the barn or house, where the rough impurities, pieces of straw, heads, and so on were removed. The riddle was made of a board bent around in a circle approximately sixteen inches in diameter and about four to five inches high with a wire mesh bottom. Mickey McGroarty of Selacis, County Donegal, born in the early years of last century, described the winnowing process for me:

> It was all clay [daub] floors in the houses that time until the twenties or thirties maybe – ye'd hardly see a cement floor in a house. The grain was swept and lifted off the floor, with a 'besom' or broom made of heather tied with a piece of wire or good strong rope, and put in bags. Some nice breezy day then ye'd take all out to the hill depending on which direction the wind was blowing. Ye'd get an old sheet and put it down on the ground with a wee flag or stone on each corner to keep the wind from rolling it over. When the riddle was filled with grain then ye held it up and kept shaking it until all the grain fell through; the corn was heavy so it fell down straight but the chaff was light and blew away through the field. Ye done that till the whole thing was cleaned. Whatever didn't clean

> from the riddling went to the hens. When ye had
> a couple of stacks thrashed then you might finish
> up with eight or nine hundredweight of corn and
> that had to go to the mill then down at Cranny
> – Glacken that owned the mill in my day.

Burning the oat sheaf to remove the grain was a practice of great antiquity in Ireland. The advantage of this method was that the threshing, winnowing and drying were done in one quick operation and the meal made instantly available. This procedure was used when small amounts were required for bread or porridge or to prepare a meal quickly for unexpected guests. Grain prepared in this way was said to be especially delicious as the burning imparted a fresh, crisp, nutty flavour to the meal.

A seventeenth-century traveller described the preparation:

> A woman sitting down takes a handful of corn,
> holding it by the stalks in her left hand and then
> sets fire to the ears, which are presently in a flame;
> she has a stick in her right hand . . . beating off the
> grain at the very instant when the husk is quite
> burnt, for if she misses of that, she must use the
> kiln. The corn may be so dressed, winnowed,
> ground and baked within an hour after reaping
> from the ground.[25]

When the grain, known as *'loiscreán'*, was removed, it was immediately ground in the circular stone quern, a common tool in country houses. In 1635 an Act of Parliament, 'to Prevent the unprofitable Custom of Burning of Corne in the Straw', was passed, forbidding the burning of the oat sheaf on the grounds that it was wasteful.

From the middle of the eighteenth century, efforts were made to mechanise the threshing process. Sufficient improvements had been made by the beginning of the nineteenth century on earlier mechanised threshers to make installation on larger farms and estates an attractive and labour-saving proposition. These machines, manufactured in Scotland as well as Ireland, made no impact on Ireland's small pre-famine farms which existed at starvation level because of economic conditions controlled by a lethal combination of foreign rule and rack-renting landlords.

Power provided by water or horses necessitated the construction of either a waterwheel or a covered house to protect the engine. Structures that contained horse-powered engines were circular as the animals moved around the centre in a circle attached to the mechanism by a long pole or driveshaft. Such devices not alone removed the intensive labour element of scutching or threshing but also increased production by a factor of five or six. Pierce of Wexford and Kennedy of Coleraine became the two biggest producers of these appliances by the middle of the last century. The further development of portable machines powered by hand or foot pedal allowed threshers to be hired out and moved from one farm to another.

The advent of these mechanical threshers caused great concern to farm labourers who earned a living travelling from place to place in teams. In the early nineteenth century bands of rioters known as Luddites roamed the English countryside smashing such machinery. They came together originally in the industrial areas in the belief that machinery was displacing their work as craftsmen. They took their name from an eighteenth-century farm labourer from Leicestershire, Ned Ludd, also known as King Ludd, who was credited with destroying stocking frames in 1782.

Steam-powered threshers were developed by 1842 and by the

end of the last century there were 500 of these in Ireland. Very few farmers could afford the investment needed to purchase so contractors became available who hired out 'threshing sets'. These became a romantic memory for many as they travelled the countryside in the months of August, September and October.

Steam threshing continued in Ireland until replaced by tractor power in the 1940s. In 1939 there were just over 2,000 tractors in the twenty-six counties. This figure increased to 13,569 in 1950 and further to 43,697 in 1960. Steam and tractor power was eventually replaced by the increasing use of the combine harvester in the 1960s.

Songs and legends were, in time, woven around the 'oul' thrashing mill' and the *'meitheal'* of men required to operate it. It was one of the biggest days of the farming year. Neighbours gathered in to give a hand. Some busied themselves taking the straw from the stack, passing it to others who untied the straps and fed the sheaves to the thresher. More gathered the grain into bags at the back where the busy monster, having digested the sheaves, spat out the grain. Others built the by-product of mangled straw into cocks. Everyone was busy.

The woman of the house bustled about the kitchen directing her helpers while she prepared a meal of bacon and cabbage or boiled chicken for the workers. In *The Green Fool* (1938), Patrick Kavanagh relates that in his district it was the marriageable girls of the area that came to do the cooking. At one threshing he counted seven of them in the kitchen. Two long deal tables were set end to end in the middle of the floor. At each of the four corners was a chair, and from chair to chair were placed long boards as seats. Twelve mugs of buttermilk stood on the table. A large pot of potatoes boiled over the fire and beside it simmered a pot of cabbage.

There was a hustle and bustle of orchestrated effort about the farm that resembled a ballet. Men moved and danced to the din and clatter of the steam-tractor and the great powering rhythm of the belt that rushed around and around in a never-ending circle between the thresher and the tractor. Puffs of steam and smoke blustered importantly skyward. Clouds of dust and chaff lifted away like swarms of bees. Good-natured banter rose above the din of the machinery and drifted across sun-yellowed fields. Indian-summer sunshine bringing the good weather essential for a successful day's threshing lit the scene with warm, slanting rays.

On a recent October day Joe Straghan drove his threshing machine across the border from Keady, County Armagh, for a day's threshing with his friend Benny Moen in Clontibret, County Monaghan. Benny clings to the old ways. In the twenty-first century, when we are all swept away on a tidal wave of technological revolution, this industrious farmer is an anachronism, but traditional methods serve him well and he sees no reason to change. Joe Straghan is an artist and, without knowing it, a natural showman, or so it seemed to me. Arriving with the thresher while the morning dew still sparkled on drumlin and pasture he backed his beloved machine in by the stooks. Standing back, he eyed it carefully, decided it wasn't level and commenced to dig the earth out from under two of the wheels. Reversing into the ruts he had just made he jumped down from the tractor seat, strode around to the back panel, pulled back a little eye-level brass shutter that hid a built-in spirit level, shook his head, and shuttling back and forth, dropped, filled, dug and checked until, satisfied at last, he beamed a wide, gap-toothed smile at us: 'She'll do at that,' he nodded.

The threshing team: Martin Murphy, Seamus Moen, Pearse Shannon, Benny and his son Enda circled at a respectful distance watching Joe practise his craft. Someone worried that the bubble still wasn't centred but: 'Aah, she'll settle herself intil that when she starts,' Joe reassured as he moved along the side of the thresher peering analytically at joints and bearings and places that he knew from experience were prone to failure. Plying an oilcan and wrench with practised ease drawn from a lifetime of experience, he inspected and tapped, torqued and tightened; he jabbed energetically with his oil can and squirted glistening streams at secret places known only to him.

Seamus and Pearse busied themselves taking ropes off rucks of corn, Benny arrived with an armful of bags and Joe commenced the final act of connecting the belt from the big pulley on the thresher to the power take-off on the tractor. This initiated another round of tightening, aligning, moving and checking until, with an apoplectic belch of smoke from the bowels of the tractor and a mighty shudder, the whole unlikely contraption shook, heaved, and burst into life. The big belt walloped around and around and around, frightening a great array of pulleys, big and small, into agitated motion. Some whirled clockwise, others pelted anticlockwise, belts drove from wheels to gears in an intricate chain reaction causing platforms to vibrate, paddles to rotate and shuttles to, well, shuttle. Shafts conveyed the energy to the other side of the thresher where more wheels, big and small, pirouetted and whirred and clanked importantly, driving each other frenetically to fulfil their part in a complex whole.

Seamus replenished the rucks as Pearse forked the sheaves up to Benny and Enda, who fed them into the churning mouth of the thresher. Drums rolled, fans blew, sorters sorted and graders graded. Checking the pickles as they flowed, Joe monitored four separate grainy rivers of oats as they funnelled into bags. He tied, carried and stacked as they filled. The fury and the frenzy ended in a great cavernous maw at the back where an array of paddles like several pairs of agitated, upside-down legs kicked and churned and ejected the chewed-up straw. Miraculously, all the spinners and shakers purred, whirred, hummed and shook in unison; order arose from disorder; a great harmony emerged from confusion – and Joe was right: in the middle of the hubbub the bubble sat contentedly in the centre of the spirit level.

Memories formed on threshing days will never dim. The passage of time can not erase them. When eyes that witnessed these scenes close for the last time, when the mind that holds these pictures ceases to be, when the rosary beads are twined for the last time about work-roughened hands, we will have lost forever the magic of the 'thrashing day'. Nothing can recapture it. Heritage parks will try, but 'vintage days' or words cannot recreate the colour and the spectacle; images imprinted on brain cells cannot be transferred; traditional memory will fade forever from knowledge.

The sense of community inherent in the threshing day and the preparations leading up to it are no more. Changes in farming practices spelled the death knell for a society at one with itself. The combine harvester provided the final *coup de grace* as it cut, threshed and winnowed in one mindless, streamlined operation. No gathering, no sharing, no cursing, no laughing. Efficiency is all!

3

—

Plain Fare and *Féar Gortach*

Bags of grain resulting from the activities of flail or thresher had to be ground in preparation for human or animal consumption. The quest for some method of processing followed the introduction of grain cultivation to Ireland by the Neolithic settlers of five thousand or more years ago. Experimentation resulted in the development of a simple instrument for grinding. Consisting of two stones, we know it now as a saddle quern. The base stone was rectangular, about twenty-four inches long and hollowed in the centre. A smaller stone of about ten inches in length was used to pound or grind the corn which lay in the hollow of the larger stone.

No matter how simple the technology, man has always attempted to advance the process and improve his lot. By the early Iron Age the rotary quern had been developed. This was a vast improvement on its predecessor. It required less labour and produced a finer, more uniform product in less time. It consisted of two circular stones, generally about twenty inches in diameter, placed one on top of the other. The upper stone revolved on a peg fitted to the lower stone which remained stationary. It was turned by means of a handle attached at the outer perimeter of the top stone. The corn was fed by hand into a central hole in the upper stone and was ground as it made its way by gravity feed to the outer edges between the two stones. From ancient times the operation of the quern was regarded as the special work of women although it was only girls of commoner rank who were taught its use. It was tedious work as it took about an hour for two women to grind ten pounds of meal. Such work was deemed inappropriate for women of the higher social classes.

Rotary querns were in common use right down to the early years of this century and can still be found abandoned near farmhouses all over Ireland. Once corn mills became established, quern grinding by the poorer people was looked upon with disfavour by the miller as it took custom away from him. Where the landlord owned the mill, people were forced to hide their querns as orders were often given to have all the querns in a locality broken. In 1802 in County Cavan, for example, 'every estate has its own cornmill and the tenantry is bound under severe penalty to grind their corn thereat and pay toll.'[26]

It was difficult if not impossible to mill wet or damp corn. Given Ireland's climatic conditions it is not surprising that the development of corn-drying kilns in the last centuries BC closely followed the introduction of the rotary quern. These kilns, as the name suggests, removed moisture from the grain prior to milling. The material used was turf. There were many kiln designs but they generally consisted of a stone-lined pit into which led a long flue. Up to Famine times every townland operated one, except in localities where the landlord owned the local mill. His mill always included a kiln and it was there tenants were required to bring their grain.

The erection of the first mill in Ireland is attributed to Cormac Mac Airt, High King of Ireland from AD 227 to 266. The story is told that he fell in love with one of his slave girls who worked for him at the quern. When she gave birth to a baby he wanted to relieve her of the heavy drudgery so he sent across the sea for a miller. As a result Ireland's first mill was then built on the river Nemnach near Tara.

It is a matter of record that watermills were in common use in Ireland shortly after St Patrick's time, both in monasteries and among the people in general. Prior to the Reformation and the dissolution and destruction of Irish monasteries, monastic sites often included a mill which served the local community as well as their own needs. A *Life of St Brigid*, written by Cogitosus in the tenth century, describes the construction of an Irish monastic watermill at her convent in late-seventh-century Kildare. Brigid is reputed to have died in the year 523.

The vast majority of these early mills had horizontal wheels and were known as 'Danish Mills' which seems a misnomer as their development is attributed to the Greeks. The earliest reference to such a wheel comes from the Greek historian, Strabo about 65 BC.

The wheels of early mills, as the name suggests, worked in a horizontal position quite unlike the image of the later upright wheel with which we are all familiar. The mill house was a two-storey structure the lower section of which contained the horizontal wheel while the upper floor held the millstones. The blades or vanes of the wheel were made of wood and turned by a concentrated stream of water directed against them. As there was no gearing, one revolution of the wheel caused one turn of the millstone overhead. It was a slow process but immeasurably superior to the old rotary quern.

It was thought at one time that vertical wheels were introduced to Ireland by the Cistercians who came with the Normans in the twelfth century but recent discoveries have shown that this is not so. A vertical-wheeled mill excavated at Little Island, County Cork has been determined by dendro-chronology (tree-ring dating) to AD 630.[27]

Watermills were developed in the early monasteries to cater

to the needs of their expanding communities. The earliest indication of the importance of self-sufficiency in water supply for domestic use and for powering machinery is found in the sixth-century Rule of St Benedict, 530. Monastic communities in Ireland used their increasing wealth to invest in water-powered mills from the seventh century onwards. Mill-wrighting skills were widely available in Irish society at that time.

The vertical-wheeled mill, as with the horizontal version, was powered by water diverted by means of a millrace from a nearby stream or river. Unlike the horizontal mill the vertical position of this wheel required gearing for the transfer of power to the millstones. Manipulation of the gearing enabled several revolutions of the mill wheel from one turn of the water wheel. Continuing improvements in mill and wheel construction meant that the vertical mill eventually replaced the horizontal-wheeled version in Ireland by the early seventeenth century. In the succeeding years steam, diesel and electricity eventually replaced water as a power source. Nevertheless, the use of the horizontal wheel and the simple quern stone survived in many places into the twentieth century.

Milling played a vital role in local economies and mills were commonplace all over rural Ireland up to the 1960s. The development of the Irish Agricultural Organisation Society by Sir Horace Plunkett in 1894 revolutionised agricultural development. Plunkett's friend W. B. Yeats, an enthusiastic supporter of the new movement, put up £200 of his own money as share capital. Another avid enthusiast encouraged by Yeats was the poet George Russell.

The availability of motor power from steam and diesel engines in the early years of this century gave independence from water-power and consequently greater flexibility in siting. Now a favourite place for positioning mills was adjacent to the new creameries which were organised by the new Coop Dairy Societies. Compulsory tillage in the 1940s created a huge increase in the amount of cereal grown with a corresponding increase in demand for milling.

There is an abundance of information on the origins and development of mills and milling for those who seek it. Conversely there is very little or nothing recorded of the small farmer, living a subsistence lifestyle, who grew, cut, threshed, winnowed and, having bagged his grain, set off for the mill with horse or ass and cart before break of day. The experience of the 'bold peasantry, their country's pride' has gone unrecorded. No first-hand account of their experiences and scholarship has ever been set down. It is time to redress that neglect.

Willie McGowan of Donegal town, in an article in a local publication some years ago, wrote that the 'first traffic jams in Donegal were caused by the horses and carts coming to McLoone's mill', near the Northern Garage on the Clar road. One of these carters, Mickey McGroarty, described for me a similar journey with his grain to another mill at Cranny, near Inver in County Donegal:

> Every man going to the mill had to bring two bags of turf for the kiln. Grain was unloaded from the cart, carried to the drying room, left down on sheets of iron and turned with a square wooden shovel about ten inches wide tapering at the end. Wooden planks separated every man's portion, and that was heated by a fire that burned in the kiln underneath. Men often worked all through the night, 'til broad daylight in the morning.
>
> When ye had one crate down and squared and levelled off ye'd see the steam and the smoke

coming up through it. There was a window up at the top to let this out. Ye'd go then an' ye'd give your neighbour a hand to spread his portion; by the time you had this done your own would be ready to be turned again. Ye'd go back and forth turning each man's three or four times, the same as for hay out in the field, till you would hear it cracking. If ye didn't keep it moving it would burn with the heat underneath. After a while at this the husks'd be all opened out ready to come off.

In the adjoining County Sligo, Bertie Monds worked at a mill in Drumcliffe. Here the system differed. Instead of each man turning his own, the mill employed a man to do the job. 'I started working there in 1942 or '43,' Bert told me. 'They took all kinds of grain in. The most thing they ground was oats and then they sold out the ground oats.

'The mill was powered by a big steam engine. The pressure from the water drove the engine and the engine drove the mill. There never was a millwheel in it although there was an old mill nearby in Miltown some time before that. It was there at the bridge at Meehan's gate an' the cogwheels that turned it are still under the bridge. There's no trace of the mill.

'My first job was carting oats to Drumcliffe. There was that much stuff coming into it from Maugherow and all over they didn't have stores enough for it! When you brought your own oats to the mill we'd dry it and grind it and give it back to you. Tuppence a stone it was that time and it finished up at fourpence or fippence. Ye might get it the same day if ye came at the right time but mostly ye brought it one day and came back another day for it. The millstone had to be set different for oats than for rye. There was only one day in the week or the fortnight that they'd grind either rye or wheat. I never seen barley ground in it. Never in my life. Mostly oats. If ye wanted wheaten meal for doing brown bread we were able to do it grand. The wheels were made of stone, not steel. Ye could grind it as fine or as coarse as ye liked depending on how the wheel was set. If you wanted it crushed green they could do it that way too. Without drying. If ye were keeping it a certain length of time an' ye had a lot of it, ye had to get it dried or it would heat.

'I worked on that kiln from six o'clock in the evening until nine o'clock the next morning with nothing on me only the trousers an' the sweat running down off me. On me own. No one with me. We used a big wooden shovel. The grain was on a wire grid, like a sieve. It was in a wee room about ten by twelve feet. Smoke an' all came up through the mesh.'

Me: 'Isn't it well ye wouldn't get suffocated with the smoke?'

'The smoke was sharp but ye'd get used to it, an' I was as sound as a horse then. When it was dry anyway ye'd take it then an' bag it. Ye'd bag it on the chute an' ye'd have to wheel it across the chute even though it was open that time. I'd have to wheel it from the mill to the kiln. An' I often wheeled it there in the middle of the night with nothing on me but the trousers. I'd have to go out an' the sweat dripping off me to bring more in for drying an' replace it as it was dried. Turf we used for fuel.

'At the top of the kiln there was ventilators, there was no windows or nothing. Grills to let the smoke an' steam out. When ye got cute enough an' ye knew yer job well enough ye left a space at the side that the smoke would go out. It would head for where it would be able to get away. It'd be getting ye but the grain would be saving ye a bit too. Aw, Jasus, the men that'd come into it – fellas often came into me at night an' they'd say, "We'll come up an' give ye a hand." I'd say, "Right, come ahead." Five minutes was as long as they'd last. The heat of the fire'd get them first thing an' then the smoke and then the sweat'd begin to come down. "Christ Almighty ye'll die here," they'd say, laughing.

'Ye didn't bag the grain there. There was a chute of about a foot square going from the drying room where the grain was, to the floor below. Ye piled yer oats over on top of that after you closed the chute at the bottom. Ye went down below then and drew this wee door an' filled the bags from the chute. Ye'd have a pile of empty bags beside ye and ye'd fill away until the chute ran out, whatever pile was over it. Then ye ran up and ye piled grain over it again. Ye might have to go up and down three or four different times for to bag the one man's oats. That was the devil. It maddened ye because ye had to go out on the street, go into the receiving room and go up three flights of stairs before ye could get back. There was no direct way of going up to the kiln fire from where ye were bagging the stuff at the bottom on the floor. Many's the tough night I put in. If ye had a helper ye'd get far more done. There was two there at the beginning before I was in it.

'Ye bagged th'oats when it was dry an' ye wheeled it out and into the receiving room an' left it beside the scale until it was weighed. There was a winch on the upper loft where it went in to be ground. Ye let down the rope and tied it to the twenty-stone bag – it wasn't a half-hundredweight ye were talking about!'

Me: 'It would take two men to lift that!'

'Well, I was well able to throw it on my shoulder an' go up the flight of stairs with it.'

Me: 'But that's two-and-a-half hundredweight.'

'Sure they don't know what work is now! There was part of my time and if I caught a young fella, like the bucks that's going now, I'd give him a squeeze like that an' that'd be the end of him!

"Twas pure savage work, of course. I'd take the twenty-stone bag of dried oats, an' if it was wantin' above an' that the winch wasn't working I'd just take it up for them. I could take it on the plank steps an' they were that straight, ye know. It wasn't the same incline as a normal stairs. I'd run up them steps with the twenty-stone bag of oats.'

The system of handling the grain in the mill at Cranny was similar to that in Drumcliffe except that each individual farmer who came with grain manned the kiln to manipulate his own share. When the grain was dry enough it was dropped down through a chute, poured into bags and left there to cool until the next day. The miller took over then but Mickey often stayed to watch. To prepare the mill for grinding the water was diverted through a sluice-way to the millwheel. Mickey remembered that it was 'about thirty feet in diameter. They'd go up then and open the sluice-gate and the water'd start to come down; the man'd go down below then and start the wheel by pulling a chain on the wall; it was fastened to a wee hook. When he pulled the chain first the wheel would go round slowly; he'd give it another notch then and it'd go faster.'

Before grinding, the husk had to be separated from the kernel and this was done by pouring it down through a shuttle. The grain was small and heavy and was gathered underneath, while the husk, being light, went on and was separated into bags. The grain was ground then and channelled into bags which were, 'pegged into a nice wooden box.' The average yield was eight stone (one hundredweight) of meal to sixteen stone of corn. Grain grown on mountain land generally yielded less, while good land required only thirteen stone to produce eight stone of meal.

Mickey recalled: 'Ye mightn't have the full of two buckets of husks in the whole nine hundredweight of corn. The meal was lovely – me mother was living that time and I couldn't wait to get home to get the farl of oat bread made. The whole family used to like to get a handful of the oatmeal mixed through the flour bread too.'

The meal, when it was brought home from the mill, was stored in a dry place, usually near the fire, for the winter. In ancient Ireland it was kept in wooden chests. Now it was put into a large bag made of several smaller bags sewn together, capable of holding five or six hundredweight, which, interestingly, retained the wooden lid of earlier times!

Mickey remembers seeing it beside the hearth fire. 'We used to have a big stool with six legs on it and this bag was put up on it, a big wooden cover put over it and the meal was dry all the time with the heat of the fire, but ye had to attend on it for the whole winter. A house that there'd be nine weans in and an old man and woman – ye'd want to have two scones made every day [four farls to a scone or cake]. Flour bread was made too with a handful or two of the oatmeal through it. There was plenty of this made so that ye'd have a bit at night or to take to school with you the next day. There was a big pot of oat porridge made for eating before bedtime. What ye wouldn't eat at bedtime that night ye'd get in the morning – ye'd boil the milk in the ponjer, go to the pot and lift a few spoonfuls into the hot milk. It was that good ye could take it any time of the day if ye got it. Sometimes there'd be a pot of spuds boiled at night and a few fresh herring, if ye had them, grilled on the tongs. Ye'd have a feed of that before ye went to bed an' I'm telling ye there was no doctor or sleeping pill as good as it anyway!'

> Packaged, pre-cooked flakes have left
> A land of that old mill bereft.

The ghosts that were so local coloured
Hiding behind bags of pollard
Have gone from those empty walls.
The weir still curves its waterfalls
But lets them drop in the tailrace
No longer wildly chivalrous.

Patrick Kavanagh
from 'Requiem for a Mill'

The staple food of the great mass of Irish people in former times was porridge or stirabout, in the Brehon Laws called *gruss*. Gruel was called *menadach*. For the poorer classes stirabout was made with water or buttermilk and eaten with sour milk or salt butter – although butter was a luxury not often available. The wealthy made porridge with new milk; if it were sheep's milk so much the better as this was considered a delicacy. The cooked meal was flavoured with honey, butter or new milk.

Mass production dulls the senses. Children reaching for a box of cereal today have no vision of the bountiful blend of field, crop and labour which fills their bowl. They are deprived of touch, sound and smell. The whole event lacks the flavour and colour described by Mickey that was so much an integral part of the life experience of his generation. Pouring cornflakes from a cardboard box carried home in a plastic bag is all our children will remember.

Like the blacksmith forges, most of the old mills stand ruined and forlorn now, where they stand at all. A few have been re-constructed as tourist attractions:

They took away the water-wheel,
Scrap-ironed all the corn-mill;

The water now cascades with no
Audience pacing to and fro
Taking in with casual glance
Experience.

Patrick Kavanagh
from 'Requiem for a Mill'

Formerly there were numerous mills in the Irish countryside. For those seeking further information, the Strafford Survey of 1632, the Ordnance Survey of 1836 or the Griffiths Valuation of 1858 are revealing sources.

Henry Viscount Palmerston, prime minister of England (1855–8; 1859–65), was the wealthiest landlord in north Sligo in the last century.[28] An absentee, he caused a four-storey corn store and drying kiln to be erected in Mullaghmore in 1829 at a cost of £340 on a site now occupied by the Beach Hotel.[29] His plan was to use Mullaghmore harbour as an export centre for grain bought in from surrounding districts. By 1841 his agent, a Mr James Walker of Rathcarrick, was having trouble convincing the farmers to do business with him. They felt they were getting a better deal if they ground their corn into meal. A generous offer of £1 per twenty-four-stone sack failed to entice new customers.

Poitín-making, which was widespread at the time, may have proved an inducement to support home industry as well. It sold for seven to eight shillings a gallon. As eight gallons of whiskey could be made from twenty-four stone of grain it could be made to yield a profit of £3/10.

A garrison of forty-six revenue police stationed at Grange, County Sligo, barracks were kept busy tracking down the illegal whiskey distillers. They were largely responsible for forty-two people being imprisoned for the offence in Sligo Jail in 1835. These numbers give us some idea of the extent of the trade.

With mills sited within reasonable distance at Ballintrillick, Bunduff, Grange, Creevy and Grellagh, farmers were spoiled for choice. Even Inishmurray Island had a horizontal mill, at Fál an Mhuilinn, but it had probably fallen into disuse by this time.

Efforts to draw Robert Culbertson, owner of the prosperous Collooney Mills, into the Mullaghmore venture failed as he judged it too risky a proposition. Walker of Rathcarrick continued in his exertions to find a franchisee on Palmerston's behalf without success but records show that the store remained empty in 1846. In 1858 Griffith's Valuation records the Mullaghmore 'House, Corn-stores and offices' as unoccupied, thus bringing to an end the prospect of yet another export venture for Palmerston's new harbour.

The most comprehensive milling enterprise anywhere in Ireland was owned by Culbertson, mentioned above, at Ballisodare, County Sligo. In 1846 he paid ten pounds per year for use of the site to Cooper of Markree Castle. It was a shrewd investment as his annual turnover was shortly to be numbered in the thousands of pounds.

This extensive operation had its modest origins in the seventh century when it was established as part of a monastic settlement by St Fechin[30]. Following the explosion in the mill on St Martin's Day, 1856, Culbertson fell into poor health which resulted in his death. Messrs Middleton and Pollexfen took over the operation of the mill in 1862. This management continued until 1883 when the mills were acquired by Messrs W. & G.T. Pollexfen & Company. The Pollexfen family was arguably the most notable to have been associated with the Ballisodare operation, if only by virtue of the fact that it was Susan Mary Pollexfen Yeats who gave birth to the famous poet and playwright W. B. Yeats and his painter brother Jack.[31]

Ownership by the Pollexfen company continued until they too passed into history with the sale of the plant in 1974 to Odlums Ltd. Fifteen years later, in 1989, the mill closed forever, thus bringing to an end an era and an industry which had been in operation in one form or another in the same location for nigh on thirteen hundred years. Only fragments now remain to show that a mill ever existed there. So too have vanished many of the immutable certainties in our generation, a period that has seen unprecedented changes in Ireland, and on our planet, in the last half of the twentieth century.

Regarding diet, an English visitor, Arthur Young, who stayed at Markree Castle during his tour of Ireland in 1776, noted that the food of the poor people was pretty much as Mickey had described it 200 years later: 'potatoes, milk and herrings, with oaten bread in summer. All keep cows, not pigs, and but a few poultry. They have an absolute bellyful of potatoes and the children eat them as plentiful as they like.' Paying a penny a pound for oatmeal, bread made from this was preferred to either potatoes or wheat bread when they could afford it. Everyone kept a plot of cabbage.

Oaten bread made good teeth and, where this was commonly used, toothache was practically unheard of. Anyone who has seen skeletons like those uncovered from Iron Age sites such as that in Knoxpark, Sligo (see photograph), will need no convincing of the benefits of a sugar-free diet when they see the strong white teeth still intact in the skull after almost 2,000 years. Examination shows that the rough diet and grit particles released from the action of the quern stone, however, had the drawback of accelerating wear on the grinding surfaces of the teeth.

William Duffy of Redbrae, County Leitrim was born in 1863.

Speaking in 1945 he recalled that in his young days there was 'no value left on milk and butter; they were very plentiful and cheap on the market.' Butter sold for twopence or threepence a pound then. 'There was as much butter eaten as bread, as a dry oatcake was supposed to be severe on the insides. You could hear the men chewing oatcake a hundred yards away. There would be dust flying out of the eater's mouth. The old people would say, "Soften your bit", meaning to use more butter or milk.' There was no toothache or bellyache then he claimed. He recalled digging graves when neighbours died and finding bones that demonstrated how strong the old people were, from their size and strength. 'Their teeth were sound and even too,' he said. 'Very big and as white as ivory even though buried thirty years.'

Oatcake was not leavened, nor was it baked in an oven over an open fire in the fashion of soda bread. The ingredients were nothing more than oatmeal with salt added as flavouring. Water was mixed in hot so as to make a paste of the mixture. When ready, the dough was rolled out and left in a slanting position on a stand or bread-iron in front of the fire to harden or cook. This stand was called a griddle in Sligo. In Munster it meant a flat iron about eighteen inches in diameter that was hung over the fire. The hardening stand for placing in front of the fire was made by a blacksmith, usually horseshoe shaped and about a foot to sixteen inches high. It had a hinged piece in the back that allowed it to stand upright. Sometimes the thrifty housewife propped a pot lid in front of the fire and left the oatcake on it. The finished bread was especially favoured on long journeys and in former times accompanied many emigrants on their arduous voyage to America.

Charles McGlinchey in his book, *The Last of the Name*, described the preparation on the Inishowen peninsula for the long ocean passage on sailing ships around the year 1850: 'The vessel had provision of some kind on board but everyone took a supply of oaten bread as well with them. The whole townland would be baking and hardening oaten bread for whoever was going away. They were baking for a fortnight beforehand. The bread would be hardened two or three times until you could walk on it. All the bread was packed in a small barrel that the coopers made for the purpose, and everyone going to America had his barrel.'

Poitín and potatoes, oatmeal cakes and porridge, salt fish and fresh milk: this was all good plain fare, highly nutritious and vital to sustain people at a time when a hard physical existence was a way of life. In the late 1930s and early 1940s transportation of goods was by ass and cart or horse and cart. Asses and creels were still in common use for many jobs such as putting up wrack at the seashore or transferring turf from the turfbank, where it was dried and saved, to the road. Not many had bicycles and those who didn't used 'shank's mare' for transport (walking). Mickey worked as a labourer on the roads in Glenties, County Donegal. He walked thirteen miles from his home in Selacis, carrying a spade on his shoulder, for work that started at 9 o'clock. His pay was thirty shillings for five and a half days and 'glad to get it'. Work of any kind was eagerly sought after. Much of this employment had to do with breaking stones for road paving.

Up to the first half of the twentieth century rock crushers were unknown. Stones for road surfacing were broken by hand with a small hammer – methods unchanged since the stone age or Roman times.

In the 1950s I remember seeing heaps of stone, crystalled white, thick-drifted with frost, piled at intervals along the roadside. My father, along with several of his neighbours, sat on little bags padded with hay on top of the cairns, each one on his own pile. Slave-chained to their burden like vassals to the oars of a Roman galley, they sat stoically, hour upon freezing hour, breaking the stones one by one with small hammers. This unusual sight, lit by a bright, cold winter sun, captured my imagination: strong men pitted against the elements pounding out a meagre existence by their own raw energy. I could not have been more than eight years old but the sight is etched forever in my mind.

In this brave new millennium, surrounded by a superfluity of comfort, it almost impossible to comprehend that, such a short time ago, work practices were so primitive and men endured such hardship. Road workers were paid three shillings (fifteen pence in today's money) for every ton of stones broken into lumps about 'half the size of an egg'. The quantity of stones broken in any one day would largely depend on the hardness of the rock. If a dense hard stone fell to the lot of a worker he would find it difficult to complete even one ton in a day. On a good day it might be possible to earn more than the three shillings and eightpence which was the County Council flat rate at the time. Dinnertime was from twelve to one o'clock; from one o'clock to quitting time at six in the evening there were no rest periods, no breaks of any kind. Men who did this work recalled being 'weak with the hunger' by the time they got home, which, if they lived some distance away, could be at seven o'clock in the evening.

The toil was heavy and continuous. Worker's rights were non-existent. Numerous accounts are related of brutish gangers, little men inflated with their own importance who used any excuse to exert their authority and have men sacked. Bernie Kelly told me of one such incident:

The ground was white with frost as far as ye could see. It never let up from freezing all day, our hands and feet were perished, like blocks of ice. There was no such thing as wearing gloves then. A couple of the men got up to warm their feet, stamping them on the ground. O——— the ganger, was down across the fields. When he saw what we were at, he came up and sacked two men there and then, told them to go home. One of the men, poor Dan McCannon, was crying for fear of what the brother Pakie would say when he got home – he was afraid he'd be knocked out of the dole and everything.

Other men told of erecting a rough shelter of twigs and *seisg* for protection against a bitter east wind. The ganger came and without saying a word set the rough shelter alight. 'What d'ye think ye're at!' he said. 'D'ye want me to lose my job if the boss comes up here and sees ye at this?' Remembering it, Bernie said, 'That was for a lousy twenty-four shillings a week!'

In the quarries where the stones for the road were dug out it was no easier. Bertie Monds of Drumcliffe remembered:

Josie Flynn's father from Cliffoney sitting on a wee bag of hay every day for five years above in that quarry turning the 'jumper'. A jumper was a heavy chisel-ended iron bar used for drilling holes in the rock that held the dynamite for blasting. 'He held it with an oul' bit of a bag or a cloth an' a wee bit of it above his hand. There was two men with two sledgehammers hitting the bar. When one hit the other lifted – you hit, I lifted – and so on every

other stroke and he kept turning the jumper for
each man. I seen Jack Cullen and one of the
O'Connors in Gleann, wee Francie Connor, sledging the jumper and Flynn there turning it. They
were able to go down two foot and a half in the
day through the solid blue rock. They never
missed a stroke. The men was that used of sledging,
they could sledge it without even looking at it.
Pure slavery, that's what it was!

Oaten bread was taken to mountain, bog and fair too. When
the fair was held in a distant town, farmers 'had to leave home
very early in the morning, five or six o'clock. Maybe stand at
a fair all day long then an' ye mightn't sell or have anything
to eat an' walk back home again in the evening. If ye had a bit
of oatcake in your pocket, there was great support in it.' Mickey
McGroarty went on to tell me about other uses to which
oatmeal cake was put:

> People going away on a journey out the mountains
> to look about sheep always put a bit of oatbread
> in their pocket – ye'd never get hungry when ye'd
> have it. The reason people took it in their pocket
> was this: ye could be up in the middle of them hills
> an' suddenly ye could drop down from hunger with
> a 'féar gortach', a weakness ye got, right all of a
> sudden.
>
> This is how the féar gortach came about: in the
> old days the houses were way far apart and the
> burial grounds was even further away. If a neighbour
> died 'way back in one o' them mountain districts
> where they were living, they were carried through

the fields, as often there was no road. A crew of
fifteen or sixteen men took turns carrying the
coffin, four men carrying at any one time. When
they got tired they would leave it down to rest and
maybe take a smoke before they went on another
bit. In the famine times they couldn't keep up,
there was that many dying. Wherever they left the
coffin down, from that time on it was known as
a stray sod so when you stepped on this you got
the *féar gortach*. If ye stepped on it at night ye were
put astray, too. It was given to that! If ye had a
bit of oatbread in yer pocket ye'd be safe.'

The *féar gortach* or 'hungry grass' was well known, not only in
Donegal, but all over Ireland. It looks no different from any
other grass but is believed to grow on the spot where some poor
person died on the *Cosán na Marbh* or Path of Death during the
Great Famine. Mickey explained that the coffins were carried
long distances across the fields for burial. Every spot where the
coffin was left down to allow the bearers to rest had, from that
time forward, the power to afflict anyone stepping on it with
the pangs of famine.

There are very few who, having worked at turf or hay, on
bog or field, have not experienced the sudden, unreasonable
craving of hunger that Mickey describes. Some attribute this to
a sudden drop in blood-sugar levels. Doctors dispute this but
cannot assign the condition to any known medical factor. If this
is so, then Mickey's explanation is as good as any. Whatever the
reason, many who feared its effects carried a bit of oat bread or
such in their pocket knowing from experience that any small
amount of food helped to relieve the condition.

My first experience with the *féar gortach* was on Cloonerco bog one spring while 'capping' and spreading turf. My father cut the dark sods with the turf-spade and slung them towards me in a steady rhythm: cut, lift, swing, catch, throw. Suddenly, and for no apparent reason, my legs became weak and shaky; a feeling of great hunger overwhelmed me. It was early in the day but I suggested to my father that it was time to light the fire and put the kettle on. He was always the final arbiter of the work and meal schedule, and fair – by his standards. 'What's wrong with ye? Sure we only got here,' he said, raising his eyebrows as he scanned an anxious face. Knowing that dinner and tea were my favourite times of day, any day, he was suspicious. 'That's the *féar gortach* ye have,' he said finally when I explained to him the ravenous hunger that had come over me. 'When ye step on the hungry grass, that's what happens. It's a bit early for eating yet, but go ahead.'

A resident of nearby Ballintrillick explained to me another method of overcoming the effects of 'hungry grass': 'If ye stoop down an' get a bit of a sally bush, ye know the *raideog*, the wee low sally bush that grows in them places, put it in yer mouth – the fact that ye chewed or let down the saliva would cure the *féar gortach*.'

Some attributed the sudden hunger to the power of the fairies. Seumas MacManus in his book, *Bold Blades of Donegal*, explained it as a bewitched grass that was once sat upon by greedy people who ate their fill without leaving a bit for the 'Gentle People'. In olden times the fairies demanded their share of whatever was going, let it be milk, or *poitín*, or in this case food.

Grains like those mentioned previously – oats, rye, wheat and barley – had been the customary food in Ireland for many centuries. On the defeat of the Desmonds in Munster Sir Walter

Raleigh was given 42,000 acres of land belonging to the native Irish in addition to a monastery and the Priory of the Black Fathers near Youghal. The terms were the same as those given to other planters: that he people his estates with 'well affected Englishmen'. His claim to a place in Irish history is that he introduced the potato to our shores in 1586, although it wasn't until a century and a half after his death that it became generally available. Sir Richard Blackwell, seeing the desperate condition of a countryside ravaged by famine in the middle of the eighteenth century, urged the cultivation of the potato to relieve the distress. His grandfather had been given some of the tubers by Raleigh. Since that time they had been grown in his private garden for the family table.[32] It is ironic then that the potato, which came from a rich man's table, soon became the main support of the Irish natives 'of the Popish parts of the kingdom, who had to take themselves to the despised wastes and barren mountains.'

By 1816 the potato had become so popular that Reverend James Nelligan, rector of Kilmactigue, County Sligo, remarked that, 'Potatoes furnish the standing dish three times a day throughout the year, except that in summer, when they begin to grow scarce, those who can save a part of their oats from the landlord's rent, make a little meal which they use either for bread or to make gruel, which they take with their potatoes.'

Things had changed so much by the middle of the nineteenth century, at the height of the Great Famine, that Alexander Somerville, reporting in the *Manchester Examiner*, wrote that, 'the people [Irish] never make use of wheaten flour except when they cannot get oatmeal. The poor man uses oatmeal for meat and drink, when reasonable in price. He has thin oat gruel and oaten bread, and he takes it out with him to the fields.'[33] The exportation of oats from Ireland during the famine years contributed in great measure to that awful calamity. Somerville reported in relation to the grain trade from Ireland that it 'was the case in 1846 and the year before; and even in 1847, oats have been sent from Westport to England, where they are in demand, at high prices, for horses; and Indian corn coming to Westport, has met them in other ships.' In an editorial written at the height of the Famine the *Sligo Champion* concurred, declaring that, 'the landlords must get their rent and their arrears of rent, so to meet their demands the grain must be sold – the grain will be sent out of Ireland to feed English horses . . . The tenant will have to make out provision for his family without money, without grain or the potato to fall back upon.'

Sympathetic views towards the Irish were not popular among the ruling classes of the time. They earned instant reprisal. Somerville's honesty brought poverty, obscurity and social ostracism when he continued to report boldly to the *Manchester Examiner* what he saw in Ireland during the Famine years. An Englishman himself, and born into deep poverty, he was finally forced to emigrate and died in destitution in a squalid boarding house in Toronto in 1885.

Prior to the introduction of the potato, reliance on grain and dairy products had remained unchanged down the centuries. Various kinds of meal or flour were baked into cakes and loaves. Flour was usually mixed with water to make dough but bread made of flour and milk was also much in use. Honey or the roe of a salmon was often mixed in with the dough as a delicacy.[34]

Old ways served successive generations well. In the twentieth century, people who had their fill of potatoes still valued the oat grain. From a vantage point of ninety-eight years of age, Maggie McGowan of Teesan, County Sligo, spoke with authority on many subjects. There was no 'humming and hawing'. Born in 1898, she spanned an era of great change in Irish life. Maggie was articulate, eloquent and persuasive. A big woman, when she conversed she leaned forward in her chair, fixed the listener with a steady blue-eyed gaze and stated her views spontaneously and forcefully. Her words exemplified her existence. A way of living only recently lost was conjured up in vivid colour as she painted realistic pictures of life in north Sligo in her time:

> We used to fill an oven – it wasn't a saucepan mind you, an oven – with oatmeal and Indian meal mixed through it. That was put down on the fire to boil; when it was boiled you'd put it out on a coal at the side of the fire and let it simmer away, mixing it now and again with a wee wooden pot-stick. When that was ready ye'd leave it out one side to cool. When it was cool ye'd go out to the creamery can with the ponjer, stir up the milk so as ye wouldn't take all the cream off it, take a ponjer of that sweet milk in with you and sit down and eat a feed of that porridge. Ye'd go into bed then and sleep as sound as a bell.
>
> The next morning there was a ponjer of milk put in on top of what was left over of the porridge from the night before and it was put on the fire to heat. That was divided around and put out on the long bowls they used to have long ago. Ye'd have a mug of tea and an egg or two after that. There never was a loaf bought in my day. Two good big duck eggs and soda bread. I often seen the men, the first thing they did when they got up in the morning was to break two raw eggs into a cup, throw a drop of milk in on that and swallow it down. They'd lift a ton weight after it! Ye had

> three good solid meals a day and nothing in
> between; they're eating all the time now but its
> not doing them half the good as the food they had
> long ago!'

She dismissed the modern woman's concern with diet: 'The bloody straps o' women that's going now takin' black tay! They wouldn't take a drop of milk in it in case it'd fatten them. Keep fit? Keep fit my eye! If they were out working hard alongside their men like the women long 'go, washing and scrubbing clothes in a tub and feeding calves, they'd be fit!'

The meals of my young days consisted of a simple diet of potatoes, milk, bread and fish as described by Maggie. Having our fill to eat was good enough. Luxuries such as raisin bread were seldom seen and all the more appreciated for that. Today, having much, we want more – and more. I can see the stone floored, paraffin-lit kitchen in our own home and a sturdy deal table where we ate the plainest of food. If I wish to recall the meal that delighted me most, I remember a simple plate of *brúitín* laced with scallions, with yellow rivulets flowing down the side from a generous gob of home-made butter melting in the middle. No haute cuisine can compare. 'Hunger is the best sauce,' said Don Quixote, a character invented by the sixteenth-century Spanish writer Cervantes!

When spuds were eaten for the main midday meal, and no 'kitchen' available, 'colcannon' or 'bruiteen' was a favourite. Potatoes were peeled, boiled, mixed with scallions and milk and mashed to a creamy texture. When served, a hole was made in the middle and filled with a spoonful of butter which quickly melted to a golden pool. Anyone having this meal on returning from school, fair, or bog will treasure the memory among their great culinary experiences. The ubiquitous potato featured too in the making of boxty, stampy, and 'pratie' bread, which were made mostly at Hallowe'en or Christmas.

Fresh herrings and other seafoods loved by Mickey played a critical role as cheap and readily available nourishment into the first half of the twentieth century. The first people to settle in Ireland eight to nine thousand years ago, known as 'hunter-gatherers', chose to live close to rivers, lakes and sea where fish and marine life provided the essentials. Up to the pre-supermarket 1950s we still knew how to hunt and gather! 'If ye had nothing for the dinner ye'd go down to the sea, pick a good can of 'borneocs' (limpets),' Maggie told me, 'bring them up and boil them, or winkles, slabhac or crannac.'

Herring could be bought near Maggie's home at Cloonagh in the 1930s for threepence a dozen or a halfpenny each and eaten fresh or salted for the winter. The simple method of cooking here was identical to the method employed across the bay in County Donegal. 'Ye put the herring on the tongs on a coal to grill them and have them for your tea as well.' When Maggie was a child, no meat was eaten on Wednesdays, Fridays or Saturdays. 'Them fast days was kept as regular as ye go to Mass now; maybe the rest of the week ye hadn't it, but if ye had it ye ate it!'

Fish 'cadgers' plied the roads in horse- and ass-carts. If they didn't own a cart, ass and creels would have to do. 'Ye never know yer luck!' With a fair wind and good fortune it might just be possible to move up to an ass and cart next year! Haddock, cod, whiting, herring or mackerel which were landed at seaside harbours such as Mullaghmore or Raughley in County Sligo were sold in season; at other times cartloads of dried fish from Inishmurray Island were brought ashore at Streedagh and Cloonagh. 'Sometimes they brought them to the fair at Grange,' Johnny McGowan told me. 'They transported them from the shore with ass-carts and creels – beautiful codfish that length. Ye'd get enough for a couple of shillings would do the house for a whole week. That's what I was reared on – that's why I wouldn't eat fish now. I got that much of it!'

When the Inishmurray men had prepared the fish by splitting, gutting and washing them in sea water, they were spread along the shore or on the thatched roof at home to dry. Preservation was achieved by repeated dipping in the sea and drying, thereby impregnating the flesh with sea salt. When ready, the fish were transported by boat for sale on the mainland. Maggie recalled that, 'at the fair in Grange ye'd see nothing only a heap of pollack and ballan that height and that breadth (indicating four feet high by six feet wide), and ye'd see different men with six or seven heaps there and an old canvas sail or such under them. They'd be sold in no time and the people glad for to get them.'

Inishmurray *poitín* was not on public display but it was just as plentiful as the fish if you knew where to go. The quality of the illegal home-brewed whiskey made on this offshore island was legendary and it was always in great demand. The whole country knew where to find it, except the RIC and Gardaí!

In Donegal, all available varieties of fish, both fresh and dried, were relished too. Mickey McGroarty told me:

> The oul' men used to go down to Inver or Mountcharles. There was a family there the name of McMonagle; they used to go down to Killybegs and buy big haddock and ling; they used to take them home and cure and salt them in a special place they had outside. Coming up to Hallowe'en my grandfather might come home with four or five of them big fish in a bag across his back. They'd be hung up on the couples about the house till

they were properly cured. They'd last the whole year round. There'd be a pound or two cut every day, put into a tin that night and soaked in water until morning. This'd be put on in the morning and boiled and ye got a feed of that and a lock of good 'Kar Pinks', a bowl of good sweet milk and a pound of country butter. When you had that ate, ye could head off for any road, I'm tellin' ye, an' ye wouldn't be hungry anyway.

4

HUNGRY EYES SEE FAR

The sun is our lord and father,
Bright face at the gate of day,
Comfort of home, cattle and crop,
Lord of the morning, lord of the day.

Lifting our hearts
We sing his praise,
Dance in his healing rays.

Anonymous

Just as Christmas had its Advent so did Hallowe'en have a similar period of preparation. The ringing of the pawl on the cogs of the hayfloat heralded the coming of this great festival of the old religion. The sound was made by two sturdy men pulling on the handles that winched the ponderous trampcocks firmly on to the flat bed.

The hayfloat was a low-slung, wheeled, horse-drawn, timber-sheeted metal frame measuring roughly nine feet wide by twelve feet in length. A long slender drum, with a length of strong rope coiled around, was fixed to the front of the cart and attached to two long handles at either end. To operate, the carriage was tipped up and the rear end eased under the cock of hay. The ropes were then drawn from the drum backwards to encircle the hay and fastened there with a clamp. Two men, one on each handle, drew the rope onto the drum, thereby winching the haycock up onto the flat bed. This technique was a great advance from the previous labour-intensive method which required the trampcock to be loaded, forkful by forkful, onto the farm cart and then brought in to the rick or haggard.

The clarion peal of this hay-float had its season and, as dependable as the spring song of the cuckoo or the flight of the first swallow, it started early in September. As clear and distinct as the angelus bell its musical toll rang across the meadow fields, calling us, not to prayer, but to work. It seems to me now as I view it from afar, for adolescent boys it represented a rite of passage too. This was hard work – men's work.

My initiation began when I was seventeen. The unplanned absence of my father on other farm business brought an invitation to pull on one of the big handles. James Gallagher it was that drew our hay in with his horse and hayfloat team and it was from James the unexpected summons came. The sudden opportunity for promotion brought a hot rush of colour to my face. Could I measure up to the challenge? Would I be strong enough? Was I ready to cross this threshold into a man's world? Heart beating faster I accepted the call, gripped the big handle and pulled mightily. The haycock shivered and jerked a small bit up the sloping cart. Pull and draw – pull and draw – pull and draw; I tried to match James's practised rhythm. Eyes twinkling mischievously he looked across at me from under bushy brows. Observing my eagerness to prove worthy he held back a grin as he gauged my fitness and stamina for the job.

If the pull was not even on both handles the load veered to the side of the weaker pull, and sure enough, with each draw the unwieldy monster inched over to me. Failure was unthinkable and I stretched every muscle beyond endurance.

'Jasus,' James said, easing back a bit, 'but that Johnnie Casey is a great young fellow. He's the best hand at winching that I ever saw!'

Johnnie was the same age as me. Although never admitting it, we were rivals. We learned how to take on the more complicated liabilities of farm life at about the same time, like driving the ass-cart. That was a big responsibility.

Asses liked to do as little work as they could get away with. That made them difficult to manage. Their main purpose on the farm was pulling the cart through rutted fields or along miles of rough stony road. It was heavy work, especially if the cart was weighted with turf or a forty-gallon barrel of water or a full load of creamery cans. Asses were not as heedless as their appearance indicated. They were very good at gauging the ability of a driver and his determination, or lack of it, to exert control. Sensing a driver's inattention, they immediately took the opportunity to slow down.

If they looked overburdened and weary that might be the case, and then again it might not. They were good at faking. It was important to know the difference. They never trotted when they could get away with walking and they never walked when they could amble. And they never, ever, galloped – except when they tried to evade capture in the morning or when they sped down the pasture on regaining their freedom in the evening. During the working day the driver had to know when slow was reasonable and when it was not. Asses were very good at feigning naivety, pretending they didn't know what you wanted. When you pulled on the left rein they needed to know that you were prepared to use the ashplant if they didn't go left. You had to know how to get the best out of them without abusing them.

Refraining from the use of harsher methods, I pinched the

short hairs on our ass's backside from my perch on the crosstrees of the cart. It had an instant effect. It may have offended her dignity as a lady, or perhaps it stung, or both. Whatever it was, she didn't like it and expressed her annoyance by putting her ears back, her head down and kicking with her hind feet. When this didn't achieve the desired result we reached an under-standing; she broke into a trot, on which I stopped plucking and we moved happily down the road at a smart pace.

Just like humans they had their paranoias, idiosyncrasies and fears. A fair master made allowances for this. They could pull half-a-ton load up a hill without a bother, yet they could take fright at a bird or a piece of paper blowing in the wind. That is why they had to wear winkers. The designers of this piece of harness knew their frailties and crafted it so the animal could see only what they had to see and nothing more.

They could cross puddles of water for miles of road on the way to the bog without blinking an eye. When they got there a water-filled boghole seemed to contain the terrors of hell for them and neither persuasion nor intimidation could persuade them to go across.

It was important to recognise their foibles and limitations and treat them with the sympathy they deserved. There were men who beat them cruelly when they rebelled. Others tried to pull them where they refused to go. It was a tug-of-war that only an ass could win! The driver who was competent in his job simply turned the animal around and backed him across the offending area. If a donkey didn't see something, it didn't exist. If common sense didn't tell you that you couldn't make an ass do anything it didn't want to do, experience eventually did.

There was nothing to match the feeling when your father first trusted you to drive the ass and cart. It was another milestone on the road to adulthood, matched only by the sense of accomplishment when ass and driver worked well together. A great sense of freedom comes with the day when you can get the ass to canter along and your balance has reached the stage when you can stand up in the cart. There you are with one hand nonchalantly in your pocket, the other holding the reins, the breeze blowing through your hair and pedestrians admiring your skill and balance as you go by. No point in being so good if no one noticed. 'That Petie McGowan's son is making a fine young fella,' they might say as you sped by. 'He'll soon be a great help to his father.'

So Johnnie could winch a trampcock better than me, could he?

James's words to me were like a red rag to a bull. At that moment I hated him. Anger swelled and adrenalin flowed. 'The smug ungrateful bastard,' I thought. I was doing my best and it wasn't good enough. I didn't like James's smirk. 'Look at the gob on the ignorant fucker,' I thought again. I didn't even want to be there. It wasn't my idea; I had better things to do.

With strength born of rage I pulled mightily. I'd show him. A few more desperate pulls and the monster was centred again. I could do it. I could bloody do it! Reassured now and confidence restored I pulled in unison with James until, lungs bursting and arms strained beyond endurance, the load tilted across the point of balance. Tipping forward it levelled off, the latch snapped into place with a gratifying mechanical click and the job was done.

'Ye'll do all right,' James said with a smile and winked. His scant acknowledgement was praise enough.

'Geddup there.' A rattle of harness, a gentle tap of the whip on the rump of the big brown draught horse and James was off down the field with his team. Aching, punished arms hung by my side as I watched James pull on the reins, driving the horse and float towards the garden where the cocks would soon be built into a fine rick. I looked at the white ring that marked the spot where the trampcock had stood a few minutes before. It would fade in time but I could not have known then that this day's experience would leave an indelible mark on my soul.

The bishop's pat on the cheek at Confirmation some years before was a symbolic thing. The pomp, ceremony, incense and vestments satisfied adult needs. It was hardly enough to turn a boy into a man. Looking back on that day in the meadowfield, I see it now as the real coming of age, a true Confirmation. A boy walked into that field; a man walked out. The broad, open expanses of meadow were nature's church. A Druid writ ran there. Providence was in the blue-hazed mountains that rimmed the fields around. It was in the blue-vaulted sky that brought forth the lifegiving sunshine and rain; it was in the bounty of the cropped fields. The lanes were the aisles of our cathedral, the firmament its ceiling, the sweet smell of fresh hay our incense. What need an earthly roof between the Lord and his worshippers?

High in the vaulted blue, choirs of skylarks sang a breathless, exultant chorus. Or was it angels? There was no bird: a carolling and singing, ascending and ringing. An anonymous tenth-century hermit, inspired by the melody, wrote:

> The singing birds of Heaven greet
> The Virgin's son with music sweet;
> One whisper of their song would heal
> The agonies damned spirits feel.

We are sprung from the clay of these fields. From this earth we draw power. In these ageless acres time and place blend and flow This very soil, these vital elements that made our bones, made too the warrior Fianna. They are not far from us. Their spirits walk with us still. They are us. We are they.

> *While Fionn was living and the Fianna,*
> *Dearer to them was the mountain than the church:*
> *Sweet they thought the song of blackbirds,*
> *Tinklings of bells they did not think sweet.*[35]

Two thousand years of Christianity is but a thin veneer. We visited an unseen and stern God in Church on Sundays but Druid and God were with us in nature's temple for the other six days – and we knew them well.

The haycocks all gathered in, October was when the ricks were made. Ricks were the huge loaf-shaped stacks of hay that held the winter's supply of fodder for the farm stock. When possible they were situated near the byres or cattle houses.

Before the advent of the hay-float, building the ricks was a laborious process. Hay was drawn by horse or ass and cart on the same day that the rick was made. On poorer farms where there was no cart, men laid the hay into rope slings. These huge wads, weighing as much as two hundredweight, were carried on their backs.

Trampcocks that had been meticulously sculpted were unroped in the field. The hay was peeled off in huge wads by one or two men on the ground and forked on to the flat bed of the cart to another man who built it layer by layer to a height of eight or ten feet. Wooden frames called 'haysavers' had been installed before setting out. Dropped into channels at the side of the cart these frames were rectangular in shape and just big enough to keep the hay clear of the iron-shod wheels that extended above the flat surface of the cart where the hay was piled. Building hay, whether on the cart or on the actual rick itself, required great skill.

Armfuls of hay were laid methodically along the front, back and sides of the cart. As this was being done each successive layer was 'tied' on the inside. Tying meant securing the perimeter with successive overlapping layers which bound the ouside to the centre. The corners required special attention, as any ineptitude in building there would cause the load to slide and collapse. If the hay was not 'let out' at the right time or the tying inexpertly done, the process had to be repeated. An expert builder could let the hay out over the horse to the 'hams' (horse's shoulders) and build the load to between ten and fifteen feet high. When complete, the burden was secured by means of a rope on either side tied from the back of the cart to the front shafts.

Adventures and misadventures during the course of a day's work made good telling later. Michael Duffy or 'Me-man's son', as he was better known, loved telling about the time his neighbours did a deal over a load of hay. Michael had acquired his familiar name from his father who got the nickname because of his habit of prefixing or ending a statement with 'me man' for emphasis. In an area where there were a number of Duffy surnames, the title 'Me-mans' was sufficient to immediately identify the family in question.

The transaction involving the removal of the hay to the buyer turned out to be no simple matter and created great amusement – to everyone but the two men concerned. Trying to control his merriment, Michael's voice rose to a soprano pitch before breaking down in great wheezy gales of laughter as he told the story. It was a cautionary tale, too, that illustrated all that might go wrong if a load of hay was not built correctly:

'Thady Leonard bought a load of hay from Big Dan Gallagher,'

Michael would begin, 'an' me an' James Rourke went down to give them a hand. Gallagher says to me, "We'll build it on Thady's cart." Thady had a horse called Bob, an' man, he thought a lot about that horse.

'Anyway, as I was building the cart of hay Thady Leonard'd say to me "Let it out, let it out, let it out." He wanted to get as much as he could for his money. Gallagher'd say to me, "Keep it in, keep it in or ye'll bring the gate with ye." I let it out an' out an' out anyway, an' it was nearly as big as Classiebawn before we were through. When we were finished we went for the gate an' what d'ye think but we got shtuck between the two posts! Thady had the horse by the head. "C'mon Bob," he'd shout. "C'mon Bob, ye'll bring it, ye'll bring it." There we were, pulling and pushing and after a while we could get neither in or out. "The curse o' God on you an' Bob," says Gallagher. At that the horse gave one plunge, took the posts with him, smashed the gate; all was smashed. Some of the stones rowlt down the hill and into the sea and that's a good quarter of a mile. Ye mightn't believe that, but ye can still see them down there below in Claddagh Geall if ye want to look!

'Big Dan was fit to be tied. The posts was gone, the gate was in bits. "Will ye give me a hand," says he to me, "to fix the gap." There was a big quoin of a stone in it anyway an' it was yon length – if it was a pound it was a hundredweight – an' Dan says, "Gimme a lift with this." I gave him a lift with it an' didn't it come down on his finger, smashed his finger, took the nail away clare an clane an' he started bleeding like a bull calf. The wife was going round in circles: "Get the doctor for poor Dan Gallagher, get the doctor quick," she'd roar. "The curse of God on you an' Bob an' the hay an' never come anear this house again," she said to Thady Leonard. I was lucky to get away with me life that day and it was months before I'd chance to even pass the house again in case I'd be murdered!'

When the cartload of hay arrived in the garden, on the day a rick was going to be made, men unroped the load and forked it up to the builders. The rick itself was the end product of a long summer of hard work often dogged by frustration and repetition when the weather broke. With so much toil invested, the final job required much planning and preparation. Some weeks prior to the big day, the chief engineer, my father, stepped the garden toe to heel, his strong leather boots measuring the outline in rectangular form. His experienced eye, practised over many years of rick-building, had already surveyed the number and size of trampcocks in the field. This determined the size of the base. There were no mathematical formulas to guide him. His instincts were all he needed.

When the layout and measuring was completed, next came the call to me to 'Go out to the "treilya" and cut a lok o' bushes.' I had accompanied him for years on this mission so I knew what was needed. The ass was rounded up and harnessed to the cart. Several loads of alder bushes were cut at a wet wooded area outside the village where they grew in profusion and drawn to the garden.

These were placed in a shallow layer on the ground inside the perimeter now outlined by logs and stones. This preparation was required to insulate the hay at the foundation of the rick from the damp ground underneath.

Making the ropes or *súgán* was the next step in preparation for the big event. The shorter days and longer nights of autumn left more free time. This was when 'ramblin' (visits to neighbour's houses to chat, swap stories or play cards) started. These pleasant evenings were subject to interruptions. At least two big clews of straw ropes had to be made prior to commencing the rick. The summons to start twisting always came as a surprise to me but it was carefully planned by my father who, for some perverse reason, regarded rope-making as a nocturnal occupation. Attendance was compulsory! Without any consultation with me he picked calm, clear, moonlit nights for the job.

These ropes, made from tough oaten straw, were used to tie down the rick and secure it from the worst that wind and weather might do. The straw was specially planted in the springtime with rope-making in mind. It had to be thin and pliable but tough and weather-resistant too, to withstand exposure to the rigours of Atlantic winters. The desired result was achieved by sowing the straw more thickly in a selected corner of the field. Being thus sown the finished product grew fine and slender while retaining the toughness of grain sown more thinly.

On the chosen evening the sheaves were brought in and the ends beaten thoroughly with a heavy wooden mallet to make the straw even more flexible. Thus prepared it was thrown at the back door where my father squatted on a low stool ready to commence operations. His agile fingers plied and fed the straw to my trawhooks or twister. He teased and coaxed the yellow skeins with expert hands as I twisted it round and round into a tough, slender *súgán*, slowly inching my way backwards out of the kitchen.

This was not a job that challenged the mind or mechanical abilities of the twister. In fact it was one of the most boring jobs on earth. The only qualification required was infinite patience. While my father might gain some satisfaction from compliments paid him by visitors on his abilities as a rope-maker, there were no such credits for the twister who, although essential to the operation, required no skill. As the rope lengthened I moved backwards through the friendly pool of yellow light that fell from the front door, out the street and on into the darkness beyond.

'Great night for the job,' neighbours might say as they came and went to the house. 'Begod, there's no one can make ropes with yer father. He can turn his hands to anything.'

And indeed he could. It took years of practise to turn out a product of uniform thickness. A good rope-maker made a product that was strong, but slender too. A thick rope made an unnecessarily bulky, heavy clew; too thin and it broke under pressure. Three-quarters of an inch in diameter was about right.

Twisting was a painstakingly slow procedure as the rope gradually lengthened across the road. Attempts at increasing the pace did no good. All it achieved was to annoy my father who just got irritated and barked at me to slow down. Feeding the straw to the twist could not be hurried; it was a careful and deliberate process.

Dowdicans' house was about thirty yards away on the other side of the road. Turning my head to look into their house to see if Kattie was sitting by the fire or if Martin, her son, might be coming in the back door from milking the cows with two frothing cans, helped pass the time. Kattie didn't mind but my father disapproved of this inquisitiveness; I was supposed to jerk on the rope before I got to the house as a signal that it was time to coil the freshly made length on to the clew. Sometimes on a mild night when Dowdicans' front door was open and my father not paying attention, the monotony was broken by stealing a bit further and twisting the rope longer and longer, through their kitchen and on out through the back door. 'Why didn't ye tell me ye were gone that far?' he would growl then, but sometimes there was a hint of humour in his face, perhaps remembering his own impetuous younger days. I don't know. He never told me.

I had mixed feelings about Martin. The milk of human kindness flowed but thinly in his veins. With no radio in our home visiting a house that had one was a great thrill. My trips to their kitchen to listen to Perry Mason were discouraged by him and I felt uncomfortable under his critical gaze.

Once, in a fit of pique, he put the Philips wireless out of adjustment, claiming that the 'trickel' was broken. *The Perry Mason Hour* was one of those cliffhanger series that left the listener wondering at the end of each episode how the hero was ever going to survive; I was devastated at the news of the malfunctioning 'trickel'. It was a matter of life and death to find out if Perry was going to escape from the criminal in his clever way or if this was the time that crime was going to triumph over good. I had to know. Mind whirling, I sat there desperately seeking a solution. Opportunity came when Martin gathered up the tin cans and went out to the byre to milk the cows. I looked at Kattie in despair. No, she didn't mind if I fiddled with the knobs, she said. I did, and soon Perry Mason's voice resonated through the kitchen. After a while Martin came in from his work and I told him with some satisfaction and pride of how I had fixed the 'trickel'. Giving me a sour look, his reaction of annoyance rather than delight at the good news was puzzling. Kattie said nothing. She looked at us with merry eyes and laughed, all her folds shaking, and I didn't understand what was so funny for a long time.

During the long, monotonous, repetitive journeys between our front door and Dowdicans' I twisted interminably around, and around and around. A study of the starry sky overhead was one way of relieving the tedium. There wasn't much else to do. The incandescent complexity of the Milky Way, Orion Nebula, the Plough. As the years went by, I got to know them well. My mind grappled unsuccessfully, as it still does, with the vastness of space. From the enveloping inky blackness I looked up at the vast never-ending cascade of shimmering light.

Could it be true that some of these bright stars in the heavens, giant supernovas, had ceased to exist long years before? Only their twinkling images that had been travelling at the speed of light, an unbelievable 186,000 miles per second, now reached us over vast expanses of empty space, hundreds of years after the star's destruction in a cataclysmic inferno. We could see them and yet they had long ago exploded into atoms! Some had flared into brilliance, lived and died long before the earth came into being. And, incredibly, we were there, in a different shape – ethereal particles floating in the cosmos. We are formed of the very stardust, molecules and atoms reconstructed by cosmic evolution from the gas and residue of supernovae. And chance assembled us here. An accident almost. A different drifting of atoms and we might have been one of those bright stars in other, grimmer skies. And the earth too will vanish. It will self-destruct in a catastrophic Armageddon some millions of years from now; burned to a crisp or swallowed by a self-destroying sun.

Other stars and galaxies will come into being, formed of our atoms, and they will know nothing of us, our civilisation, or a place once called Earth! And will other humans grow there formed in the image and likeness of God the Creator? We in Him and Him in us? Or are we creatures in His dream? Is nothing real? Is it true that for space-travellers time stops as they approach the speed of light and keeps them forever young? Could it be possible that our sun and solar system is only an insignificant entity in an obscure corner of that myriad, luminescent mass of stars and light, a galaxy we call the Milky Way?[36] The Milky Way itself lost and tiny in the immensity of never-ending space. Surely God created us and everything else in the universe is secondary to our existence. Black holes? Invisible objects in space weighing ten times more than the sun and collapsed into a volume the size of a football field; their gravity so immense that not even light can escape their pull. Enter there if you can, if you dare, and emerge somewhere else in space, or someplace else in time. Is this the answer to the enigma of space travel by 'warp factors' like those used by the captain of the Starship Enterprise? 'Warp factor 3, Mr Spock, if you please.' No fool him! Could black holes serve as time machines carrying us to the distant past or the unknown future? If I could travel backwards in time and kill my father or mother would I be born anyway? If there was life out there on other planets among the myriad stars were there other young people up there on one of those pinpoints of light twisting ropes too? Parallel universes? Red giants? White dwarfs? Novae? Supernovae? Neutron stars? Neutrinos? Quarks and quasars and . . .

'Slow down on that bloody rope,' my father shouted in exasperation. His concern with earthbound things was not going to let my preoccupation with the heavens interfere with his reputation as a rope-maker. A well-made rope would serve us better in a winter storm than any starry-eyed contemplation of the mysteries of the night sky.

Northwards, in the direction of the vast Arctic wastes, barrages of luminescence shot skywards. Travelling at the speed of light, long incandescent curtains of fire painted a majestic, rapidly shifting backdrop to the canopy of stars. Shimmering draperies of pulsing brightness swept the contours of the abyss.

Kerry people called them the 'Borey Dancers'. We called the display the Northern Lights. The older people of Mullaghmore sometimes watched and marvelled with us at this 'murmuring of the solar wind'. They thought the effect was created by sunlight reflected from the ice and snow of the frozen plains of the Arctic. One of our neighbours, Michael, had been to America, and consequently knew everything. 'That's the Rory

Bory Alice,' he said with a knowledgeable air, but few believed him, thinking it another one of his many fanciful concoctions. But Michael was right and indeed it was the Aurora Borealis[37] in Norse mythology identified with the ride of the Valkyries. My feet might have been fixed to the ground on those starry nights, but in my mind I was elsewhere, and rode across the bright speckled sky with those Norse warriors who rushed into the melee of battle selecting those whose fate it was to die.

An Chaor Aduaidh

olagón bog na cruinne
ag casadh ar a fearsaid:
sioscadh na gaoithe grianda
os cionn folús an duibheagáin;
dán mascalach an domhain, a phaidir gheal,
ag soilsiú an mhaighnéadasféir . . .

(The Northern Fireball

the soft wailing of the world
turning on its axis:
the murmuring of the solar wind
over the vacuum of the abyss
a masculine poem of the world, its bright prayer,
lighting up the atmosphere . . .)

Nuala Ní Dhomhnaill
ó 'An Chaor Aduaidh'

On such clear star-clustered nights, from the dark outline of the Bluestack mountains of Donegal, the faraway St John's Point lighthouse winked at me like an earthbound star – a bright jewel of hope glistening in the dark, a shining beacon of life and hope for souls a-wander at sea. Further out along the ocean where Slieve League sloped to the horizon, Rathlin O'Beirne lighthouse, another watchful sentinel of the night, conversed busily in answering flashes with St John's Point. Beside the byres, ramparted turfstacks stood silhouetted by a luminous sky. Up and down our little stony road the bright lamplit windows, starlit windows, strung under the bushy-browed, thatched eaves, reflected the lamp-strewn canopy overhead.

Cold, calm nights magnified the plaintive conversation of the swans on Bunduff lake, giving the sad-sweet notes a melancholy unworldly expression. It carried to me, singsong, swan-songed, on the frosty air; unearthly music that wafted and fell gently from the sky as the graceful guardians of the lake kept their lonely vigil. So sang the children of King Lir sent on a nine-hundred-year exile by their witch stepmother, Oife, when she turned them into four swans. Regretting what she had done, and unable to recant the spell, she gave them the power that, 'There shall be no music in the world equal to yours, the plaintive music you shall sing.' And indeed I have never heard music to match the bewitching beauty of swan song carried on the still air of a frosty night.

Each October approximately 12,000 of these whooper swans return here from Iceland. Making a landfall near Malin Head, they fan out all over the country. High above in graceful V-formations they bugle in long-necked flight calling encouragement to each other as they pick out their favourite lakes: Lough Foyle, Lough Swilly, Lough Neagh, Bunduff Lake and further on to other winter quarters. Here they will stay until lengthening days and warming sun call them away again to their breeding grounds.

For the old people there was a story to match every occasion. Rope-twisting was another opportunity to perpetuate yarns passed on to them and entertain the listener. A good *seanchaí* gripped the attention of everyone present. Younger listeners would, in time, retell the tales etched on their minds on long winter nights. Like the conversation between Mullaghmore man, Dan McGovern and Tawley man Pat Wymbs:

A group of men stood chatting near Summershill. From its height, on the northeastern flank of Mullaghmore, they looked out for miles on a commanding view of land and sea, from Glencolumbkille in County Donegal to Knocknarea mountain in Sligo. Thinking to take a hand at Wymbs and the inhabitants of his area, McGovern, looking over slyly in the direction of Tawley some five miles distant and winking at the other men, said 'I can see the Tawley men stirring their pots of stirabout away over there in the bogs.' This caused great hilarity among the group as they enjoyed a good laugh at Pat's expense. Pat was not amused as stirabout was a mean food enjoyed only by those who couldn't afford better. When the laughing died down he took a thoughtful pull on his pipe and eased a leisurely cloud of blue tobacco smoke into the air. 'Well, y'know,' he said slowly, turning to McGovern with a critical gaze, 'hungry eyes sees far.'

How 'Red Willie' got rid of the tinker was another favourite: Willie McGloin was a bachelor and a 'returned Yank'. He lived alone in a small, thatched house in Bunduff on the Sligo-Bundoran road along the Leitrim bank of the Duff river. Willie, as was usual at that time, left the door unlocked when he went ramblin' to neighbours.

One night, on his return, he found a travelling man or 'tinker' by the fireside who, unbidden, had taken shelter from the night which had turned wet and stormy. Willie didn't like the look of the man but, thinking discretion the better part of valour, chatted away and made him a cup of tea, hoping he would leave shortly. The night grew wilder, the tinker was comfortable by the fire, and they chatted on. Willie's concern increased but still he said nothing. When it got very late and there was no sign of the visitor leaving, Willie hit on a plan. He suggested to the tinker that they should make a hay rope to secure Willie's rick. He explained to the stranger that it was in danger of being knocked down by the wind that was still rising.

Fetching an armful of hay and a trawhook he asked the visitor to twist the rope for him while he, Willie, spun it out. The man agreed and they commenced to twist. The visitor twisted on down the kitchen floor, out the door and on to the street. When he was a short distance away, Willie jumped up, shut and bolted the door, put out the light and went to bed, leaving the surprised stranger out in the cold. We are not told what happened to the tinker afterwards but that's the story that has come down to us about the clever way Red Willie managed to get rid of his unwelcome visitor.

One of W. B. Yeats's short stories, 'The Twisting of the Rope', from 'The Stories of Red Hanrahan' in *Mythologies*, tells of an incident during which Hanrahan was tricked in a similar way when he became a nuisance to the woman of the house in which he was staying. Yeats loved to listen to the stories told by the people of the countryside. Much of his writing was inspired by information gathered from them. Could it be that his idea for the story of Red Hanrahan came about when he heard of the adventure of Red Willie of Bunduff and how he got rid of the tinker? Perhaps he got the story directly from Red Willie. We shall never know!

There were other ways in which the unwary could be bested by a clever manoeuvre. Charles McGlinchey in his book, *Last of the Name*, related that Eoin O'Kerrrigan of Inishowen was a shrewd individual and a difficult man to best. However he acknowledged that, in his travels around Ireland, he was once outfoxed by a Sligo woman. Arriving there late one evening he called for lodging at a house in Gurteen where the landlady lived alone. Eyeing her visitor and regretting she had let him past the door, she said she wouldn't put him up unless he could beat her at three standing jumps. When Eoin agreed to the challenge she stood at the back wall of the kitchen. Facing to the front door she reached the doorstep in three jumps. Eoin tried next and his third jump took him out a couple of feet beyond the door onto the street. When he turned around the cute woman had slammed the door and bolted it, leaving her unwanted visitor to find accommodation elsewhere. We have to guess why this cautious Sligowoman felt she had to resort to such a trick to outsmart the Donegal man. Eoin wasn't telling.

Following several nights of twisting, stargazing and storytelling we had two golden clews of ropes, each about thirty inches in diameter. This brought an end to the annual ritual of rope-making and heavenly contemplation.

Events so far were the prelude to an orchestral composition that had its grand finale in the making of the rick. A summer's work was at stake in making the right decision to choose the perfect day for the job. Every evening now the old men scanned the sky and setting sun with anxious looks. The general consensus was that no one in their right mind would depend on weather forecasts heard on the wireless.

The Meteorological Service[39] was in its infancy then and many a man who listened to and acted on their advice had reason to rue his trust. Worse still, defective information gathered in this way and passed on to a trusting neighbour invited ridicule or worse. Willie was one of the first men in our village to get a radio and from that time forth assumed a new importance as an authority on the weather as well as a valued source of information on national and world affairs.

Up to the 1950s newspapers were not the casual purchase they are now. Money had to be spent on items of greater importance. Every penny counted. 'Look after the pennies and the pounds will look after themselves,' was good advice. On the infrequent occasions when the *Irish Press* or *Irish Independent* was bought it was read very carefully. The *Irish Times* was regarded as an organ of the ascendancy classes and rarely purchased by country people. If the newspaper was not hoarded because of some item of special interest it was passed on to grateful neighbours. Petie Tehan remembered that in Tawley, County Leitrim, in the 1930s, the paper was purchased by one family or another almost every day when other business, such as selling a cart of turf, brought the purchaser to town. Five or six neighbours gathered in that night to a house with a good oil lamp where the news was read and debated. Some readers were known to make up their own stories as they read the paper, giving the listeners a mixture of invention and fact! Information on a regular basis from the radio was something new and greatly valued.

Willie's next-door neighbour, Patrick, trusting the new technology, abandoned the old way of studying nature and signs to predict the weather. He took to enquiring of Willie at important times, what the weather forecasters said. Once when Patrick intended to 'let out' a field of hay to dry prior to 'tramping', Willie confidently advised him that the weather forecast was good. There would be no rain that day! Reassured, and with the sun warm on his back, Patrick went to work and shook out his field of hay. By noon, clouds had rolled in from the Atlantic, the sky became increasingly dark and before long the rain came dropping down. It increased to a downpour and continued all day.

It wasn't the first time this had happened. Patrick, arriving home in a black humour and soaking wet from his attempt at haymaking, had strong words for Willie, believing that he had been led astray on purpose. They didn't talk for years afterwards, and it was through experiences like this that we gradually came to know that the Met Service was no more reliable than the old way. In fact it often could be dangerously misleading. It was just as unsafe to rely too heavily on the new technology as it was unwise to close up the old spring wells when piped water was introduced to the countryside or to throw away the oil lamp and candles when electricity came.

On a harvest day long ago, after weeks of waiting and anxious watching, the morning dawned bright and clear. All indications had looked good the previous evening, and now my father stood with a group of his friends and neighbours in the middle of the road. Faces angled solemnly at the sky, they circled and scanned with seasoned eyes the four points of the compass, carefully studying the prospects for their venture. A cloud settling on Slieve League or Sean Gleann indicated bad weather before evening, a rising cloud-cap was a very good sign. A robin singing high in the bushes or on top of the *péacán* ('shoot') was a very good indication indeed, but singing lower down or in the middle of a bush, a bad sign.

> *This time of the year mind worried*
> *About the threshing of the corn and whether*
> *The yellow streaks in the sunset were for fine weather.*
> *The sides of the ricks were letting in; too hurried*
> *We built them to beat the showers that were flying*
> *All day. 'It's raining in Drummeril now,'*
> *We'd speculate, half happy to think how*
> *Flat on the ground a neighbour's stooks were lying.*

Patrick Kavanagh
from 'Temptation in Harvest'

The voice on the wireless had spoken with authority that morning. It was hard not to be convinced. 'Showers and bright periods clearing to fine weather,' the voice said confidently. 'I don't care what he says,' Bernie Kelly said, shaking his head. 'I didn't like the look o' that moon last night. There's nothing but bad weather on it.'

'There was a touch of frost all right,' another ventured, 'an' I never saw it yet but there'd be a cuttin' after it.'

He was echoing the distrust of all farmers on the western seaboard. Bad weather, wind and rain was their lot; good weather was treated with suspicion. It triggered a sense of foreboding, a feeling that there would be retribution. The gods were only playing with them. Punishment would come, swift and sure.

'Feel the heat in that sun; ye couldn't trust it,' Martin Rourke opined. 'I'm afraid it's only boilin' rain!'

'Do you know better than the wireless?' someone else asked. 'Isn't that their job to be able to tell the weather?'

'It's all right about that but I'm afraid I don't give in to them no matter what they say,' Martin Dowdican said with conviction. 'Look what happened to Pakie McCannon.' This brought a few rueful smiles.

'Aye, there's no doubt about it: there'll be a cuttin' all right but I think we'll get the day out of it,' Johnny Barry ventured. And so it went.

'There never was confusion till then,' one old man recalled, referring to these early attempts at weather forecasting on the wireless.

Disillusioned with the new technology, many went back to the old lore. Swallows flying low or cricket song in the hearth meant rain; a new moon lying on its back held the water, upright it would spill rain. A 'weather gall' or 'dog' (short horizontal rainbow segment) to the left of the setting sun meant broken weather; ahead or to the right it meant northerly breezes and good weather. The wind would blow to it or from it within twenty-four hours. Mare's tails and goats' hair in the evening sky brought wind. Lightning to the north meant the weather was going to take up; if it flashed towards Inishmurray, it was going to break. Pigs became restless when wind was on the way.

> Loud quacks the duck, the peacocks cry,
> The distant hills are seeming nigh.
> How restless are the snorting swine;
> The busy flies disturb the kine.
> Puss on the hearth with velvet paws
> Sits wiping o'er her whiskered jaws.
> 'Twill surely rain; I see with sorrow
> Our jaunt must be put off tomorrow.

Anonymous

The Sheerin family in Rossinver, County Leitrim, took no chances. When it was vital to have good weather, as on the day of a wedding or a rick, the little statue of the Child of Prague, normally kept in the house, was moved out and placed in the hedge as a supplication. Every home had a statue of the Child of Prague. In our house its duties were different. That statue was our investment bank. My mother always kept a halfpenny wrapped in brown paper tucked tidily underneath it. Even to a child's eyes this seemed strange behaviour. When I asked her why she did it she told me that the Holy Child would see to it that 'the house was never without money'. Her mother did it before her and the old people believed it.

Not having any money, we thought a lot about it. The Child

of Prague's commitment seemed a lot to me like the promises of the Sacred Heart to the house where his heart was 'exposed and honoured'. This contract was on the wall of every Irish home. Only with the Child of Prague it wasn't in writing. Maybe it should have been. But it wasn't. It was handed-down information. There was nothing you could point to and say, 'See! This is what you promised.' With the Sacred Heart it was reassuring to have it in print. When things weren't going well you could go and read it again to make sure it wasn't a misunderstanding.

My mother was prepared to take help from wherever it came. When we had nothing else we had hope – and promises. 'Have the name of it if ye never had it,' she declared defiantly in bleak times.

In the evening's gathering dark, when the day's work was done, we often walked along the path that ran through the meadow, cans in hand, to get water from the well. Sometimes we saw a new silver moon suspended in the sky. When this happened and we stopped to admire, the Druid spirit of pagan ancestors stirred in my mother's soul. Following a custom as old as the rocks themselves she turned a small flat stone on the ditch three times while saying, 'I see the new moon. The new moon sees me. God bless the new moon and God bless me.' This, she said, was to bring good luck and money until the new moon came again.

As the years went by even I could see that our house never had any money, so I often looked under the little metal statue to see if someone had taken the halfpenny. But it was always there, and my mother always believed, and still we never had any money – not for long anyway. We owed the price of the calves before they were sold. The creamery cheques disappeared as soon as they arrived. So I stopped believing. 'Oh sure, g'wan with ye,' I said to her when I got older. 'Sure, we always have money in the house; we always have a halfpenny.' She looked at me, and smiled, her faith indomitable, and prayed for my unbelief. We didn't know little Jesus could be used to influence the weather. If we had known she might have changed its duties and spent the halfpenny.[40]

On Inishmurray it was said that when the wind blew strong from Glengarragh, near Benbulben, it wouldn't settle until the witch who lived there had something to eat. 'If it was at night fallin' that storm would never stop till the mornin', till she had her breakfast', the islanders insisted. We knew there was rain on the way when big lumps of soot fell down the chimney and rolled out onto the floor. There was no surer indication. The absorption of the moisture-laden air when rainy weather was on the way loosened the soot's grip in the chimney. My mother's mortification was complete when the chimney spat its accusing message at a time when friends or neighbours visited. She took it as a reflection on her abilities as a housekeeper but deftly shifted the blame onto my father: 'I told that fella to clean the chimney,' she would complain, 'but you might as well be talkin' to the wall.'

Soot had its uses as a potash fertiliser in the garden or, spread on a toothbrush, it kept our teeth healthy long before toothpaste became available or affordable.

Every area had its own weather indicators. 'Bad luck to that oul' "whinaforlia" wind,' Petie Rooney of Glenade in the neighbouring county of Leitrim would say when the wind blew from Crumpaun Mountain. 'It's rain any hour from it.' A bright morning was a fool's guarantee of a good day. Shakespeare, well aware of traitorous dawnings, acknowledged this strange fact when he declared:

Full many a glorious morning have I seen,
Flatter the mountain tops with sovereign eye . . .
Anon permit the basest clouds to ride
With ugly rack on his celestial face . . .

Sonnet 33

Moisture gathering in the air had an optical effect, bringing an intense clarity to the view; distant places seemed nearer. When the hills and headlands of the north Mayo coast rose blue and shimmering behind Inishmurray Island, when every house and squared field between our hill and Benbulben Mountain stood out sharply, when the ravines and purple slopes of Benwiskin towered radiant and supreme, when you stopped to admire the changes and clouds of midges ate you alive, when the old people felt the rising damp in their bones and the mist's soft wind-borne bouquet brushed your face and nostrils: it was then you knew that the air was water-laden and the rain close by. It was not necessary to sit in an armchair and listen to the weather report. It was forecast in every one of the five senses.

Clocks too, like thermometers and wireless broadcasts, were scarce and unreliable in olden times. In farming communities where work was dictated by climate and seasons, dark and light, this was not as big a disadvantage as might be imagined. Circadian rhythms were felt in rural areas long before the term was coined. The farmer went by the demands of stock rearing. He obeyed not clock and calendar but the pulse of nature which dictated a time for planting, sowing and reaping. The fortunes, hopes and fears, the very luck of the tiller of the soil was, from prehistoric man, bound up in his relationship with the natural world.

It was industrialisation that regulated time and forced men

and women to punch clocks. Factory workers wake to the alarm and count the hours. From the middle of the nineteenth century the industrialised parts of the north of Ireland operated to man-made schedules: more cheerless taskmasters than the lord of sun and sky. In towns like Belfast, Lisburn and Banbridge, in Newry, Armagh and Dundalk, the first timepieces were made. In an earlier era when survival was no mean achievement a clock was not first on a list of necessary items! Farmers, on having to rise early for fairs or other essential occasions, often brought the cock indoors, so reliable a herald was he. Imprisoned under a creel in the kitchen, his loud 'cock-a-doodle-do' anticipated the dawn.

Chaucer, author of *The Canterbury Tales*, gives many clues in his writing as to how time was told in medieval times. One tale, 'Man of Law' describes how the shadow of a person, or any standing object, could be used similarly to a sundial. When:

> . . . *the shadow of each tree*
> *Had reached a length of that same quantity*
> *As was the body which had cast the shade;*
> *And on this basis he conclusion made:*
> *That on that day, and in that latitude,*
> *The time was ten o'clock.*

When the railroads came, anyone within sight or hearing of the tracks could tell time by the passing of various trains. Only the trains that had to make connections were reliable, however. Others started when the driver felt in the humour. Their most important connections were the pubs, where the driver, fireman and guard quenched their thirsts. It was important to know the difference.

Our clock was a 'Baby Ben' that we got in a parcel from

America. After a few months in Ireland it lost its American habits and adopted the native disposition. Even so, it kept reliable enough time, and was never more than fifteen minutes slow or fifteen minutes fast. As it grew older it became more temperamental. It wouldn't keep time at all if it was left standing up. It only tick-tocked away contentedly when it was put lying on its face. But hours weren't that important. In between the rising and the setting of the sun there was time for everything!

'I was a man before we had a clock,' Patrick Doherty of Glenade, County Leitrim, told me. 'Me father had a watch but when it was broke there was no way to fix it except you went to Sligo, and in the thirties that didn't happen too often. They'd tell time as their people did before them; ye knew the time by watching the sun. There's a big lump of a rock on the mountain we call "Peak-a-Dhaw" (Peak-at-Two) – when the sun was over it, we knew it was two o'clock.' At night the time could be told from the position of the star group Pleiades as it moved across the sky. Every area had its own way of telling the time and with practice a great degree of accuracy could be achieved.

A man from Grange, County Sligo, recalled arriving on Inishmurray Island in 1943. When the islanders came to greet the visitors the first question they asked was: 'What time is it?' 'But clocks were scarce then anyway,' he recalled. 'The first time we had one here, a German came round selling them, little square clocks. Me grandfather would know by the sun coming in the window what time it was!'

The sun's progress across the kitchen was an indicator too. In *The Green Fool*, Patrick Kavanagh relates that when he went to Pat the Hack's house to rouse him for the fair at Carrick in County Monaghan, Pat was unperturbed. He looked at the dresser. 'It's not six yet,' he said. 'It's not six till the sun shines on the second of them blue plates.' In the 1930s alertness to every detail mattered.

Of all the autumnal endeavours, making a rick was the most formidable. It took a team of six to eight men all day. Only a perfect day would do. A sudden downpour of rain or a rising wind would have disastrous consequences. Some prepared for rapidly changing weather by having on standby a large cover made of bags sewn together and sealed with several coats of whitewash. If rain came on suddenly the 'heart of the rick was rose' and the home-made tarpaulin tied on. Raising the middle section ran the water off and made it possible to keep the half-made rick dry for seven or eight days.

Ready for the worst, the assembled men were of the opinion that, barring the unexpected, the indications looked good.

'It looks like a wee smur o' rain out the back of Inismorra but it might go 'round,' Martin Rourke said.

Bernie Kelly agreed and added, 'I've been watching the cloud risin' on Slieve League all morning and no lie nor doubt about it but I'd give in a lot to that. That day'll improve. Ye'll see it yet.'

It was my father's rick; the risk was his – and the loss too if the day deteriorated. Protocol and common sense required that he make the final decision. 'It might only be a pet day but Columbus took a bigger gamble,' he said carefully, scratching a wire-stubbled jaw. 'We'll chance it!'

Some men looked to the heavens for guidance: 'The last Thursday of this moon was on the seventh of the month', Johnny Barry said. 'It was a good day like today so we had a fortnight of good weather. The moon will be full next Tuesday night, if this keeps up till then ye'll have it good right up to the end of the moon.'

The others nodded in quick agreement, and moved off

purposefully. There was no time to lose. Word was sent out, rakes and forks gathered and pretty soon a *meitheal* (work-party) of men strode determinedly about the garden.

The youngsters were kept home from school on that day. Hearts light with the vision of free time dancing in their heads they busied themselves untying ropes from cocks of hay. The older men set about building the foundation; huge wads of hay were lifted and, arching through the crisp morning air, left sun-blazed streamers behind. Communal work was a form of relaxation for them, a welcome release of energy and anxiety. A buzz of conversation hung over the garden as they chatted animatedly of cattle prices or bad days formerly experienced at making ricks, their talk punctuated occasionally with instructions: 'Let 'er out a bit on this side here.' or 'Make sure you tie that corner over there.'

When the rick got a bit higher the younger helpers were allowed to walk on top. Climbing the ladder we paced back and forth, compacting the layers laid down by the older men. It was great fun at first as we viewed the world from this new perspective and jumped about playfully, turning somersaults and tumbling through the soft, sweet-smelling hay. A few sharp words of rebuke from the older men reminded us of the dangers of falling off and of what we were supposed to be doing. Johnny Barry smiled indulgently at us. 'Ye can't put an old head on young shoulders y'know,' he said as he nodded and smiled to the other men. Chastened by stories of men falling off, or of an Inishmurray man killed by sliding down onto an upturned pitchfork, we soon settled to a dutiful parading back and forth.

As the years went by we gradually learned the art of building from these men and, in time, replaced them in the serious work of planning and constructing the hayrick. Such knowledge had been refined and handed down over the millennia. This and other expertise passed on to so many of my generation resides within us still. It will die with us.

When the rick progressed to the half-way stage it was 'let out' to form a pregnant bulge along its sides, then gradually 'taken in' two thirds of the way up until it acquired its distinctive loaf-like shape. The younger helpers were summoned to assist the men on the ground at 'pulling the butt'. This required trimming and removing all the loose hay around the foundation. The builders on top beat the sides with pitchforks. They raked and combed, shaped and sculpted the rick into its final loaf-like shape.

In earlier times, buttermilk was the most common refreshment to slake thirsts. In the 1950s nothing but 'porther' would do on this day to satisfy the drouth generated by such hard work. Bottles of the black Guinness stout were sent for and handed to the workers during brief rest periods once or twice during the day. If money was scarce, and it generally was, the drink might be got 'on tick' but the farmer's reputation for hospitality and family honour depended on doing the decent thing. Maintaining place and status was essential. Loss of face on matters of such social importance was unthinkable. The day of a rick and the waking of a family member were two of the special times when topers and abstainers alike expected their special due.

The men paused now and again to quench their thirst, drinking the black creamy liquid out of the bottle with smacking of lips and satisfied expressions that spoke of a reward well deserved. Hayseeds speckled the sweat of honest labour that shone on their brows and necks and glistened on sun-browned, sinewy arms. I don't remember any fat farmers on our road. A life of unremitting toil and Spartan existence saw to that. There was no welfare state. Recognition and reward was earned. The clumsy, the lazy and the foolhardy survived at the bottom of an

'You are a queen by your own fireside as much as any monarch on her throne': Cervantes, 1605. Brigid and Mary Kate Duffy at home in Mullaghmore, County Sligo, 1990

Jimmy Flynn, Laughy Barr, County Leitrim, sharpening a slash hook in his kitchen, 1994

Ignatius Maguire mowing a field of oats at Latoon, County Fermanagh, 1992

Thomas Boyce cutting rye with a sickle at Mullaghmore, County Sligo, 1989

J. McGowan

The reapers rose with the blink of morn
And gaily stook'd up the yellow corn,
To call them home from the fields I'd run
Through the blowing breeze and the summer sun.

'The Reapers', William Allingham

Reaper and binder at work on Benny Moen's farm, Clontibret, County Monaghan, 2000

A horse-drawn reaper and binder, c. 1905

Weather prognosticators. Will it be a good enough day to make a rick?
L to R: Joe McGowan, Bernie Kelly, Petie McGowan, Paddy McGrath,
Johnny Barry

End of an era: Coen family erecting the last hay-rick built in County Sligo, 1992

Bernie and Alice Kelly twisting hay ropes at Mullaghmore, County Sligo, 1991

Joe Mc Gowan, Mullaghmore, County Sligo, off to the seashore with ass and creels in 1959

J. McGowan

Wheelwright Paddy Clancy with Jimmy Boylan, Ignatius Maguire and Paddy McMorrow 'shoeing' a horse-cart wheel at Latoon, County Fermanagh, 1994

J. McGowan

'Hands moving with the practised rhythm of a concert pianist, he twisted, wove and fashioned the pliable rods': Brian Gilroy making a creel at Agharrow, County Leitrim, 1994

J. McGowan

Michael Bruen, Maugherow, County Sligo, fishing lobsters off Inishmurray
Island, summer 1999

R. J. Welch, Courtesy of Ulster Museum

Baiting longlines on Rathlin Island, 1889

Hugh Barry with captured hare, 1989. The witch hare was immune to everything except a silver bullet

impassive social order. The only fat was on the bullocks and cattle that grazed the fields in oblivious tranquillity, heedless of all the labour exerted on their behalf.

The youngsters drank lemonade, a rare concession and a very special treat. We looked enviously at the older men as they nonchalantly 'heized' the dark bottles of Guinness onto upturned heads and glugged down the dark elixir with practised ease. Ah, it was a poor thing to be so young! The years passed too slowly then and it seemed the day when we could partake of the privileges enjoyed by adults would never come.

The woman of the house prepared a good dinner for the workers about noontime. It could be potatoes with bacon and cabbage or turnips, and many were the unfortunate farmyard hens that never lived to see the rick finished, having provided the main attraction at the midday meal. In the evening the men were given a pot of tea and home-made bread and jam.

In earlier times, 'there was tea but the people didn't have the money to buy it,' one old man related. 'Willie M—— made sure to have tea for the evening meal but that's the only time they got it. They had twelve men at the rick this day and in the evening when they were finished they were all put sitting around a big table in the middle of the floor. Mugs was all they had that time and every man got a mug o' tay.

'The man sittin' next to Pat at the table looks into his mug an' throwing a look at Pat he says to him, "That's light stuff, Pat."

'"Damme but I think you're right," says he, looking into the mug, "for I can see Belleek on the bottom of it."' Belleek Pottery in County Fermanagh, where farm delft was made, always stamped their name on the bottom of their product.

An article on the 'delft woman' in an *Irish Times* article of 1930 reported the attraction this travelling woman's 'gaudy selection of cups, saucers, jugs, bowls, vases and holy water fonts' had for the country buyer. There was an especially brisk demand for earthenware mugs as many farmers and labouring men would not enjoy tea if served in the choicest china cup: 'They considered that tea tastes nicer when taken in a mug. Moreover, nobody would dream of drinking buttermilk out of a cup or glass. A mug is the only satisfactory vessel for a good draught of this refreshing beverage!'

The priest's breakfast, which was given after the station Mass in country homes, was an important occasion. Only the very best in the house was good enough for this distinguished guest. If there was anything new and fashionable the improving woman was going to be ahead of her neighbours in providing it. An old man of south Sligo, born in the nineteenth century, remembered such a breakfast when tea was used for the first time in Cloonagh: 'There was to be a station in John Brennan's house, RIP, and they thought they'd have tea for the priest's breakfast. When the woman of the house boiled and stewed the tea she served up the tea leaves on a plate dressed with butter. The priest smiled and enquired, "*Cá bhfuil an subh?*" (Where is the juice?) She told him she left the *subh* in the sgillit (little pot, skillet) so the priest explained to her how the tea was to be made. Tea was used only at Christmas and important functions and taken with oatcake. Up to about fifty years ago [1890] very little flour was in use, a half-stone at Christmas and another at Easter.'

Blasketman Tomás Ó Criomhthain remembered the first time tea was introduced on his island in the late 1800s. A shipwreck occurred and dozens of tinfoil-lined boxes were washed ashore. The men, not recognising the strange substance, emptied the contents and broke the containers for firewood. A few stray boxes remained and one of the women noticed the deep colour that came from the leaves when they got damp. She tried dyeing her petticoats in the peculiar substance. Normally they would be coloured with woad. The black liquid worked. 'It was a complete success,' she reported afterwards, 'for no colouring matter ever went so deep into a petticoat as that did.'

The clever woman continued her experiments and was the envy of the island when she uncovered this additional use for the brew. When a jealous neighbour went to see what she was up to, the woman, 'had another story to tell about the stuff – she had two ravenous pigs that were dying of hunger, and since she started boiling the stuff for them, mixed with a handful of meal, they lay at their ease, belly upwards in the yard. "And pretty soon they'll be fine and fat," said she.'

Her friend, who had two famishing pigs in her own house, 'ready to eat the children with hunger – all skin and bone though they're nearly a year old', went home in a rage to her husband. He was one of the men who had dumped the contents and kept the box. They got into a big fight and she, 'made him so savage in the end that the neighbours had to come and separate them.' He rose early the next morning on the pretext of going into Dingle to buy food for the pigs. Some relations paid his fare and he was never seen afterwards.

Following a strenuous day's work, the rick was topped by late afternoon and a protective cover of thatch applied. The rushes used had been carefully selected and cut for the purpose some days or a week before. We gathered ours from the farm of Thomas Wymbs in Bunduff where they thrived in the marshy conditions by the lakes below his house.

Such ventures were never merely commercial transactions between vendor and purchaser. The commerce of country life was more than just a trade of goods and services; it was an affirmation of friendship, an exchange of courtesies, a drawing together of the human strands of small communities. Thomas was my mother's cousin. Like most countrymen, he 'could turn his hand to anything.' He shared her love of life, of dancing and music. He sang the old ballads: 'The Boys of the Old Brigade', 'Kevin Barry' or 'The Secondhand Trousers I Bought in Belcoo', at country-house gatherings or anywhere else a few people might listen. Rattling out hearty reels and jigs on his 'melojin', he was a welcome visitor when he came to dances in our house.

When I arrived with the ass-cart for a load of rushes, he put aside whatever he was doing, picked up the scythe and mowed away for hours. He didn't like the changes he saw closing in all around and complained loudly as he worked that the country was 'gone mad'. I gathered and strapped the sheaves and listened and smiled. I was young and didn't care and thought the country was fine.

There must have been times when my visits were an imposition but, mad world or no, he always made me feel welcome, and I looked forward to his inevitable invitation to pull up to the fire and have a couple of thick slices of his home-baked bread and a mug of tea. Thomas was a widower with two young girls to look after. They sat across from me on the long 'furm' beside the fire. People admired him, for he looked after his family well. They praised him for his diligence. I heard them saying things like, 'he could make a cake as good as any woman' or that he was so good-natured, 'he'd share his last crust with ye.'

Thomas's green rushes were now ready to grace our haystack. Thatching with these was a job for a few select men with the necessary experience and skill. It was crucial that the rick should be well sealed so that it would not 'draw' water during the long and wet winter months. It was a slow, tedious but essential job begun in late afternoon and not completed until dusk. Every square inch of the top third of the rick was covered with a glossy layer of fresh rushes. Each handful had to be placed securely, and skilfully interwoven with the hay, row by row, all along the sides and top.

As the evening shadows lengthened the enterprise was ready for the finishing touches. The huge golden clews of straw ropes were rolled out and tied on from end to end starting low on the sides and continuing in parallel rows, about ten inches apart, all the way to the crown. These were then criss-crossed from side to side across the top at twelve inch intervals to form a pattern of neat rectangles. The finished product with its handsomely sculpted shape, golden hay-combed sides, green rushes and rectangular lines of bright yellow was elegant indeed.

In a week or two the ropes were tightened as they became loose when the hay compacted and settled. My father spent several evenings 'cobbering' or 'muggling' the ropes: taking the cross pieces and interweaving them with those that ran lengthwise in a network pattern that gave further security and prevented them from slipping out of place.

When the day's work was done the new creation was appraised. The men stepped back and with experienced gaze ran critical eyes along the sides to gauge whether it leaned to one side. They scanned the upper part to see whether there were any weak spots in the thatching that might take in rain. If it inclined to one side or another props made of strong wooden posts were applied to force it into an upright position as it settled. Decisions were fraught with responsibility as the winter storms would find any weak spot. The men's faces showed fatigue from their exertions but contentment too as their judgment of the weather had been vindicated and the day's labour brought to a successful completion. Tools in hand, ready to head homewards, they paused to discuss the prospects of whether wind and rain would hold off long enough to make a start on Bernie Kelly's or James Rourke's rick the next morning.

Evening fell and darkness crept stealthily about us. We watched the sinking sun call the stars, one by one, into the air. Gradually the men traced tired steps home to their own farms where anxious cows lowed to be milked. Hungry calves bawled at the gate, impatient and worried by the delay in their normal routines.

In the dim-lit dusk, bats darted to and fro, swept and squeaked and swooped in shallow curves around the house and rick. Tonight I was too tired to indulge in the game of trying to sweep them out of the air with a broom. A soft meadow-scented breeze wafting from the sea carried the promise of another fine day. Its gentle zephyrs whispered around the quiet garden and stole between the familiar house and byres. It caressed the curves of the new built stack.

Here, in this peaceful place, among the shadows, I sensed the whispered presence of rick-makers of long ago reincarnated in age-old routines. I dallied in the hay-sweet garden imagining their ghostly appraisal of our craft . . . *No, nothing had changed; nothing at all; not in a thousand years.*

Towards the east the full yellow globe of a harvest moon cast soft shadows as it ascended through the pink-tinted, mare's-tail clouds over Truskmore. Like a night lamp, it rose with unruffled calm, tracing a silvery passage across the perilous sea. Its glittering allure beckoned, calling me to faraway, mysterious places.[41] In the kitchen my mother lit the lamp. Eyes alight, she sang one of her silly songs for me that we only heard when she was happy:

> *Oh the cat had a kitten,*
> *And the dog had a pup,*
> *And sez I, 'Oul' woman,*
> *Is yer rhubarb up?'*

5

WINTERING IN

We sleep and wake and sleep,
but all things move;
The Sun flies forward to his
brother Sun;
The dark Earth follows,
Wheel'd in her ellipse, and
human things return upon themselves,
Thro' all the circle of the golden year.

Alfred Lord Tennyson
from 'The Golden Year'

As the lengthening nights stole the daylight hours, the summer-sleek cows, swollen bellies heavy with calf, grazed ever closer to their winter quarters. In the quiet harvest evenings they waited patiently near the gate at the bottom of the lane that led towards the byres. Contemplatively chewing interminable cuds they seemed to know instinctively that it would not be long now before the hinges swung and they were allowed into the warm shed. Calves bawled impatiently, hungrily, as the grass grew scarcer and less sweet.

The cow byres that stood deserted and bare during the summer months took on a new life. Stone floors were scrubbed, sod and wattle roofs brushed, and walls whitewashed. Spiders scrambled for cover as the heather besom reached every corner. Its bristles demolished summer homes and tore away the intricate lace of delicate strands that had captured many an unwary fly. Of all such creatures the spider was regarded with benevolence: it once spun its web to hide the persecuted Christ. At another critical time in history it concealed the entrance to a cave where the Scottish patriot Robert Bruce hid from pursuing English soldiers. A fistful of spider web gathered from the rafters staunched a bleeding wound and had antiseptic properties too.

Care was taken not to interfere with the array of Brigid's crosses and blessed palm stuck into the sods in the roof. These were a testament of faith, a protection against evil. They brought blessings and good fortune to the animals and the work. The magical elfstones, tucked into the space between thatch and wall, were left undisturbed too. When God and the vet failed to bring relief, otherworld forces waited!

Jeyes Fluid was sprinkled on the flagstones and a fresh covering of hay scattered about the 'sink' and floor where the cows would soon be tied. Vertical posts, ropes and chains by which they were tethered were checked and renewed. Outside, a saffron-bright coat of new-laid thatch gleamed over white-washed walls.

When the cows were allowed indoors they exhaled heavily, contentedly, in great snorts of steam. Each one was tied to a stake in its own place. Munching armfuls of fresh hay piled under their heads, their hot breath brought warmth and new life to the building. Cows are not ambitious creatures. It doesn't take a lot to make them happy. A full belly is usually enough. They looked around languidly, placidly chewing the cud. Winter had commenced and these were familiar sounds, reassuring the household that all was well as we moved smoothly through the cycles of the seasons, adapting to the demands, submerged in the work.

Cows can lose the cud. Willie Foran of Breaghwy, County Sligo, told Maggie McGowan that, 'If ye see a beast failing and if they're not chewing the cud ye'll know they've lost it'. On the strength of this advice Maggie took a cud from a neighbour's goat and gave it to her cow, on which it regained its former good health. 'J.M. came up to me here the next day crying about what I did to his goat. He thought it'd die! He didn't know that a goat has two cuds until I told him and he went away happy then.'

> And the rain coming down, and the rain coming down!
> How lovely it falls on the rick well headed,
> On potato pits thatched, on the turf clamps home,
> On the roofs of the byre where the cows are bedded!

Patrick Kavanagh
from 'October 1943'

In country places a farmer's worth was measured not by the acres he owned but by the number of cattle he possessed. The quality, not the quantity of land, determined how many animals it could support. A farmer with fifty acres of bad land might only be able to support three cows with calves, whereas a landowner with thirty acres might comfortably fodder four or more. A man might have 'three-cows place' or 'five-cows place'. Acres told little.

A headcount of livestock was a very sensible (and age-old) way of determining the measure of a man's wealth and his place in the community. In ancient times it was a general standard of value not only in Ireland but in the entire civilised world.

In this country a cow was equal in value to one ounce of gold. As an article of payment a cow was called a *séd*. Cows or *séds* were very often used both in actual payments and in estimating amounts.

The next unit of value above the *séd*, termed a cumal, was equal to the value of a bondmaid. A *cumal* was worth three *séds*, therefore a bondmaiden was equal in value to three cows or three ounces of gold. A sack of corn was also used as a standard of value called a *miach*. In the Brehon laws this was the universal standard in estimating fines for trespass and payments for grazing. One *miach* was worth a *screpall* (scruple = 1.3 grams) of silver. It would be interesting to know what price a feminist might bring then!

In recent times a man with ten-cows place, or more, could be classified as a 'strong' farmer, especially if he could afford a servant boy. If a man was mentioned in conversation as having two-cows place, it immediately conjured an image of a man of modest means indeed. In the rural Ireland of long ago ownership of land implied means and a degree of wealth. A man having no land or less than one-cows place was 'a man of straw'. The implication was that unless he had a profession or special skill he was a person of no consequence.

If John B. Keane were to write his play *The Field* today, *The Site* would be a more appropriate title. Small farms and farmers are being wiped off the map. Houses and housing estates mushroom everywhere. Cows and cowslips, meadow, hill and glen disappear under bulldozer and concrete. Farms, sites or fields, it is no matter! Cattle and possessions have to be protected and nurtured.

Having housed the livestock in their winter quarters, preparation of fodder was added to the evening chores. Turnips and mangels had to be cut before being fed to the animals. This required slicing a full bucket of turnips or mangels for each cow as additional nutrition to their diet. The extra nourishment should result in bigger and creamier yields of milk.

We didn't have the cast-iron mechanical slicers of the wealthier farmers but what we had plenty of was muscle power. Our cutting was done sitting on a 'furm' in the kitchen. Balancing the turnip or mangel on the end of the stool we used a sharp knife to slice them into a bucket underneath. Anyone who has done this will not forget it, as several tons of turnips were cut over the course of a winter. Yes, tons!

When full, each bucket was topped with a shake of the yellow 'Injun' meal and fed to the cows before milking. As an alternative, and depending on the farmer's preference, potatoes were sometimes 'scalded' by pouring hot water over them and fed to the cattle instead of the other root crops. After scalding, the potatoes had to be cut in half as there was a danger that the entire article, because of its smooth contours, would catch in the animal's throat and choke it.

When growth stopped and bare fields provided little sustenance, the rick in the garden was 'benched' for pulling, that is, a small platform about eighteen inches deep was started from the top of the rick and the hay pulled from this for feeding the cattle. This was an arduous task, as the hay was so compacted at this time that it was difficult to extract. Broken fingernails and aching wrists resulted from the struggle.

Some farmers used hay knives to cut the bench as a labour saving alternative. Others considered this wasteful as the sharp blade cut the hay into short 'tráithníns' which blew away or fell to the ground. Other thrifty men would not see sense in spending money on a tool when the job could be done by hand.

Small birds gathered around at hay-pulling time. The hayseeds that accumulated as the hay was pulled were a favourite food, especially of the pied wagtails. When these 'willie wagtails' showed up in numbers, snow and frosty weather could be expected.

With the arrival of the cows to their winter quarters, the byre became communal property. The ass remembered her own corner and trotted there jauntily to be tied to a stake. A kick from her hind feet deftly planted, accompanied by a barrage of noisy farts quickly settled any objections from the cows. Preferring a quiet life, they stayed out of the way.

Space was at a premium on small farms so provision was made for two roosts in the cow byre that provided perches for the hens all year round. Hay-lined wooden tea chests along the wall provided comfort for them when they laid their eggs or felt broody.

On finding new lodgers installed in what they considered to be their exclusive property, the hens expressed their disapproval of the new arrangement by kicking up a racket. They stalked in indignant circles at the entrance casting sidelong glances at the cows inside. How dare they! The air shrilled with a cacophony of outraged squawks as they cackled their objections to sharing lodgings with the winter visitors. Led by their strutting leader, the cock, they kept up their noisy protest, until the gathering darkness and fear of predatory foxes eventually forced them into a wary acceptance of the new order. They retreated hesitantly indoors where they kept up their raucous protestations as they hopped uncertainly, one by one, on to the wooden roosts. From here they stared sulkily at the offending cows who looked around at them with expressions of mild curiosity.

The perches were installed five feet high over a stone-lined 'sink' or drain. The drain ran behind the cows, so droppings from hens and cows were caught in one efficient channel. This amounted to a lot of manure in a short space of time. Cleaning it out with a graip and throwing it through a little opening in the back wall to the 'dunkle' outside was laborious work which had to be done every day. As the winter lengthened it became necessary to build the dunghill at the back of the byre as it grew, and grew. In the springtime it was an important fertiliser for meadows and crops. It seems strange now but not so long ago a man's wealth – and indeed his prospects for marriage – were measured by the size of this dung heap!

Hens are fractious creatures at the best of times and always seem to argue among themselves before settling down for the night. Relative newcomers to Ireland, some believe their disputations are about the rain and constantly wet feet. Their evening debate is about whether to leave Ireland altogether and go back to their home in Norway in the morning. In the end they are silenced by the rooster's advice to wait one more day in the hope that the weather will improve!

Sharing quarters with the cows was not the only indignity inflicted upon hens. Besides being pounced on from time to time to provide variety for the dinner table, working hens were 'tried' on occasion too. 'Trying' was the process of determining whether the hens really were working, that is, laying eggs on a regular basis. It required poking an exploring index finger up the hen's back entrance to determine whether there was an egg in the making. One of our neighbours who exhibited an extraordinary diligence at examining his birds in this way was nicknamed 'Try-the-Hens' – but not to his face, of course.

When the woman of the house was endeavouring to make up a package of four or five dozen eggs for market, it was important to know what tomorrow would bring. A hen that was 'tried' and found wanting too many times was placed high on a shortlist for the dinner table. No idlers were allowed on small farms where every penny counted. Of course the farm manager wasn't altogether unfeeling. Allowances were made for the occasional respite required to cope with their annual bouts of hen troubles such as 'pinfeathers' (moulting) or 'clocking' (broody).

The exploratory finger was an indignity that didn't have to be suffered by the proud cocks that strutted about the yard. But then they had their own worries. A high mortality rate was their fate as only one rooster was needed to service a large flock of hens.

Indoor plumbing had not yet arrived so the byre, especially in the wintertime, served as an outdoor toilet for the householders as well. In the summertime, hunkered close by the privacy of a sheltering ditch, surrounded by the sights and sounds of creation, nature's call, where and when it came, was answered in nature's way. Summer breezes wafted where summer breezes would, while at a safe distance, heads angled, eyes bright, hens circled attentively. A handful of soft green grass provided the final flourish; it was 'kitten soft' for thousands of years before toilet paper was conceived. In the byre a neat portion of hay served as a satisfactory, if coarser, substitute. It was the natural way and environmentally friendly aeons before the term was invented. All beaches were blue-flag beaches then. Pollution wasn't a problem.

Recycling too was practised before the term was invented. As recently as the 1960s, town dwellers, having read their local newspaper, the *Sligo Champion*, the *Clare Herald*, the *Roscommon Herald* or the *Cork Examiner*, cut it into squares and hung it on a hook in the toilet. For those with a telephone, the directory was a softer option. For all, the coming of wrapped bread and the sliced pan was a boon in more ways than one. The paper packaging was de luxe and much sought after as a tender replacement for the harsher and unbending newspaper. In the 'big houses' soft sphagnum moss collected from the bogs was applied to posteriors more used to pampering![42]

With the cows closer to home it was easier now to get the day's round of work completed. For one thing, we didn't have to trek out to the fields when milking time came. In addition, the animal was tied which meant the bored creature couldn't just walk away when she lost interest in the process or decided she had had enough, as she often did in the field.

Now, at milking time the glimmer of the cart-lamp candle shed a dim yellow light on the interior of the byre.

> *Outside in the cow-house my mother*
> *Made the music of milking;*
> *The light of her stable-lamp was a star*
> *And the frost of Bethlehem made it twinkle.*

> Patrick Kavanagh
> from 'A Christmas Childhood'

Cows munched and nuzzled hay with steamy breaths. The whish-whish of the twin streams of milk that squirted rhythmically into the can as we squeezed the cow's teats – these were comforting sounds. A creamy froth built on top as the vessel resonated from a tinny high pitch at first to a mellow bass as it filled.

Sometimes we squeezed a thin arching white stream towards the waiting cats and laughed as they licked and darted with little pink, open mouths trying to catch the milk that squirted all over their furry faces. At other times we engaged in forbidden milk fights using the cow's teat as a natural water or, in this case, milk pistol. Looking back it's not difficult to understand why such irresponsible behaviour must have been a great source of frustration to hard-working parents!

Milking cows meant more than just an efficient extraction of product. The unruly, motorised, mechanical rattle of milking machines was a long way off then. Commercialisation had not yet stamped out tranquillity.

One of the hazards of milking was the ever-present danger of a sloppy slap on the face from the cow's tail as she flicked it around. Sometimes the misbehaving appendage got wrapped about the milker's head and face. This was unpleasant at any time but particularly disagreeable when it was laden with a thick brown, mucky coating caused by an over-indulgence of lush aftergrass digested and excreted onto the cow's tail. Looking back I believe it was this experience that provoked my first exasperated experimentation with expletives I had heard the older men use! *'Shit!'* I howled in frustration and shit indeed it was.

Cows differed very much in temperament. Some were patient, others were not. Some seemed to understand they should remain still during milking; others had different priorities. They regarded the two-legged creatures pulling at their teats as an unfair imposition at worst or somewhat of a nuisance at best. Quite often a full can of milk went flying when a nervous cow lashed out with her foot. Or worse still, when she lifted a shitty, hairy hoof and put it down, right in the middle of the can. When this happened it took some explaining to parents whose existence depended on every drop of milk they could send to the creamery.

My father generally blamed me when things went wrong. Believing the cow to be at fault, I felt this was grossly unfair but there was no persuading him. Having to take the rap for the cow's transgression didn't help my relationship with the beast at all. Very soon the rapport between man and beast needed for a smooth milking operation went from bad to worse. Cows rely on instinct and are not persuaded by reasonable debate. You can't make a deal with them. Their inherent sense told them I was getting very annoyed at being blamed for their bad behaviour. And they were right. This made them even more nervous and more likely to upset the can, and anyone who thinks that these jobs are all part of pleasant and placid pastoral pursuits is wrong!

Cow's teats differed in size and varied in the ease with which the milk could be drawn. Modern machines don't care about such things but back then it made a difference. Some cows had teats that would fill the milker's fist. With these it was possible to get a good grip and milking was almost always easy. Others had small teats that had to be milked by a stripping motion, using the thumb and two fingers lubricated by dipping the fingers into the milk. Regardless of teat size, some farmers could not milk with dry hands although milking wet was condemned as unhygienic by dairy inspectors. Then there were cows that could hold on to their milk, especially if they checked and didn't like who was doing the milking. They had their favourites too! The practice of singing to cows while milking was common up to recent times. It had the effect of soothing them and allowed the milk to flow more easily. At one time girls employed for work in the dairy with good voices got better wages than those that could not sing!

Fynes Moryson writing in the early seventeeth century knew about headstrong cows: 'The Irish cowes are so stubborne', he wrote, 'that as many tymes they will not be milked but by some one woman, when, how, and by whome they list. If their calves be taken from them, or they otherwise grew stubborn, the skinnes of the Calves stuffed with strawe must be sett by them to smell on, and many fooleries done to please them, or els they will yeilde no milke.' Equally unimpressed by the rebellious Irish he observed that the, 'inhabitants of that time were no less froward in their obedience to the State, than their beasts were to them.'

There were cows with which, even though the teat size was adequate, great force was required to squeeze the milk through the opening. Sore, tired wrists we called *'thaulac'* resulted from the effort. The condition, common to farm workers, could also be brought on by repetitive use of a lanspade or turfspade. Some wore leather straps to support the wrist thereby preventing or alleviating the problem.

There were other, stranger forces at work too that could cause disruption. Before starting to milk it was customary for some to squeeze the first few drops on the ground as an offering to the fairies while saying, 'In the name of the Father, Son and Holy Ghost'. Feeding the fairies while calling on the Holy Trinity may seem a contradiction but it's a wise man who keeps all sides with him! If the cow kicked and spilled the can of milk in the course of milking many old people would remark: 'Ah, take it for luck; maybe some poor creature wanted that!'

Enid Porter in her book, *The Folklore of East Anglia*, attributes the origins of a similar custom there to the influx of Irish immigrants during the famines of the nineteenth century. When the first lamb of the season was born Norfolk shepherds poured some of the ewe's first milk on the ground, 'as a gift for the fairies who, if denied this, might cause later lambs to be stillborn.'

Seamus Moore of Drumfad, County Sligo, recalled the experience of a Cliffoney woman some years ago while milking her cow on a summer's evening near Áth Sluaigh fort near his home. When she commenced her work she could hear crying but couldn't identify the source. When she had finished milking, the cow kicked the can spilling the contents on to the ground.

It was only then, when the crying she had heard just a short while before turned to laughter, that the woman remembered she had forgotten to pay the fairies their entitlement. The *sidhe* will have their due!

We spilled the first few drops on the ground too but it was for reasons of hygiene – I think. Perhaps it was a forgotten remnant of an ancient belief. 'God bless you, Polly,' we said as, the milking finished, we dipped a thumb into the froth and traced the sign of the cross on the cow's hindquarters or 'elder'. It was a symbolic gesture to ensure continued good luck, and an expression of thanks too. Hopeful cats in tow, the full can of milk was brought away to be strained, cleaned and deposited into the waiting churn.

Until recently the woman of the house or her daughters took charge of milking and the dairy. Up to the early decades of the 1900s, this as well as other farm work was done in bare feet. Shoes were a prized commodity that weren't worn except when absolutely necessary.

The division of work that left milking to women is a very old practice. Farm work began at first light long ago; it is recorded that the bondmaid of Dubthach, St Brigid's father, milked her master's cows at sunrise. When the sixth-century St Molaise of Inishmurray was asked why he wouldn't allow cows on to the island to supply milk for the religious community he replied, '*An áit in a mbíonn bó, bíonn bean, agus an áit in a mbíonn bean bíonn miostan.*' ('In the place where there are cows, there are women, and where there are women there's mischief.') No doubt this learned man was very wise to keep his disciples out of the way of temptation!

Being a good milker was an essential skill for a young woman on the lookout for a husband. A Ballintrillick farmer, now in his eighties, told me how it was when he was a young man.

'These girls'd be on the market for a man anytime from twenty on. If they didn't know how to milk, it was a black mark against them. A girl had to be three things: a good milker, good with the needle and good with the churn-dash. It was all women that milked cows! The men wouldn't mind helping, but they wouldn't be let! I remember me mother milking the cows and me father looking after the child; she wouldn't trust him with the cows at all. It had to be done right! There's a woman up the road there in Grange, Mrs Rooney – well that woman could go out an' milk six cows in the byre while ye'd be sayin' Jack Robinson.'

The dairy being such a central part of farm life, it's not surprising that there's a rich lore of stories attached to cattle and milking. One such relates that the first cows which came to Ireland were as a consequence of the capture of a mermaid. On the May Eve after her seizure she requested to be carried back to the strand where she was caught. Before she returned to the sea she told the assembled gathering, who grieved to see her going, that they should gather there in the same spot on the following May Eve, that three magical cows would appear from the water. When the twelve months went by a great crowd, having heard of the amazing prophecy, gathered by the shore. Shortly after midday three cows emerged from the water: *Bo Fhinn*, the white cow, *Bó Ruadh*, the red cow and *Bó Dhubh*, the black cow. When they came to the road they took different directions, the black cow heading south, the red cow northwards while the most elegant one, the *Bó Fhinn*, made her way to the royal residence at Tara. It is from these three cows that all the cows in Ireland are descended.[43] There are many places named after the *Bó Fhinn* such as the island of Inishbofin, off the coast of County Galway.

According to accounts, Inishbofin was at one time enchanted, invisible, and hidden by a thick fog. Two fishermen lost in a mist at sea stumbled on to the island. Delighted to have reached the safety of land, they went ashore and lit a fire to dry their clothes and cook a meal. Unknown to them the lighting of a fire was the signal that broke the spell that held the island. When the flame hit the rock the fog lifted and the solid island materialised around them, as it has remained ever since. As the mist cleared the fishermen saw an old woman drive a white cow down to the lake. When it reached the water she struck it with a stick and it was immediately transformed into a rock. One of the fishermen, angry at what he had seen, struck the old witch and they were both instantly turned to stone. The three stones are still to be seen: the white cow, the fisherman and the old woman. From this magical incident and the white cow, Inis Bó Finne, or Inishbofin, acquired its name.

There are echoes of this legend in the story told to Francis Crean of Ballintrillick, County Sligo, by his grandmother:

> Once upon a time there was a great scarcity of milk in Ballintrillick and Glenade. It was a time of great hunger and famine in Ireland. During that time a white cow used to come out of the sea at Mullaghmore and make her way to the stricken townlands. She gave an endless supply of milk until each house had received enough for its needs. This continued over a long period of time, the white cow returned again and again to supply the whole area with milk.
>
> Eventually a selfish woman in the townland of Drinaghan, wishing to have all the milk for herself, decided to milk the cow dry. After she had taken enough milk for her own needs she proceeded to make sure that no one else would have as much.

She continued milking, and milked, and milked
until the milk overflowed and ran into the local
stream. Still she continued to milk until the
stream turned white and after a while contained
more milk than water. The greedy woman milked
on until finally the cow ran dry. Immediately
following this the cow returned to the sea at
Pollyarry in Mullaghmore and was never seen
again.'

This story of the benevolent milk cow is a variation of a legend
well known in England and Scotland as well as Ireland. The
Irish version tells of the *Glas Ghoibhneann* (the grey of
Ghoibhneann, the smith-god) a famous cow of plenty that
appeared in times of crisis to provide poor people with a supply
of milk. She is often associated with holy wells, some of which
are called *Tobair na Glaise*. An enchanted cow arrives mysteriously
and gives milk to all who need it until someone annoys her or
abuses the privilege, on which she departs and is seen no more.
This otherworld cow is said to have appeared at a holy well in
County Donegal called *Tobar Bride*. She gave a quart of milk
to everyone there until people quarrelled about who should own
her, at which she went away and never returned.

The legend of another such fruitful cow is recorded in
Leamonaghan, near Ferbane in County Offaly. St Manchan,
who established a monastic settlement there in the seventh
century, owned a cow which gave milk, not alone to the saint
and his community but also to all the poor of the district who
came to milk her. Tradition has it that the people from the
neighbouring town of Kilmonaghan, hearing of this wonderful
beast, stole her. The saint set out and tracked his missing cow
by the mark of her hoofprints embedded in the rocks. By the

time he discovered the culprits, it was too late – the cow had been slaughtered and was cooking in the pot. Undaunted the saint worked a miracle that restored the cow to good health, except for one of her thigh bones. He brought her back to Leamonaghan where she continued to give milk as before. As living proof of the veracity of the legend, one of the rocks used to track the cow could be seen at the local school until recently.

This fantastic animal was so highly regarded that, as a mark of respect, no one in Leamonaghan produces milk for sale to this day. If there is surplus milk, they will give it away, but will not accept payment for it. To do so would dishonour the memory of the saint. According to recent newspaper reports, a man who moved into the area in the 1940s, seeing no logic in adhering to such a superstitious belief, set up a dairy herd. He was forced to abandon the venture when eleven of his cows died overnight for no apparent reason and calves were born on the farm with heads like sheep!

St Manchan's shrine, which is believed to contain the saint's bones, is preserved in the National Museum. Curative powers and prevention of disease are attributed to the waters of his holy well in Leamonaghan. The saint's memory is still held in great respect there. In his memory the well continues to be visited by the faithful of the area on his feast day, 24 January.

The onset of shorter days brought changes too for the thirty or so turkeys we reared for the Christmas market. They were rounded up and housed earlier now. Weighing twenty pounds or more, these were large birds that required a lot of space, so they had their own quarters.

Industrious foragers, they scavenged meadow and stubble methodically during the day. They were the show-offs of the farmyard. On fine evenings, craws stuffed, and puffed up with turkey importance, the cocks strutted about importantly in proud and ostentatious displays. Guldering loudly, wings stretched to the ground like Spanish galleons at full sail, they took off in short but quick bursts of speed across the farmyard. Red necks ablaze in fiery splendour, they made a fine spectacle. Unimpressed, the turkey hens looked on. Maintaining their dignity, they took no part in these intemperate exhibitions. 'Boys will be boys,' they seemed to be thinking as they looked on indulgently.

One of my jobs was to round up this rowdy flock and house them for the night. My chief interest in the evenings at that time was to get the chores done so I could go off 'rambling' to a neighbour's house for card-playing or conversation. Unmoved by these turkey-world displays I hurried them with undignified haste to their night quarters. Sometimes their wild, tree-bred, turkey instincts rebelled at any kind of confinement. They were the bane of my young life as, on fine evenings, some notion of a formerly wild and free existence awakening in them, they made defiant bids for freedom and staged periodic turkey rebellions.

Showing no deference to my authority, or my plans for the evening, first one bird, then another, and then the whole flock took to the air with a wild graceless flapping. All I could do was watch helplesly while they circled around to land on the highest point of the byres. Safely out of my reach, the turkey rebels perched aloft. Red necks stretched and swivelling, they looked down at me defiantly as if they were thinking in their turkey minds, 'What are ye going to do about that?' Carried away with the moment, they couldn't have given any thought to the inevitable consequences of such subversive behaviour. With gay abandon they risked all for a wild moment of illusory freedom. Living for the moment, nothing was learned from other ill-considered experimentations at resisting the inevitable – and I didn't have time to waste on pondering the philosophy of turkey minds.

Luckily for the mutinous birds, my mother was around most of the time to protect them. When she wasn't, I pegged clods of turf to knock them down. Well-aimed shots dislodged them from their lofty perches without injuring anything but their pride. A good shot and a direct hit forced an undignified surrender and a dizzy return to earth.

My mother had a sixth sense for this sort of thing. She had an intuitive perception of the danger to her charges no matter where she was and invariably rushed onto the scene shortly after hostilities commenced. Her irate 'What in God's name are y'at there?' meant other ways had to be found to bring the birds down. Persisting in my method of turkey control only meant that hostilities would open on another front and this time I would be on the receiving end. Where my mother was concerned and it came to a choice between me and the turkeys, I knew I was going to lose! They were an important source of income so no irresponsible or cavalier treatment of such a vital asset would be tolerated. As well as that she had a real fondness for them. Having coaxed, nurtured and fed them through sickness and health from the day they were hatched, they were like children to her. She was strange like that. She became genuinely attached to cows, calves and turkeys, yet her affection didn't extend to any prolonged grieving when the calves went to the butcher or the turkeys to the Christmas table.

When she was around, gentler, albeit slower methods of persuasion had to be found. Coaxed and threatened by turns, they were eventually talked down and shooed into their house. Here they showed no such inclination for high places. Now, when they were wanted to fly, they didn't. Subdued but still contrary, they had to be lifted up onto their roosts, poles that stretched from wall to wall at about three feet from the ground. I wouldn't care where they spent the night but allowing them to indulge their preference for lying on the ground caused deformed breastbones that for some reason, known only to the buyer, resulted in downgrading and lower prices when they went to market.

When the work was done, my delight was to go rambling to McGraths' home for a game of cards. There was no television then and very few radios. Rural electrification wouldn't arrive until the late 1950s, so those that had a radio used it sparingly. The complicated system of wet and dry batteries used to power it had a limited and expensive life. My father ruled the apparatus with an iron hand and while *Ceolta Tíre*, a programme of traditional Irish music, was his delight, my requests to listen to Radio Luxembourg, a pop music station, fell mostly on deaf ears – and leathery ones, I thought unkindly.

The radio at that time was, for some reason, called a wireless, which was strange, as to receive any signal at all it was necessary to have lots of wires. One wire was strung from the back of the set to intersect with another wire that was strung from the chimney overhead to a tall mast about fifty yards away. Other wires went to wet batteries and still others to dry batteries.

Once, in a fit of pique, on being refused permission to listen to my favourite station, I experimented. Bored and sulking outside by the carthouse I shortly discovered that a pin stuck through the aerials had the effect of knocking out the radio signal. I went indoors to check and sure enough there was my father, glasses perched on top of his nose, fiddling frantically with the knobs on the set. 'What's wrong with this bloody thing?' he bleated impatiently as he checked the wires back and front. I could hardly believe it. It was true. The pin worked like a charm. I had woven a mysterious, magic spell just like the Druids in their great contests of wizardry with St Patrick. And no mean feat it was to beat this relentless man at anything!

My friends and I rolled around outside in fits of laughter at his frantic efforts to discover what had gone wrong with the radio. This was more fun than listening to Radio Luxembourg. Served him right, I thought – after all, it was me that had to carry the bloody heavy wet batteries on the bike to Timoney's shop in Cliffoney for charging. This meant two trips, mind you, not one, as the charging took two days. A blow had been struck for the underdog – if not for freedom then at least against injustice! When we had had enough fun we removed the pin from the aerial, thereby restoring the signal. Over the years, I don't believe my father ever associated my disgruntlement at his choice of stations with these strange interruptions to his favourite programmes.

In the absence of the great electronic passions of this modern age, card-playing was an all-absorbing pastime; the lengthening nights at this time of year marked the commencement of the season. The older generation often played for buttons when they had no money. 'What money?' Maggie McGowan exclaimed when I asked her. 'There was no money! They played for buttons! Some of the men wouldn't have a button on their good trousers if they had a run of bad luck. The swearing would start with the wimmin when they went home then and they had to sew new buttons on! "The divil shoot you an' the cards! What happened to the buttons?" was the cry.'

Card-playing was a nightly observance, eagerly looked forward to and religiously kept at various houses: McGraths', Leonards' or Pat Kelly's, where ramblers as well as card-players were welcome. The game was 'Twenty-five' and only men played. It could be a boisterous pastime. Because of the rough-and-tumble nature of the game, women rarely participated.

To pass the long nights the older females visited neighbour women, sometimes taking their knitting with them, busily making socks or jumpers, knitting intricate patterns while they chatted the night away. Crochet, too, was a popular pastime for women in the home, young and old, which brought in a modest income. 'They were better times long ago,' Maggie told me. 'There was respect for old people then. There was no one left on their own. Wherever there was an oul' woman, all the neighbour women would gather in and bring their knitting with them and chat and knit and keep the fire going all night. I don't see one here in this place apart from me own family from one end of the week to the other.' 'Home help' put in place by government policy means well, but nothing can replace the camaraderie of friendly neighbours that Maggie remembers.

Sometimes when there was a heavy workload, the women spent the night at home crocheting, sprigging or patching the family clothes. Because of the heavy spadework involved in planting crops, maintenance of the men's trousers was something that required constant attention. Holes were worn very quickly in the fabric above the knee where the forearm levered the spade. When the trousers were patched the clever woman prepared another neat rectangle of cloth. This was fastened over the freshly sewn patch with a safety pin to protect the new repair when the man of the house went back to work with his spade.

Such economy is a far cry from the present craze among the younger generation, who now wear torn jeans as a fashion statement! Long ago it was a shameful thing to be seen with torn trousers – no house-proud woman would allow her skill at needlework to be brought into disrepute in such a way. Clothes may not have been new, but no matter how poor a family was, they were always neatly patched. Everyone could afford that.

The serious card-players went to Leonards' or Kellys' where the hard men of the First Division smacked the table triumphantly with mighty thumps when sporting a winning card. At other times they roundly abused anyone who 'reneged' or 'let the game out'. Scattering cards about the place, they dispensed insults and abuse with unrestrained abandon. 'Ye bloody eejit ye! What did ye do that for, or d'ye know how to play cards at all?'

'Six o' them was there playing cards every night, a few pence a game,' Bernie Kelly recalled. 'Great players they were: Jimmy McGowan, one of the best in Mullagh; Pat Kelly and Patrick, Jamesy 'Charlie' Gallagher, John 'Tailor' Leonard, Willie Duffy, Jim Gilroy an' yer uncle Patrick McGowan was a great man for playing. That'd be back in the '30s. They played every night except Saturday when they had to wash and get ready for Sunday. There was no card-playing in the pubs then or money for drinking. It was all country houses they went to.'

My choice was a gentler game of 'Twenty-five' played at McGraths' where the cards were dealt on the 'furm' close by the warm blaze of a log fire. We played for money when we had it, pennies and halfpennies and a big game we called a 'rubber' at the end of the night for a threepenny bit. 'Play wan an' ate th'other', was the harshest reprimand heard here as Martin Rourke laughingly chided a player who dallied too long over the choice of a card, or 'I'm tellin' ye, ye're in for it now', he would threaten with a chuckle when dealt a winning hand. 'There'll be nippin' an' natchin' of teeth this night, an' the man has no teeth'll have sore gums.' His misquoting the Bible always got a good laugh.

If someone lingered too long over a difficult choice of card, the solemnity was soon broken – 'Arsh hole winkin', Kitty got a clinkin', up in the blinkin' hole', dropped into the silence, to the tune of 'The Girl I Left Behind Me'. It was enough to shift the focus and we all collapsed into fits of laughter at this crude interjection of salty humour.

Those of us who were adolescents and prone to a budding curiosity about such hidden female parts might ponder walking home on starlit nights what was meant by the words of the jingle and Kitty's unsung response to the 'clinkin'.' This was long before sex education. For those who had no sisters at home to spy on or any other revealing source, a woman's anatomy was a great mystery. Such things were taboo subjects, a forbidden zone, familiar to and entered only by adults. You didn't ask. Information on these hinted adult activities could only be gathered from veiled references, ribald humour, smirks and schoolyard gossip.

When the reality of what men and women did in their passionate moments slowly unravelled it seemed absurd. Not the friends and neighbours I know. Think again. One day on the way home from school one of our pals declared that even the King and Queen of England did it. This was the last straw. Shock and disbelief reigned briefly. Surely not! Surely they didn't engage in such incongruous behaviour.

City dwellers believed that country children had an advantage, that they were introduced to sex in a natural way, that it happened as a normal interaction in their daily environment. We didn't see it like that at all! The cock did it with the hens out in the 'dunkle'. The dogs in the street did it with gusto. The ram engaged the sheep with frenetic enthusiasm. The bull did it with the cow in the field. But they were only animals. Neither inspiration nor education was acquired by such observation. You wouldn't be surprised what the lower orders might get up to. Cows ate grass in the field. Humans didn't. Somehow we didn't apply animal behaviour to anything that people might do. Some degree of decorum was expected from them.

It was rumoured for a time that one of our schoolmates, Pat, had confided about a chance meeting with Miriam over behind the woods one day. A combination of warm sun, inviting grass and licentious hormones nourished conversation and curiosity to an enthusiastic discussion of regions normally protected from light of day or heat of sun. The conversation ended in mutual agreement to 'show me yours if I show you mine'. And they did. Or maybe it was lies. Bragging, bravado and lying were all a part of those years. But it could be true, and other hopefuls waited for their chance. For some of us it never came and we nodded knowledgeably and laughed with the older men when these subjects came up in conversation, disguising our ignorance as best we could. With such complexities are a young man's adolescence littered! To paraphrase Patrick Kavanagh, our sexual education then was 'part of the usual barbaric life of the Irish country poor'.

Some of the boys made a fist with their thumb sticking out between forefinger and middle finger, smirking shamelessly as they gestured at each other or at some of the girls. The embarrassed response of the girls and the sniggering of the boys indicated some secret sexual connotation but for the life of me I could make neither head nor tail of it. To ask invited ridicule. So, again, not wanting to seem different, I went along and laughed and pretended I knew. When enlightenment came I couldn't see what was so funny. Perhaps by then I was too old to understand the joke!

Knowing glances and chuckles accompanied the cryptic advice that, 'there's no use getting off at Mullingar if you're going to Dublin, ye know.' Another puzzle was the risqué greeting, 'How's the man in the boat?' that certain of the older men in the village called out to some of the women. Today such comments would be enough to bring on a sexual-harassment case but, at least for some of the cruder characters in the community, this ribald repartee was a way of village life and no one took offence. Country people had a primal appreciation of female parts long before feminists demanded their recognition. Sex excited more than political correctness. The only fear of harassment came from the priest!

The card-players' equivalent of the World Cup were the games played before Christmas. Here a goose, a duck, or a plump turkey was the prize – or a skinny reject with a crooked breast that couldn't be sold at market. No matter the trophy, the contest was all, and these marathons were eagerly anticipated:

> My name is Pat McGovern, in Culreawach I do dwell.
> I had a clutch of turkeys but one I failed to sell.
> This turkey I will raffle, the country for to crown,
> And every one that enters in must pay me down a pound . . .

The tournaments were held in country houses, with as many as twenty or thirty crowded into a small kitchen or spilling over into an adjacent room. Six men sat to a table with every two players paired together in a game of 'partners'. Sometimes nine players sat, three against three, the winners going on to the next heat. Great feats of memory were needed as it was necessary to keep a running count of the score as well as anticipate what cards your own team might hold as well as your adversaries. Tea and cake was served sometime during the night or early morning for the hungry players. Local musicians often attended and smoke and ashes whirled from the hearth later in the night as the card players took to the floor and the whole affair ended up in a dance into the small hours.

Everyone knew that, despite their popularity, cards was the devil's game. 'They wouldn't carry the cards in their pocket at night,' one ex-player told me. 'They were too much afraid. They'd always throw them on the table before they'd go home. I wouldn't like carrying them at night! They're all right if they're played right but how many plays them straight? A crowd of fellows used to play cards at Y—— Harrisons in Cliffoney,' he continued. 'The cock and a few hens used to roost over a big stone flag that was at the back door of the house. This night, didn't the cock come down and crow on the table where the cards was being played. That finished it, the cards was gathered up and everyone went home. There was someone cheating.'

A rooster crowing at night was a bad sign at the best of times and people didn't like it. The cock coming down and crowing on the card table was a message that was too clear to ignore! There were other, more honest ways to influence fate: some men wore a darning needle hidden in their clothes to bring good luck.

'A whistlin' woman and a crowin' hen drags the devil out of his den,' my mother often said. There was nothing worse than a crowing hen. It went against nature. In the middle of a hot August afternoon a hen on Neddy Brien's farm at Cnuckeen in north Donegal jumped up on the ass cart and began to crow. The woman of the house, Peig, had gone to the shore some time earlier to gather seafood. By eight o'clock in the evening her dead body was carried on a door to her house to be waked. She had slipped on a rock and was drowned in a deep pool.

On the Inishowen peninsula in Donegal, Charles Mc-Glinchey recalled another such incident in Paddy Roddy's house. There was a roost for the hens near the door here too. One night at bedtime the rooster began to crow and flap his wings. This frightened the people of the house: 'The old man was lying in the kitchen bed and he asked the young people what direction the rooster was facing. They told him he was facing in his direction. Then he told them to feel the rooster's feet, were they cold or warm. They told him they were warm, so Paddy said the thing would go past without a death. That same night a son of Paddy's nearly died with a colic but he pulled out of it next day and got all right.'

Some card-players, as in any game of skill, were naturally better than others. There were still more who were known to have sinister powers. A man called Sean O'Neill who lived in Carns, County Sligo, always carried a pack of cards about with him, as his companions often remarked. One day at Mass, he is said to have taken 'the joker out of the pack of cards at the time the priest was consecrating the bread. He could never be beaten at cards afterwards but neither could he ever again be in the chapel at the time of the consecration – he would get weak and have to leave. I saw it meself!' While gaining in some mysterious way a special power at the card game, he lost the privilege of attending this most sacred part of the Mass.

Coming home from a night's playing, enveloped in foreboding darkness, we tried to put such strange stories out of our minds. Tales of challenges to roadside card games made by dark strangers on lonely country byways were common.

Listening to these yarns on nights when cards were put aside there was no fear on us as we turned our faces to the cheery warmth of McGrath's wood fire. Pine logs crackled and spat arching comets of light; resin sighed and sizzled out of the wood as we sat listening to the old men, to Jimmy McGowan or John Rogers. Their weather-beaten faces solemn, they terrified us with tales of encounters with ghosts and fairies. It was a delicious, spine-tingling dread and, fascinated, we hung on every word. The pallid glow of the flickering oil lamp lit the faces of the storytellers and wide-eyed listeners. It brought an eeriness to the shadowy corners of the house as, card games forgotten until another night, experiences of strange happenings were told.

'There was this man, Michael 'Johnny Nappy' Rooney was his name,' Jimmy would start:

He lived up near Glenade in the County Leitrim. He was out 'til all hours every night an' he nearly couldn't be bate at playin' cards, he was that good. People thought he cheated but he never could be caught at it. When he was on his way home from a card game about two o'clock on a winter's night didn't he see a small table on the side of the road with a pack of cards and a candle on it. There was a well-dressed man standing beside it and damned if he didn't challenge Michael to have a game with him.

Well, they started playing anyway an' Michael couldn't get a game off this fella. After about an hour of this Michael started to smell a rat and hit on a plan. He fumbled and dropped a card on the road when he was shufflin' the deck. When he bent down to pick it up what did he see under the table, but the devil's foot on the man – the cloven hoof.

Well, I'm telling ye Michael often told me that when he seen this he broke out in a cold sweat an' 'cut his stick down the road as fast as he could. As he was leaving the stranger shouted after him, 'Ye may thank what ye have 'round yer neck or I would have kept ye.' Ye see, Michael was wearing a brown scapular an' the devil had no power over

him when he had it on. That finished Michael
with the cards an' from that night on no one ever
saw him out late at night again.

The devil might have been a fearsome character to some but
not everyone was afraid of him. A local man married a woman
who was well known to the neighbours as 'a terrible scald' – he
had no peace with her. After years of nagging, he finally took
to the bottle to drown his sorrows. He went out drinking almost
every night to forget his misery and came home oblivious to all
abuse heaped on him. His wife wasn't pleased at all with this
new turn of events so she hatched a plan to keep him at home.
Dressed up in a white sheet and hung down with chains she hid
in the bushes at a lonely place on the road and waited for his
return from the pub.

When she saw him coming she wailed and groaned and
rattled the chains like a mad person. The husband took no
notice – he just passed on as always. Desperate to get his
attention now she rattled harder than ever and called out in a
strange voice, 'I'm the devil. I'm the devil, do ye know me? I'm
the devil.' He looked back then, steadied himself and beyond
fear, squared up to the strange apparition. 'Why wouldn't I know
ye,' he said wearily. 'Amn't I married to yer sister!'

Had he lived in earlier times he would have had recourse to
other remedies. J. B. Doyle, writing in his *Tours in Ulster* in
1854, noted regulations on the statute books in Carrickfergus
dealing with the 'noisy nuisance of women scolding'. It read as
follows:

> Ordered and agreed by the whole court: That all
> manner of scolds which shall be openly detected
> scolding, or evil words in manner of scolding, for

the same shall be condemned before Mr Maior, shall be drawne at the sterne of a boate in the water from the end of the pier round about the Queen's Majesties Castle in manner of ducking; and after when a cage shall be made, the party so condemned for a scold shall be therein punished in the manner noticed.

Town Records

6

—

HEARTH AND HOME

As the days grew steadily shorter all the farm business was put in order. Turf saved with back-breaking care in the long summer days were taken home by ass or horse and cart, and built in strong, brown stacks ten feet high. Often positioned to give extra protection from strong winds, they had a permanent, fortress-like appearance. Building the turfstack required a certain skill as it had to withstand the worst that winter gale and driving rain could do. The outer layer or 'free' had to be constructed in a particular manner. There was only one right way to do it. Longer sods were used and built with their ends facing out and sloping downward to throw off the rain. For stability it was desirable that this outer wall slope inwards about five degrees off the vertical.

When summers were wet it proved impossible to save or dry turf sufficiently for burning. Then we picked the driest and took them home before winter. The remainder were built into small stacks or 'clamps' and left on the bog. Drying breezes, when they came, wafted through the 'free' to dry the turf on the inside. We returned to draw these from the centre later in the year and cart them home as the need arose.

In such years it was necessary to supplement the supply of turf with timber from the nearby woods. Half a crown or five shillings to the local gamekeepers on the Classiebawn estate secured a tree. It was marked, cut, sawn into manageable lengths and carted home. My father was a proud man and regarded this as a last resort. Timber was normally procured only by those who, to put it delicately, did not manage their time well enough to save turf when the summer sun was high. No one spoke about it but there were two classes of people: those that burned turf and those that burned 'sticks'. A nod of the head, a facial expression told the story.

Chainsaws did not exist then. Crosscuts were used: long, deep-toothed saws five to six feet long with a handle at either end. Two men pulled alternately on each handle. Sawdust spat at either end as the sharp teeth see-sawed back and forth, biting deep into the trunk with each tug.

As was the case with much of what I was called on to help with, I wasn't too good at that either. An ineptitude born in part of youthful exuberance and partly of impatience to be done with the job caused me to push as well as pull. All that was accomplished by this excess of zeal was to bow the blade, making it harder for the man on the other handle to draw the implement to his side.

'Pull! Pull! Don't push!' my father barked at me in exasperation, interrupting bouts of daydreaming brought on by the monotony of the work. Once, unsupervised by him, my brother and I struggled for days in an attempt to saw a big log. We sawed and sawed with raw enthusiasm and little skill as the blade went round and round in a never-ending corkscrew. Despite our best efforts the twain never did meet until my father came and, taking charge, redirected our energies to a more useful end.

People with no land, or those who wished to supplement their farm income, cut and saved turf for sale. It was big business. Cartloads were sold to neighbours or brought to market in Bundoran or Sligo town. In normal times imported coal was used by the creameries to boil and sterilise milk. Increased demand for milk products during the war years meant more coal was required. Disruption of shipping led to increased difficulty of supply, thereby creating a greater demand for home-produced turf. Ballinfull Creamery paid two shillings and sixpence per barrel of peat to local suppliers in the early '40s.

A 'barrel' was the unit of measurement used in selling turf. It consisted of a volume of four feet by two feet by three feet. Eight of these made up a horse cart of turf 'crivened' (layered) in rows six to eight sods high over the top of the crib. When the load was brought a long distance by road, it was secured by placing a bag on top which was fastened to the cart with a rope.

On bogland, where use was controlled by the landlord, tenants paid two shillings and sixpence for the right to cut two hundred barrels or about thirty-three cartloads of turf per year. Persons not living on the estate paid ten to fifteen shillings for the same right. Although no one was allowed to cut more than they could use, many contrived to produce up to fifty cartloads for sale. According to a report by the Congested Districts Board, one shilling and sixpence to two shillings was received for an ass-cart load in 1895 and three shillings to five shillings and sixpence for a horse-cart. Two shillings was still the usual price up to the 1930s.

Horse and cart was the most common transport for hay, turf, potatoes and other farm produce sold to nearby towns on market days. In addition, carters hired out their services to businesses when required. In the '30s they were paid eight to ten shillings to take a load from surrounding districts to Sligo town. On the quayside there were no derricks or hoists. Coal boats were unloaded by shovelling the coal from the hold up onto the deck, and from the deck onto trolleys which in turn were pushed across the gangway to waiting carts on the quay. Carters engaged in hauling from the ship to the storage yard in the 1930s thought themselves very well paid at one pound per day.

Farmers from the surrounding countryside were sometimes pressed into service to help unload the ships. Even though the wages were an inducement, those with horse-carts were reluctant to take on the job because their animals were prone to take fright in an unfamiliar environment.

Those who were tempted by the rewards often brought home funny stories of life among the 'townies' working on Sligo docks. Marty Nicholson of Maugherow, County Sligo, often worked through the night to meet contracts in order to have ships ready to sail on the morning tide. 'They were tough men,' Marty recalled, speaking of his workmates, 'They had to go down into the hold of the ship to start, and shovel the coal from the hatch up onto the deck and there was men there then that put it from that into these bogeys.

'There was great rivalry among the townie carters. They liked to brag about who had the best wives and homes and so on. When it came to dinnertime, the Sligo boys could see when they were driving up the street whether there was smoke coming out of their own chimneys or not. They were always pulling this fella's leg – Jack was his name – bragging about the grub they used to get at home: "My Maggie now, d'ye know what she'll have for me? A big steak about that thick" and so on. Another would say, "Well my one, she's mad on puddin's; it's this puddin' she makes an' it's that puddin' she makes." The way the townies'd talk ye'd have a job to follow them, rale townie talk!

'Anyway one day they were all driving up the quays talking and codding. Jack was fed up to the back teeth listening to them. When he got as far as his own house he jumped off the cart and started rappin' on the front door. There was no smoke in the house and the other boys was all gigglin'. He was hoppin' mad. "Fire, fire," he shouts! After awhile anyway his wife puts her head out the upper bedroom window an' she says, "Jack, where's the fire?" "It's in every fuckin' house but mine," he says. Well, we were laughin' for days!'

Hay was bought by firms in Sligo for horse teams engaged in carting and deliveries around the town. Companies such as Hunter's Coal kept six to eight horses; Hanley's timber yards kept five. A load of hay that weighed one ton was worth one pound in money in the '30s. As it was a cumbersome burden, cart, horse and load were driven onto a weighbridge in order to calculate the weight.

Travelling by horse and cart from the Maugherow hinterland into the nearest market town, Sligo, took three and a half to four hours. This allowed time for a brief stop at the 'Maugherow Looking-glass'. Men left at five in the morning to be in the marketplace before nine in order to sell their load of hay or potatoes. The womenfolk followed a couple of hours later, reaching town by midday just in time for the sale money to be handed over for the shopping.

When potatoes were sent to market, carts were loaded on Friday afternoon with up to one ton weight of the tubers which were held in bags weighing twelve stone (168 pounds or a hundredweight and a half) each. The vehicle was then propped with a length of timber to the back-band so the horse could be easily backed between the shafts in the morning for a quick getaway. The procedure was second nature to George Siggins of Cloghboley, County Sligo:

> All ye had to do then was connect the draught
> chains in the dark of the morning and away ye
> went. It was a flinty road as far as Drumcliffe so
> the horse had a good footing. When ye got that
> far you had to jack up the shafts again to take the

weight off the horse's back and put a stone to each wheel so it wouldn't roll down the slope. Ye had to take out two nails out of each front shoe and put in what we called frost nails. They had a special shaped point to give the animal a grip when they went on the tarmac. Other than that they would slip and fall on the tarred road. The frost nails weren't kept in all the time because they would wear out too soon.

When ye got to the Market Yard in town ye had to wait there and sometimes ye wouldn't sell the spuds at all. If ye sold them ye had to deliver to a radius of a quarter of a mile from the town, that's if ye didn't sell to Blackwoods or some of the shops in town. I remember carting Aran Banners into town at thirty-five shillings a ton. That was all, an' all the work ye had with them! When ye were finished then ye had to make yer way home again, another four hours an' take out the frost nails again as soon as ye went off the tarred road.

What was the Maugherow looking-glass? It was a clear pool of water on the river at Teesan bridge just outside of Sligo town. Here, people going to market paused to put on their shoes and gaze in the crystal stream, using the reflection to comb their hair and arrange their clothes before proceeding further. Mirrors or looking-glasses, as they were called, were a scarce commodity, not regularly found in homes until the early years of the twentieth century. In their absence, people used clear pools or window-panes to see themselves.

Nature provided hundreds of these 'looking-glasses' all over Ireland. Although they have long since gone out of use, the memory of their importance remains. Near the chapel at Kilteevoge, Glenfinn in County Donegal is Lána na gCos Dubh (Blackfeet Lane). Ard an Coirithe (Dressing Hill), outside of Glenties, County Donegal served the same purpose.

Ireland's faces mirrored in her rivers – what would we see today?

There was great competition to determine who would be first into market in the early months of the year with the new potatoes. The farmers went with asses and carts or horse-carts to O'Connor Bros, Stevensons, Bellews or to the Market Yard selling their wares in boxes of one hundredweight or half a hundredweight! In later years when enterprising hauliers acquired lorries to transport goods, the people were slow to hire them: 'They'd rather go in themselves and save the few bob. The lorries was too expensive.' Bringing potatoes to market in Sligo suffered a serious setback in the 1950s when graded potatoes began to arrive from Dublin and from abroad, cheaper than they could be produced locally. It signalled the loss of native fruits and vegetables and 'people grew them less and less.'

As previously mentioned, it was quite common, into the early decades of the twentieth century, for people travelling to town on business to go in their bare feet. In 1798, the year of the French invasion at Killala, more than half the Irishmen who came from the countryside to march with Humbert against the English went barefoot. It was customary at one time, not only in Ireland but throughout Europe, for people, especially women, to go their whole lives without ever wearing a shoe. In the early years of the twentieth century, when footwear became more common, the first pair was often bought by a young couple prior to their wedding, almost as a symbol of adulthood. Following the occasion they were worn only at special times such as weddings, fairs, trips to market or such. On Sundays people often went barefoot to Mass, put on the shoes before entering the chapel, took them off when they came out, and carried them home over their shoulders. Being unused to footwear, many were probably more comfortable without the constricting leather!

Recalling the first time he wore shoes as a young man, Tomás Ó Criomhthain related: 'Everybody marvelled at my getting boots so soon, for in those days men and women alike didn't usually put on boots until their wedding day'.

Within living memory, children going to school rarely wore shoes. Most farm work was done barefoot. On trips to market involving ten, fifteen or more miles on the road, precious footwear was tied and carried around the neck. Illustrating the value placed on a good pair of boots the story is told of a man walking into Sligo carrying them under his arm. Stubbing his toe off a stone in the roadway he looked down at the bloodied digit and, turning to his travelling partner, exclaimed in relief, 'It's a good thing the new shoes didn't get that!'

Footwear was not bought in shops but made by local shoemakers, of whom there were many in every locality: Tivnan in Grange, McGowan in Bunduff, Gillen and Clancy in Carns, the Mac Partlands in Ballyfarnon – they were among the last of the old shoemakers in County Sligo. They measured the foot, bought the material and made a custom-fitted shoe. Patrick Kavanagh's father was a shoemaker, 'in the good days when a pair of shop boots were an insult to any decent man's feet'.

The footwear made by local craftsmen was rugged and sturdy but their strength, so to speak, could also be their weakness, as they were stiff and uncomfortable to wear, especially on long journeys into town. Another good reason to go barefoot! Eventually, mass-produced factory shoes became plentiful and affordable. Skilled local craftsmen were reduced to making a living by repairing shoes and boots bought in shops. Another unique talent contributing to the hardy texture of rural society disappeared.

Tailors, boatbuilders, weavers, coopers, shoemakers, native and itinerant, plied their lifelong trades supplying local needs as their fathers and grandfathers had done before them. Their crafts were primitive but their place was assured. Slowly, one by one, most of these men, who had been an integral part of rural life, were swept away by the skill of townsmen and factory. When their trade was no longer viable they became wanderers, like the nomadic singers, scholars, fiddlers and beggars who crowded the roads of Ireland.

During my growing-up many homes had a shoemaker's 'last'. In an era when economy was essential and thrift a virtue, the man of the house repaired and half-soled the family shoes. Rugged work made tough footwear a necessity. Prior to use, boots bought in shops were put on the last and fortified with steel toe- and heel-plates. Serried ranks of strong studs were hammered into the perimeter of the sole and up the centre. Durability, not fashion, dictated. 'Have you any idea of the young fellas that grew up long 'go?' Maggie McGowan exclaimed to me during one of our conversations. 'They had neither a bicycle nor a horse, only their two feet with two big strong shoes on them and there was as much iron on them as there's not on a horse now!'

Robust footwear was indispensable up to the 1950s. A stinging clip on the ear was my reward when, in protest at their weight and clumsiness, my father caught me making a pantomine out of walking with a new pair of boots which he had just ironclad. He was quite proud of his handiwork and I was quite indifferent. It was the beginning of a new era. Elvis Presley was singing about 'blue suede shoes', narrow-legged trousers called 'drainpipes' were the fashion of the day. Style, not sturdy, was what I craved!

My father, like many men of his time, could make a go of most jobs. There was no spare cash to pay tradesmen. When shoes needed repair he set up shop with last and hammer, usually on a Sunday or on a wet day unsuited for working outdoors. Square portions of leather about a quarter of an inch thick and as big as an A4 page were available in shops in every locality. These all-purpose shops sold groceries, boots, drapery, dried fish, cattle feed etc. Many served as undertakers too, making money on your going as well as your coming. Life and death were all one package.

When there was mending to be done my father bought a piece of leather, soaked it overnight, pulled up the multi-purpose long stool that we called a 'furm', planted the shoemakers last on it, and went to work. Cords made of several strands of hemp twisted together and coated with a black sticky substance called 'wax-end' were used for stitching harness as well as shoes. Shortly, with great pride and very few tools, he had transformed an old worn pair of boots to almost new condition. With a fresh pair of studded half-soles and skilfully stitched uppers installed, he had cheated the shoe shop out of a sale for at least another year. The craft of the old generation stemmed from necessity. Self-sufficiency meant survival.

Change came slowly and local shoemakers held their own against the factory product into the early decades of the twentieth century. One of these factories, Martin's, in Carrigans, County Sligo, came into operation in the early 1900s. It had, in addition to local markets, a contract to supply institutions such as the County Home, formerly the Workhouse, now St John's Hospital. They wholesaled their products to shops in Sligo, Leitrim and Mayo as well. Marty Nicholson of north Sligo recalled his father fitting him with a pair of shoes at Martin's factory in 1920. He paid two shillings for them. '"Martins for

Everything" was written on the gable,' he recalled. 'It was a bakery too. Stephen Doherty and Martin Banks were shoemakers in the area. Martin's factory was cheaper than them because he was turning them out in mass production. There was fourteen girls sewing tops. The shoemakers managed to compete with Martin because, even though they were dearer, their shoes were a much better quality, and better leather. They made good strong boots too.'

John Martin was a prodigy, his feats legendary! People still recall with pride and wonder how he was a 'boon to the whole country'. It is worth pausing here to contemplate his genius. People who knew him say he was born a dwarf, that he was 'absolutely deformed'. His torso was a normal size but he could touch the ground with his hands. His legs were only six or eight inches long and looked like 'two sods of turf'. He pulled himself along with the help of two blocks of wood attached to his hands.

Even by today's standards he was a shining example of the adage that where there is a will to succeed, handicaps are merely obstacles to be overcome. In addition to a shoe factory he developed a hotel with a pub licence. The pub was noted for the high quality of its Guinness. 'It was twopence a pint and ye could be drunk that time on two shillings. He came into the bar one night: "Men," he says, "I think it's for snow." One of the fellows had a few drinks on him. Turning around he looked down at Martin and said, "It wouldn't snow very much until you'd be up to your neck in it!"'

A separate section of the building held a bakery and in another several women were employed at dressmaking. Not alone did he supply local markets but he exported his products 'all over the world'. He was the first in County Sligo to install a vacuum/gravity cashier system to route transactions at the counter through an office in another room. 'You'd unscrew the ball, put the money in and it sped through this system to the cash desk. The cashier'd write it up and back it would come again.'

He did the architectural work on the stone building and, unbelievably, built much of it himself – often at night! Given his handicap, people were baffled at his abilities and success. Some explained it by speculating he had a pact with the devil, others said he was in league with the fairies. No mortal man could accomplish what he did! He was the first in the area to have a lorry on the road. George Siggins recalled that it was a kind of hybrid car/lorry with a little cab on the front of it. 'When I was going to school in Ballinfull you could hear it coming from miles away; there was no silencer on it.' When it broke down there was no mechanic to call on. 'He got out the instruction book and read it from cover to cover. When he had tested and eliminated everything that might possibly be wrong with it, he discovered a fault in the magneto. And that was a time when most people wouldn't know a magneto from the man in the moon!'

John Joe Herrity of Raughley recalled one of John Martin's business trips to Liverpool to upgrade his operation and procure modern machinery in order to increase production at the shoe factory. 'When he went into the big plant,' John Joe recalled, 'they saw the wee dwarf coming and they were firing sixpences and shillings at him, thinking he was in begging. He went up to the reception desk and asked to see the general manager, that he wanted to buy new machinery for his premises. That took the talk off them. He wasn't in begging!'

Ironically, the downfall of John Martin's empire came about as a consequence of his greatest success, the securing of a large contract with the British government to supply boots for the army. He completed and delivered on time but they refused to pay, claiming he had used inferior leather. He was shattered! He had borrowed money and invested heavily in time and material to fulfil the order. Faced with ruin he promptly brought court proceedings against them – and lost. That was the beginning of the end. He lost heart. Having married some years before, domestic problems now also beset him and his business declined. When he died some years afterwards, there was no family left to carry on. His wife was unable to keep the business going, so one of the most remarkable and unlikely entrepreneurial adventures ever undertaken anywhere in Ireland passed into history.

A few ruined walls are all that now remain of John Martin's shoe factory to remind us of the small man with the heart of a giant. There is much we can learn from his example. The memory of his deeds will remain as a lasting monument to his struggle and the triumph that the human spirit can achieve over adversity and encumbrance.

Transport improved gradually in the first half of the last century but a trip to Sligo was still an adventure: 'I was the first in my town to get a bicycle,' Maggie McGowan told me. 'Paid for it out of the eggs. When I had the bike I'd share it with my friend and pal from next door. I'd start away and cycle two mile of the road, lave the bicycle up to the ditch an' she'd come along an' take it an' go on two mile more. Ye'd walk that two mile an hop on the bicycle then and go on two more. We were in Sligo in an hour's time. When I had to walk it, it took me three an' four hours. It was ten strong mile from the house I was reared in 'til ye got to Sligo. It was a great rest when ye came up to Tully Hill an' pulled off th'oul shoes to rest yer feet. Ye can believe that now.

'Before I got the bike I often got a lift from Jack Harte. His father Jim Harte had a pub in Lislarry. A jennet they had. The

body of the cart used to hold six half barrels. When ye'd be at
Connolly's he'd be coming along, he'd be half drunk but that
made no differ to you whether he was drunk or sober, as long
as ye got up on the cart. Ye had nothing to sit on only the barrel
an' there wasn't as much as a bag under ye. An' yer basket of
stuff with ye, whatever ye had. He'd draw a shkite on that poor
jennet when he'd be halfway out the road an ye'd be hoppin up
an down an there'd be a ring on yer backside for weeks. But ye
didn't heed that, ye got carried home anyway. Ye got as far as
the "Cottage" in Lisadell. Later, when times was good, we got
two bicycles.'

Much of the harvest work had to do with digging potatoes. In
reasonable weather these were gathered and stored in pits by
early November. Sombre, earth-blackened fields stood out
where formerly gay-blossomed green foliage bedecked sun-
showered acres. Long, black heaps of pitted clay sheltered
summer's bounty and winter's salvation. Bleached, bone-dry
stalks lay strewn in ragged skeins about the dark rectangles:
gathered into piles and burned, pillars of smoke, signals to the
gods, ascended skywards. Answering columns came from neighbouring fields and hills, declaring a victory, connecting the
communities. Yellowing autumn days were spent astride potato
ridges peeling back fat-hen, chickenweed and withered stems.
With dogged determination, through good weather and bad, my
father persevered through shortening daylight hours, digging out
Kerr Pinks and Aran Banners from the rich black earth. A live
turf coal burned behind him to light his Woodbine fag. Twopence
was better spent on a loaf of bread for hungry children than
wasted on a box of matches.

When wind-blown showers beat in off the Atlantic, he
hunched tightly to the shelter of the sod ditch at the bottom

of the field. A coat thrown over his head and shoulders, he waited patiently for nature's onslaught to pass. There were few intimacies between us that I remember. Now I recall the acrid smell of lingering cigarette smoke, soft aftergrass and musky black earth when he pulled a corner of the coat around me.

Long lines of freshly dug, earth-mottled potatoes waited for us when we came home from school during the digging season. A quick dinner of raw egg mashed through boiled spuds, *brúitín*, or just plain potatoes and buttermilk, and we were off to the field, buckets in hand. Already an area of ground designated for winter storage had been marked out in the loose earth. We gathered bucketful after bucketful, shaping a triangular ridge about two feet at the base, two feet high and ten to fifteen feet long. The smaller, damaged, sunburned potatoes and 'poheens' we gathered into another pit to be kept as fodder for the hens and turkeys.

Kerr Pinks were the favourite eating variety and these were kept in separate pits from the Aran Banners, which were grown exclusively for the farm animals. They were not as dry and floury as Kerr Pinks but they grew bigger, therefore producing a higher yield per acre. The mounds of potatoes were left to dry and then thatched with a thick coat of rushes or rough grass ('spret') to repel the rain. This layer was covered with six inches of clay, a natural cold storage effectively preserving the crop from winter frosts, wind and rain.

When bouts of bad weather or bad health slowed down the harvesting, neighbours gathered in to give a hand. Then we were kept at home from school as there was a full, hard, back-breaking day's work ahead, gathering the long lines of potatoes. In rural communities national and secondary school pupils were often kept at home during the course of the year to help out with the various tasks on the farm – setting potatoes, cutting turf, gathering seaweed and so on.

The concept of state control of education came into existence with the formation of the Board of Commissioners for National Education in 1831. It wasn't, however, until the School Attendance Act of 1926 that it became compulsory for children between the ages of six and fourteen to attend school. A previous attempt to enforce attendance in 1892 had proven a failure. Following the legislation of 1926 it fell to gardai to monitor school attendances in their respective areas. Summonses were issued to parents responsible for children's non-attendance. In country districts the law was, more often than not, interpreted with reason and liberality and, in the words of a local garda, 'Nelson's eye' applied at crucial harvesting times.

Gathering potatoes and footing turf are two of the most back-breaking occupations known to man! For those whom the muse called, even the mundane was poetry. When Patrick Kavanagh picked up the tubers (as he related in *The Green Fool*), 'the smells rising from the dry brown clay were a tonic to revive the weariest body, the loneliest spirit. Turning over the soil our fingers were turning the pages in the Book of Life. We could dream as we gathered the potatoes, we could enter in the secret places where all unwritten poems lie.'

Good man Patrick! Weren't you the lucky lad to have had time to dream. Tedium, not lyricism, ruled in our cabbage patch. If you had been working for Petie McGowan or Pat Kelly in the stone-free sandy soil of Sligo they'd soon have knocked the poetry out of your head!

Despite his musings, Patrick admitted that it was not possible to be a poet and a potato-picker at the same time: when someone suggested that he was leaving half the crop behind him he admitted that his 'metaphysical wanderings had a bad effect on my skill as a potato-gatherer.' Mullaghmore raised no poets but many potato-pickers: it was the skill that was most in demand at the time!

For ordinary mortals any diversion from the sheer drudgery was welcome. Where there was a number of young gatherers, potatoes were a tempting size to make handy missiles. One mischievous blow provoked a flurry of retaliation. A hit from a potato stung but did no lasting damage. The fights were brief and suppressed as soon as they came to the notice of humourless diggers who had serious business on hand and little time to waste with childish games on short harvest days.

The pits of potatoes had a special attraction for greedy eyes that knew instinctively what delicacies they contained. The cows looked across the fence at our labours with great interest. Their placid expressions belied a thieving intent. When we left the field temptation often proved too much to resist. Charging through the fence, they abandoned their peaceful manner to bore madly into the protective covering. Gorging on the raw potatoes created gases in their stomach which would expand to kill them if the break-in wasn't detected. When potatoes were fed to cattle, the deadly effect was neutralised simply by scalding the tubers with hot water. Eaten raw they meant almost instant death for the greedy animal as their bellies immediately bloated into great swollen balloon shapes. If a vet could not be found at once their fate was sealed. Failing salvation from a professional there were a few who knew how to use a sharp knife. Locating the vital spot they plunged the blade deep, thus releasing the killer gas.

Another hazard when they broke into the pits was the possibility of the animals choking if a potato caught in their throats, as it often did. This emergency had to be dealt with instantly or death came quickly. A bare arm or, if time allowed, a tongs was thrust down the cow's throat to try to dislodge the potato. Butter could be used to help lubricate the area, thus facilitating the removal. When all remedies failed, the death of any animal was a big loss on a small farm. It was a huge financial blow and cast a pall over the family.

Newspapers recently reported a study by a United Nations Disaster Management Team on the affect of drought and cattle deaths on the Mongolian steppes. I was reminded of the reaction to similar fatalities in our village and on our farm in the 1950s: 'Herders and their families are emotionally attached to their livestock,' the report stated. 'Deaths of their animals affect them almost as deeply as the death of human friends.' Mongolia, Mullaghmore or Ballybunion, the feelings and human emotions are the same. The relationship between farmers and their animals on small farms in Ireland in the last century was identical to that experienced in Ethiopia or Mongolia today, an interdependence inextricably linked in success or failure, life and death.

By November, with the crops gathered in and the winter routine established, work gradually moved away from the fields and centred around the farmyard. Thatched houses required continuous observation and frequent maintenance. The average dwelling was a good, sturdy, stone-built structure. Of necessity, it provided basic shelter and answered the practical needs of the occupier. One storey high, a bog oak framework of sturdy beams and latticed timber formed the roof of these simple homes. A layer of sods cut from a suitable field was laid on top and finally a thick coat of weatherproof thatch. Underneath, three compartments, a kitchen in the middle and a bedroom at either end formed the living quarters. Each room had a fireplace, the biggest and busiest in the kitchen.

There were no hallways and one window provided the light for each room. These openings, generally small, linked to memories of bad times and taxing landlords, faced away from the prevailing wind. The other sidewall, windowless, hunched its blind and rugged shoulder to the Atlantic. Lime from kilns that abounded in the countryside ensured a plentiful supply of whitewash for the exterior walls as protection and decoration. The scarlet flowers and bright green foliage of fuchsia hedges gave a splash of colour in summer. Bees hummed there constantly and sometimes we took the flowered pendants, pulled out the long centre stamen, and sucked the sweet sugared essence that so attracted the bees.

Strictly functional, these dwellings were Spartan and had little ornamental beauty. However, the simplicity of design with its balance of door, windows, chimney and roof imbued these houses with a natural elegance, classical in its purity. All of the materials were drawn from the locality: stones prised from a local quarry, roof scraws dug from the field, thatch harvested in the cornfields. Rafters and purlins rough-hewn of bog oak were dowelled together without a single nail and stained naturally by smoke and age. Constituted of indigenous materials, they sat comfortably in their surroundings, rooted in the landscape, something that the modern bungalow does not. Today, when they can be found, painters and photographers strive to capture the bare essence of these buildings. The sight of a man on a ladder thatching a roof was once so common it would not attract a second look. Now it is so rare a sight as to draw tourist and local alike with camera in hand. The thatched roof will soon be the sole preserve of the 'folk museum'.

Patrick Kelly lived in such a two-roomed farmhouse in Mullaghmore. Growing feebler as time gathered him to herself, he spent the last years of his life in a losing battle to keep it thatched and repaired. All about, a new wealthy class moved in and built luxurious holiday retreats. Around his home the old Mullaghmore faded away but Patrick, a contented bachelor, smoked his pipe and watched, amused by these opulent displays.

'I see them all with grand new houses,' he said to me one day with a laugh, 'but when someone wants to take a picture it's to my house they come! How is that?'

Patrick could not withstand the winds of change that swept through Mullaghmore and Ireland. His time came, he passed on, the auctioneer's sign went up and shortly thereafter mechanical diggers levelled his cottage in an hour. Not a grain of dust now remains to show where his house once stood. Not a shred of evidence abides to prove he ever existed. There is no testimony to a lifetime of struggle.

A gaping crater is all that remains to mark a spring well, crafted long ago with care into solid rock in the shape of a K, on his land where crystal waters once surged. The desecration mocks a sacred, life-giving fountain that nurtured countless generations of Kellys and McGowans, Gilmartins and McGraths, Currids, Rourkes, Barrys and Leonards. A shrine to a unique existence, brutally and senselessly ravaged. A thousand generations of memory obliterated in an instant of time.

Lord Palmerston, on visits to his lands in north Sligo in the nineteenth-century, admired the thatched cottages of the countryside. Selling lime he produced himself at tenpence a barrel he required that his tenants whitewash their homes twice annually. The neighbouring landlord, Sir Robert Gore-Booth of Lisadell, owned forty townlands in the parishes of Ahamlish, Drumcliffe and Rossinver. Not to be outdone by his neighbour he issued an order that his tenants, too, were to have their properties whitewashed by the first day of April each year. To accomplish this so early in the season often presented difficulties for tenants vexed by spring cropping and bad weather.

To ensure the order was carried out, Sir Robert sent his agents, under the notorious Captain Dodwell, on tours of inspection. Johnny Rooney of Coolagraphy, Ballintrillick had managed to coat only the front wall and gables of his home in time for one of the captain's visits. Dodwell dismounted from his carriage, walked around the house and discovered that the back sidewall was left undone. Demanding to know the reason why, he reprimanded Johnny for his carelessness:

'My good man,' he said, 'don't you know you are supposed to do every part of the house?'

Harassed with spring work and the cares of a large family Rooney applied indisputable logic to the distinguished visitor's query: 'Look here, Mr Dodwell,' was his reply, 'every time you wash your face, do you wash your arse?'

When mild days came, prior to the onset of winter, thatch was inspected, strengthened, patched and renewed where necessary. If a new coat was required, the netwire was rolled back and a fresh application laid. This was another talent that each small farmer acquired over the years. 'Scollop thatching' was a special skill practised by tradesmen, of which there were one or two in every locality. This method of thatching was rarely used along the west coast as it would not withstand the fierce winter gales that hurled in off the Atlantic. One such experiment in Mullaghmore ended in failure when a complete roof was lifted off in a gale and deposited in a neighbouring field. Only when his thatch was secured with ropes or netwire tied firmly to pegs in the sidewall and gable could the Atlantic dweller lay his head to rest at night.

'Down by the sally gardens my love and I did meet,' go the words of an old perennial which refuses to die. The 'sally gardens' held no romantic associations for most smallholders who grew a small coppice of sally bushes, sufficient to supply rods for their needs. They were sometimes grown as a cash crop to be sold to basketmakers or at fairs and markets. They had their own peculiar unit of measurement: A 'hand' consisted of three rods. A 'hundred' was made up of forty 'hands' plus a 'tilly' of eight rods.

Harvested in the autumn, they were made into scollops to secure the thatched roofs but they had other important uses too. Skilfully woven together, they were used in making the big oval baskets that held the longlines required by fishermen. Baskets of a similar style were fashioned for teeming the big three-legged cast-iron pots of spuds. When the potatoes were cooked and the pot emptied onto the loose weave the boiling water flowed through onto the cobbled street. Huge clouds of steam spiralled aloft, leaving the potatoes in the basket to cool. The clever householder did this in a different place each time, thereby employing as an extra benefit a very efficient method of weed control!

The supple reed had harsher uses. Half a century later it requires no feat of memory or imagination to recall its ruthless imprint; burning hands and welted legs still carry the sting. Wielded by disciplinarian parents and teachers, it was an unsparing instrument applied to exert control and beat knowledge into countless generations of Irish children. Rod-wrought retribution was inevitable as a punishment for homework undone or transgressions committed. Fiercely wrought the staff of wisdom! Anyone who felt its humbling lash on smarting flesh will not mourn its replacement by gentler methods of persuasion and control.

The tyrant teachers in our school, shapers of future generations, were not content with flaying tender palms and legs. They inflicted on us the final indignity, insisting that we, the recipients of the lash, replenish the instrument of torture as the need arose. On the side of the teachers it must be confessed that at an early age one is not easily convinced of the importance of a good sound education. The world at hand is a much greater wonder.

Gentler methods of persuasion took up little time in our school. A healthy respect for Sister de Pazzi's prowess with a cane, wielded at the end of a strong right arm, commanded greater attention than any intrinsic appreciation of the three Rs. Her discovery that my father owned a thicket of sally bushes used for scollop thatching resulted in my reluctant participation in her mastery of the unruly and the unwilling.

This uneasy cooperation was punctuated by a subversive defiance when on some occasions a faulty set of rods was delivered. They were carefully nicked halfway through under the bark with a sharp penknife so that they would snap on being used. Colm was my schoolmate and sometime leader of the resistance. He had convincing ways, but I placed no confidence in his much-discussed theory that, if a hair was placed across the palm of the hand immediately before it was slapped, the offending rod would break in half. This theory lasted all through my school years due, no doubt, to the practical difficulties in testing it. I even went so far as to carry a hair in my pocket once or twice. The prospect was as tantalising as it was simple and occupied much of my thinking time, especially when nursing throbbing palms after a particularly bad day at school.

A successful attempt would baffle and unnerve the nuns. It would put the enemy into disarray. The triumphant pupil would become a folk hero. He would undermine a loathsome punishment and subvert this repugnant aspect of schoolgoing days forever. The emancipation of the underdog was within our grasp. But these dreams remained just that – dreams. They were never realised, as I could never quite figure out how to get the hair in place before Sister de Pazzi pounced. She was quite unpredictable in these matters.

Born in 1898, Maggie McGowan recalled her schoolmates getting, 'a box on the ear' in addition to the sally rod as punishment during her schooldays. 'A full clout,' she told me. 'But it done them all the good in the world, meself included. I got more boxes in that school it was surprising I had an ear at all! Miss Higgins from Carns, she'd draw the full shkite, she had a big hard hand, harder than me own. She drew it across the ear, there'd be bells in yer lugs for ever so long. Ye got hit with a ruler then for a minor offence. Other times if ye did anything wrong ye got the sally rod. She'd go out to the garden an pull it herself – an' they grew for spite. There'd be welts on yer hands with the beating ye'd get.

'I hated the livin' sight of me school days. I had to do all the work in the mornin' before I left for school. An' bring two sods of turf, one under each arm. An' carry them down to the school. A slate under th'other arm. No books, nothing, a slate. Ye wrote all on the slate an' ye spat on it an' wiped it off with yer elbow. That was the teaching, an' still, they turned out the best of scholars. An' the best of children!'

The history of basket-making, and for all I know, the use of the rod as an incentive to good behaviour dates back to the Ice Age and was until recently an essential element of country life.[44] In ancient times people lived in wattle huts woven of sally or hazel. An early sort of boat consisted of nothing more than a wicker frame covered by horse or cow hide. The Boyne coracle is a survivor of this method of construction. More recently, wattle coated with daub or plaster served as a partition between rooms. Early in the nineteenth century wickerwork was put to use in the making of beds, cradles, chairs and even doors and windows. Wicker doors were lined with straw mats for warmth.

Most such primitive applications had ceased by the advent of the twentieth century but baskets for household use and as containers for such diverse items as potatoes, turf and longlines for fishing were still much in demand. These simple items were often made by the homeowner. Ass creels and 'pardoges', were mostly woven by specialised creelmakers, of which there were a number in every district.

There is little or no use for creels now except as curios and souvenirs of a bygone age. No one beats a path to the door of the few survivors who retain the old skill. Demand for this age-old craft disappeared in a relatively short space of time. It ended suddenly in one generation of rapid change. If you go to the few creelmakers who still practise their trade and ask them about their craft they will display their skill with reverence and pride. One of these, Brian Gilroy of Augharrow in County Leitrim, demonstrated the art for me some time ago. His hands moved with the practised rhythm of a concert pianist as he twisted, wove and fashioned the pliable rods; hands that were the last in these parts to be called upon to fashion a creel for a donkey's back before they become the preserve of the folk museum. When men like this pass on they will close another chapter on country life and take with them an ancient profession, a human accomplishment drawn from necessity. It rests now, fragile and tenuous, in their capable hands.

Creelmakers held exhibitions of their expertise from time to time. Far away from his native Mullaghmore, sitting in an apartment in Flushing, New York, Mattie Joe Barry told me about one of these fairs held about 1915. His mind travelling back in time, his face alight with pleasure, he recalled for me one such demonstration:

Word was sent out through the village that Brian McCannon, a creelmaker from nearby Creevykeel, was going to demonstrate the making of pardoges at Pollyarry. Pollyarry was a busy place then where wrack, washed ashore by wind and tide, was harvested for use as a fertiliser for crop and meadow. Ordinary ass-creels were used by the local men for bringing the wrack up the steep path from the 'claddagh' or shore to the road above. The heavy creels were then lifted off, one side at a time, in order to tip the seaweed onto the roadside for removal later by ass- or horse-cart.

Advances in technology which he felt should be brought to the attention of the local farmers had come to Brian's attention. Having given the matter some thought he decided the time was right to do it!

Country villages in Ireland were thickly populated then. Mattie Joe reeled off the names of the young men that assembled at Pollyarry on the appointed day in 1915. 'They came in from all over,' he recalled. 'John 'Taylor' Leonard was there and Paddy Barry, Jamesy Charlie, James Rourke and John Kelly on the Hill. Your father was there and Owen McGrath and old Pat Dowdican, God be good to them. They're all dead an' gone now. There was so many there I couldn't name them all. It was like a fair day!

'Well anyway, Brian called for attention and started to explain to them about the pardoge and showed them how it worked. You see the pardoge was just like the creel except the bottom was hinged, you pulled out a rod and the load of wrack fell through the bottom to the ground. There was no more need for lifting the heavy creel. They were all impressed with this and I can tell you, Brian was busy for months afterwards – you might say that day at Pollyarry, in its time, was like the big trade fairs they have now!'

Solutions weren't packaged then. Individuals had to rely on their own ingenuity.

As with many of the world's great inventions, this innovation seemed to develop spontaneously in more than one place at the same time. Bertie Monds of Drumcliffe, County Sligo, remembered a similar occurrence in the village of Glencar. A man there named Allingham independently produced a similar labour-saving method: 'He lived up on the upper road above the Glencar lake. He had a son and the son was supposed to be an awful clever young fella. He used to have to work a creamery can when he was putting out manure in the fields. The creamery can was put under one creel to balance the load while he emptied the other one. So he invented the pardoges. He didn't see them anywhere, he just thought of it himself. He put square bottoms on the creels and hinged them so that they would drop simultaneously when he pulled a rod.

'The first day he went out with them there gathered nine or ten lads to see the pardoges working. He loaded up the creels and went out on top of the ridges where he already had the potatoes set and drew the two sticks. Down came the bottoms and out went the manure. Everyone was greatly impressed. Turning around to go home one old man, shaking his head, said to the watchers, "That's it, lads! Ye can go home now; science has gone as far as it can go."'

Like the creels, creelmakers, pardoges and trade fairs at Pollyarry the thatched house too is now a rarity. Not so forty years ago when scollops and thatch, netwire and rye straw were made ready for the mild, wind-free day when essential mainten-ance could be done. Sally rods were cut to about thirty inches long, pointed at each end, twisted in the middle and bent double to make to make scollops or 'keepers'. When finished they resembled large hairpins. With scollop-thatching, the securing rods were hidden, except for a row at the ridge, eaves and gable, and some decorative work. This method is said to be very ancient, reaching Ireland and England with the coming of the Celts. Even the word 'scollop' is derived from the Gaelic.[45]

When netwire was used to secure the thatch it was fastened to a slim length of timber lath or bullwire stretched about ten inches along the length of the eaves. This in turn was secured by keepers driven into the thatch. In addition, it was tied down with ropes to pegs driven into the sidewall and gables. Scollops were driven in here and there over the expanse of the roof to provide extra security as well as to draw the netwire close to the thatch.

Prior to the use of netwire the thatch was firmly tied down with ropes made from twisted oaten straw or bog fir. These were drawn horizontally from gable to gable and vertically from eaves to ridge in a network similar to that described previously for the hayrick. These ropes were also secured to stone or iron pegs driven into the sidewalls and gable.

The replacement of the labour-intensive ropes with netwire in the 1930s was a boon as it cut the time and labour needed for roping in half. It did not need to be replaced every year, as with ropes, and, in addition, provided much greater security against high winds. With its closer weave it had the added advantage that it kept blackbirds and thrushes from their destructive habit of destroying the thatch by digging into it for worms and other insects.

Wheat and rye straw were preferred for thatch because of their greater durability and longer lifespan. Flax, where it was available was also highly valued. In the northwestern counties rye was specifically grown for the purpose. Although rye bread is now a popular choice in a healthy diet, the grain was used then for cattle feed.

The decrease in the number of thatched houses is paralleled by a dramatic reduction in cereal planting and a resultant higher price for suitable straw. Consequently, reeds or *seisc* that grow wild in lakes and rivers, and even plastic reeds, are now often used as an alternative. In seaside areas bent or marram grass provided a long-lasting alternative. Less suitable were rushes, which, because they were so soft, had a very short life. Heather was used too, particularly in Donegal.

Straw which was to be kept for thatching was preferably cut with a hook or sickle, then scutched and cleaned by hand. When cut by mowing machine or scythe the product was inferior. It was untidy with rough and uneven ends.

Before applying the thatch some tradesmen steeped the straw in a solution of 'bluestone' (copper sulphate) to prolong its life. Having a caustic effect on the hands, it was uncomfortable to work with. Some sprayed it on the roof when the thatching was complete. The tools of the thatcher's trade were special needles, used when the thatch was sewn on, a mallet, a sharp trimming knife, special rakes or combs, and 'spurtles' used for patching.

Thatched houses, despite the flammability of the material and its proximity to chimneys, very rarely caught fire. One of the disadvantages of this kind of roof was that it was impossible to gather rainwater from the eaves. It flowed off and down the cobbled streets. Our neighbours who had slated roofs with eave-runs, positioned barrels under the downspouts to catch water for domestic use. This water was rarely used for drinking but it provided a ready supply for ordinary domestic use at a time when water was drawn in tin cans from spring wells in distant fields.

Science had not yet alerted the public to the risks of asbestos. No one, to my knowledge, has ever recognised this danger or advised consumers of the hazards of using water that ran off the asbestos-impregnated slates that had replaced the quarried natural slate of older roofs.

Long before the benefits of insulation became known, the thick thatched roofs kept country houses warm in winter and cool in summer. One of the most familiar features of the Irish countryside was the three-roomed farmhouse with bright whitewashed walls and amber thatch blending naturally and picturesquely into a landscape of meadows, pasture, tilled fields and stone walls. Being frail, they were built where shelter could be found, cuddled into the earth safe from the ravages of wind and weather. In *The Western Isle*, Robin Flower observed that they 'kept faith with their surroundings', contrasting sharply with the newer constructions which, 'stand in a perpetual contradiction of the whole environment of hill and sea and sky, in which they are so violently set down.' Solid and efficient, the older houses sheltered countless generations of Irish men and women who went forth from their simple interiors to build nations.

As with most farm work, thatching was a time-consuming, labour-intensive task in competition with a host of other jobs that had to be done on dry, calm days that were all too few. The expression '*Ní hé lá na gaoithe lá na scolb*' ('The day of the wind is not the day for thatching') was good advice. On our small farm I learned the skill from my father as he had learned it from his father and so on back through successive generations over the centuries, and millennia. It was the poor man's roof, fashioned by a skill born of necessity, not choice. We looked with envy on the labour-free slated house. Illustrative of the great changes in country life, the thatched house has today become, with some exceptions, a showpiece, and a luxury the poor man can't afford.

We may look back on thatching and thatched houses with nostalgia, but how many who were a part of that world would want to swap slate for thatch and return to the simpler way of life? Why do we regret losing something we don't really want? Why do we long for a way of life we wouldn't return to: an austerity that was sustained by penury, not by anyone's wish for it to be so? What is it that attracts us to open fields, dangerous seas and rustic hearths, despite remembered toil and discomfort?

Perhaps we miss the intimacy of a society where neighbours depended on each other, needed each other. Unrelenting elements and never-ending work did not prevent the older generation from putting down sheaf, spade or bucket to exchange banter and conversation with a neighbour, or a stranger. Mechanisation of labour, automatic appliances and jet travel have not bought us more time. They have increased the pace, stolen the serenity.

An elderly neighbour, Georgie McLoughlin, spoke to me one day of the lack of friendly contact in modern living. Neighbours who once stopped to chat when passing on foot or by ass and cart now waved from speeding cars. 'Ah, I don't know who they are half the time,' he said wistfully. 'They look to me like birds in cages flying by.'

Birds in cages we are indeed, and in cages of our own making!

7

TRICK OR TREAT

By Hallowe'en the farmhouse was flanked with castellated stacks of brown turf, the garden abundant with ricks of golden hay, the infields lined with towers of corn and stooks of straw. The pressures of harvesting behind us, air and land reposed. Or so it seemed. It was a time to give thanks, a time to pray and reflect, as it always had been, even before the arrival of Christianity. The replacement of the Celtic New Year or festival of Samhain with Hallowe'en and All Saints' and All Souls' days was merely a part of the Christianisation of the old religions.

The Celts divided the year into two halves: the dark half from Samhain to Bealtaine in May, the light half from Bealtaine to Samhain. Samhain, which fell on 1 November, was their New Year, a pastoral festival marking the passing of summer and the beginning of winter. It was a time of great celebration, feasting and merrymaking, just as our Christmas/New Year period is now.

On the Isle of Man, isolated from the changes brought to the English mainland by the Saxon, 1 November was regarded as New Year's Day down to relatively recent times. Manx Mummers went around on Hallowe'en singing a holiday song in Manx: 'Tonight is New Year's Night, Hogunnaa!' The word is very like the Scottish 'Hogmanay' where children there went around on New Year's Day begging and rhyming, 'Hogmanay, trololay, give us of your white bread and none of your grey. Get up and gie's our Hogmanay'.

In ancient times the great assembly of the five provinces of Ireland took place at Tara on Samhain. The festival was celebrated with horse racing, fairs, markets, debating, political discussions and the formulating of new laws. The festival of All Saints wasn't introduced by the Church until the seventh century. It was finally moved to 1 November in AD 835 to take the place of the pagan cult of the dead. When, over a hundred years later, it had failed in its purpose, All Souls Day was introduced in 988.[46] Its position in the calendar year, as well as that of other festivals, was displaced by Pope Gregory XIII in 1582 when he decreed that ten days be dropped from the calendar. Hence the continued observation by many, on November 11, of what they hold is the real Hallowe'en, sometimes called 'Ould Halloweve'.

There was concerted and deep opposition by ordinary people to changing the calendar year, a reluctance to interfere with nature's eternal cycles, to alter time. This was not something that could be decreed by an act of parliament, they protested. The citizens of Malwood Castle in Hampshire, England set up an experiment to determine if God and nature were on the side of the legislators. In the village there was an oak tree which always bloomed on Christmas Day in honour of Christ's birth. They would observe it on the new Christmas Day to see if buds appeared. If they did not, there could be no doubt that 'the new style was a monstrous mistake', another Popish plot. They flocked to the tree and, when no buds appeared, the opponents of change claimed a victory – their view had the endorsement of God Himself. They were confirmed in their view when buds appeared on the tree on January 5th, old Christmas Day.[47]

Today the Church feasts of All Saints and All Souls have largely displaced the old customs. But beneath the veneer of Christianity, some vestiges of pagan ritual still survive. Old convictions manifested in numerous practices endure to the present day.

Our ancestors believed that on Hallowe'en or the eve of Samhain the spirit world opened and became one with us. The barriers between the supernatural otherworld and our world disappeared; the forces of light and darkness merged. The souls of departed relatives returned to their old homes to sit by the fire and accept the hospitality of their family. All things were possible. At the exact hour of twelve o'clock, a time that belonged neither to the old year or the new, phantom figures of those long dead came forth. Boundaries dissolved. Humans too could pass into their world.

Many believed that not only could the ghosts of the dead return to their earthly homes on that night, but the fairies, underground hosts of the Tuatha dé Danann, also wandered freely. They traipsed between our world and theirs, the ancient ringforts wide open and a hive of activity. Lights were seen going from one fairy fort to another:

> Out in the boglands of brown
> In a maze of silver white,
> Over the bawn and the clover fields
> In a whirling wild delight,
> A woman latches the door,
> And signs the cross on her brow,
> For, Glory to God, the lights are near,
> And the fairies passing now.

Nora Murray
'Will-o'-the-Wisp'

Some held that the fairies could turn the *buachalán buí* (yellow ragwort) into horses and travel about all night on them.

Sometimes they took mortals along, but when this happened, they had to abide by certain rules. If these fairy rules were disobeyed the enchanted world was closed to the culprit at once.

Charles McGlinchey in his book *Last of the Name* describes such a journey experienced by one of his neighbours. 'I heard a story of a Magheramore man called Sean the Tailor, long ago, who was coming up Skeeoge Brae late one Halloweve night, when he saw a crowd of fairies riding about through a field on their horses. They called on Sean to come along with them, that they were going to Scotland. The king told him to jump on a white calf that was in the field but warned him that he was not to open his mouth or say a word till they came back home. They all set off, with Sean on the calf, 'til they toured Scotland and then came across the Moyles to Malin. When they reached the Knockamenny Bens, the horses all jumped over the bar mouth of the Isle of Doagh, the calf as well as the rest. When Sean saw the way the calf jumped, he could keep his mouth shut no longer and shouted out, "I don't care what happens, but that was a great jump for a calf!" With that the fairies and horses and calf and all disappeared, and Sean was left by himself down at Lagahurry in the bottom of the isle. By the time he got back to Magheramore it was milking time next forenoon!'

No one dared approach a graveyard on that eerie night. Anyone hearing footsteps might not look behind them for it was the dead on their track. Should they behold someone from the spirit world face to face 'the earthly gazer will surely die.' In Ireland and in Brittany, food was laid out on the eve of All Souls for the dead who came to visit the houses in the stillness of the night. It was believed the Holy Souls in Purgatory were out and about seeking the assistance of mortals, so the Rosary was said after supper for their relief. Doors were left open for them and particular care was taken that no dirty water be thrown out for fear of drenching them.

The water used for washing feet should never be thrown out after dark at any time. It was believed to be endowed with a peculiar quality that made it the agent of supernatural powers wishing to exert control over the washer. However, putting a live coal into the water before disposal neutralised the attraction it held for evil spirits – another example of the purifying action attributed to fire. The belief was widespread and recorded in the Schools Manuscript Collection of the Department of Irish Folklore, UCD, in areas as diverse as Tonranny, County Galway; Achill, County Mayo; Clonakilty, County Cork; Ballynagaul, County Waterford and Tourlestrane, County Sligo.

It was usual for country people, prior to throwing water out at night, to say, *'Chugadagh, chugadagh, uisce amach!'* ('Take care, take care, water going out!') or *'Seo chugaibh!'* ('Here it comes!'). This was a warning to avoid drenching or giving offence to ghosts or fairies that might be passing. It was recommended to do this at any time but particularly on Hallowe'en. The practice undoubtedly saved some few mortals from a drenching too! Some farmers took the custom further and would not clean out the cow byre after dark on this night.[48]

In these days of piped water it is necessary to explain that, up to the 1960s, before running water was introduced in rural areas, dishes were washed in basins filled from a can of spring water drawn from the well and heated from a kettle of boiling water. The basin was used in the same way for shaving, washing feet and all aspects of personal hygiene. As there was no sink or waste pipes, the dirty water was then thrown out of the open door. Many houses had a cobbled area outside inlaid with an intricate system of channels and drains to take away such waste. It served too as a runoff for the rainwater that came off the eaves.

Stories of unnatural and bizarre occurrences at this time of year come from all over Ireland. In Rathkeale, County Limerick, a woman was sentenced to be hanged for murdering her husband. The crime was carried out in the hope of marrying another man. On the eve of her execution she sent for her lover. When he came she held him close and whispered that she would come to marry him on Hallowe'en:

> She was duly put to death: it was remarked that in her last moments she paid the greatest attention to her dress, wearing a pair of fashionable brogues with silver buckles. Neighbours remarked that when the young man went out at night for a walk the sound of those brogues was always heard on the road beside or after him.
>
> The last day of October came and the young man, as in a trance excited, dressed himself carefully in the evening and towards midnight listened for the steps outside. They came, to the horror of his friends in the house, and like one enraptured, he broke away from his sister and brother, who heard the steps of two people fading in the distance. Next day he was found drowned.[49]

It was not unusual for someone passing by a ringfort or other fairy place on 31 October to see lights or hear sounds of merrymaking inside or indeed to see a relative or friend long dead:

> It is considered that, on All-Hallow's Eve, hob-goblins, evil spirits and fairies hold high revel and that they are travelling abroad in great numbers. The dark and sullen Phooka is then particularly mischievous and many mortals are abducted to fairyland. Those persons taken away to the raths

are often seen at this time by their living friends, and usually accompanying a fairy cavalcade. If you meet the fairies, it is said, on All Hallow's Eve, and throw the dust taken from under your feet at them, they will be obliged to surrender any captive human being belonging to their company. Although this evening was kept as a merry one on farmsteads, yet those who assembled together wished to go and return in company with others; for in numbers a tolerable guarantee, they thought, was obtained from malign influences and practices of the evil spirits.[50]

At all times throughout the year it was customary to give children sent on errands at night a cinder from the hearth to hold in their hand or put in their pocket to keep the fairies from them. It was especially important on November Eve to heed this precaution. A small piece of iron or a cinder was put in the cradle to ward off evil. In Derry, 'oatmeal and salt are put on the heads of the children to protect them from harm.' In Kildare and other parts it was customary to make a cross similar to the St Brigid's cross and set it up for the purpose of 'warding off ill luck, sickness and witchcraft'.

As children we were told that after Hallowe'en blackberries or other wild fruit must not be eaten as on that night the Phooka pissed on them. This was a language children could understand. Any other advice about seasons and they might still be tempted to eat fruit that, while luscious on the branch, was overripe or rotten at this time of year.[51] A Pooka's piss was a greater deterrent than a parent's advice!

The lighting of bonfires at Samhain has diminished now in most parts of Ireland but was a common practice at one time:

Bonfires were formerly kindled at this time as well as at Midsummer. When the embers had partially burned out, those who assembled were accustomed to cast them about in various directions, or sometimes at each other, with no slight danger to those who were not skilful at parrying or escaping from the burning brands. Among men and boys this was regarded as an amusement only, however dangerous it might prove to individuals; but it is thought to have been connected with former Druidic or Gentile incantations. The high streets or market squares of towns or villages, or fair greens and crossroads in the country places, were usually selected for kindling this Samhain pile.[52]

The seventeenth-century Irish historian Geoffrey Keating recorded that in the pagan era Druids used to assemble to make human sacrifices to the gods by burning their victims during the celebrations.

Fires were an important part of Druidic ceremony. On the Royal Hill at Tara King Laeghaire and his followers, surrounded by Druids and nobles, Bards and Brehons, worshipped their gods and carried on the old beliefs by lighting a beacon pyre. Pagan custom dictated that all other flames must be extinguished and rekindled only from this Samhain fire. St Patrick caused consternation in the old order when, disregarding authority and tradition, he lit his paschal blaze on the Hill of Slane. The light of a new faith:

> On Tara's hill the daylight dies –
> On Tara's plain 'tis dead;
> 'Til Baal's unkindled fire shall rise,
> No fire must flame instead.'

'Tis thus the king commanding speaks,
Commands and speaks in vain –
For lo! A fire defiant breaks,
From out the woods of Slane . . .

Denis Florence McCarthy
from 'The Paschal Fire'

The custom of quenching hearth fires at Hallowe'en and rekindling them from bonfires outside, survived in Celtic countries until recently. In Scotland, farmers walked around their fields in a sunwise direction holding brands from the bonfire in order to destroy witches. The ritual had the added benefit of averting all malevolent forces, particularly those loosed at this dangerous time of the year. It was a custom to light Hallowe'en fires in the English countryside of Lancashire and Derbyshire. Here the people knelt around the fire to pray for the dead; as in Ireland, bunches of blazing straw were then carried about the farm property to bless and fertilise the fields.

Bonfires survive in England but have now a more sinister connotation. Following Guy Fawkes's endeavour on 5 November 1605 to blow up the English House of Lords in protest against anti-Catholic laws, the lighting of bonfires was moved to this anniversary. Effigies of the unfortunate conspirator are still burned on top of the pile.

The word 'bonfire' is believed to derive its origins from 'bone'-fire, as in pre-Christian times the fires were most likely sacred ones at which bones were burned. The practice of burning bones was carried out at Hallowe'en celebrations in more recent times in Dublin and in Scotland. They may well be a remembrance of early human and animal sacrifices.

In Ireland, the Hallowe'en fire survives primarily in Dublin.

Gardaí and fire brigades are on full alert preventing damage to property and persons. Many injuries are caused to youngsters from firecrackers and rockets exploding prematurely in their hands despite warnings of the risks on TV and radio.

Until recently, young people in country places went out on November Eve leaving a trail of mischief as they impersonated the capricious spirits of folklore – a twentieth-century vestige of the old beliefs. Now, on Hallowe'en, Irish housing estates and villages turn into imitations of US suburbs as children dress up and go from door to door in imitation of the American 'trick or treat' they see on television. This practice is a conglomeration derived from Hallowe'en pastimes brought across the sea to the US by emigrants from Irish and other European cultures. Black cats and pumpkins, which have nothing to do with Samhain, are the most recent importations, a typical American 'mix and match' derived from a melting pot of Norse, French and Scottish traditions formerly practised at several different times of the year. A peculiar example of an old tradition exported and later reimported! Strangely, television, usually the death knell of many old customs, in this instance may have been the instrument of this one's resurrection, albeit thoroughly Americanised.

Years ago there were no 'trick-or-treaters' in Sligo. But the spirits were out! Evidence of the previous night's activities greeted churchgoers as they walked to Mass on All Saints' Day: carts left with one or no wheels, gates missing, cabbage-strewn roads. Worshippers kept a sharp lookout and were seldom disappointed! As rascality was traditional on this night there was a more lenient attitude towards the rascals if they were caught – as long as the pranks didn't go too far and there was no excessive damage to person or property. Mercy depended on the eye of the beholder and the good or bad humour of the victim.

A favourite trick was to fasten the front and back door of

a neighbour's house from the outside and then climb up on the roof to block the chimney, sending clouds of smoke into the kitchen below. If there were ramblers in the house, so much the better. With the doors tied there was no chance of the hooligans getting caught.

The school gate, symbol of incarceration for successive generations of young people, was always a target. It came off the hinges easily and was sure to be missing on the morning after Hallowe'en. Retribution from outraged nuns was just as certain on the next school day. The first morning after the fairies had been out was taken up with detective work. Dire consequences were promised if the missing gate was not returned forthwith. Some of the more audacious boys looked forward to the encounter. Pacts were made or threats imposed to draw the weaker souls into bonds of silence.

Sweaty palms betrayed fearful hearts as we filed into our seats. Clad in voluminous black robes, girdled at the waist with a stout leather belt, Sister de Pazzi was an imposing figure of authority. Attached to the belt was an oversized rosary, with a strong steel cross and beads as big as marbles, that hung to the ground. Her seven-stone, five-foot-and-a-bit presence swelled with righteousness; her frame and rosary beads pulsed with the compressed energy of a cobra about to strike. Scandalised at the damage suffered by Church property and insulted by the impertinence of the nonentities who inflicted it, her face made even more severe by the starched white headdress and black wimple that encased it, she drew herself up to her full height and turned to face her charges.

Anything she lacked in stature and bearing was made up for by three feet of wooden pointer menacingly poised in front of a baleful countenance which left no doubt that the wand would be vigorously employed. Standing there, a beacon of Christian virtue in a sea of vice, the merciless glare of offended society shone fiercely through her steel-rimmed spectacles. Like the ferocious gaze of Balor of the Evil Eye, it pierced the bravest heart and chilled the most innocent bone.

Although filled with foreboding, we put on as confident a face as we could. Mustering our courage we looked back at our accusing Boudicca with bland expressions of offended virtue. From where she observed our quaking flesh we must have looked a pretty unconvincing lot indeed. We knew the promised storm was no idle threat and would soon break over our heads if the truth was not forthcoming without delay. In the arsenal of methods used by this saintly woman to instil knowledge, inspire fear and nurture respect for authority, the virtues of patience and gentle persuasion were not found.

Inevitably, one of the perpetrators, singled out for cross-examination, broke under pressure, confessed the crime and revealed the whereabouts of the gate. Everyone breathed a sigh of relief. Sooner or later, it always turned up. And why not? Sure, it was all in a night's fun, and Hallowe'en would come again.

Older and more energetic pranksters indulged in more complex tricks. A favourite was to take a neighbour's ass-cart, dismantle it, and then reassemble it inside one of the outbuildings. Everyone got a good laugh the next morning when the unfortunate owner, having searched for the missing cart, discovered it in such an unlikely place. It took more than one man to put it there and it would take more than one to recover and reassemble it. Assistance had to be sent for to accomplish the job. Often it was the helper who joined most enthusiastically in the scolding who had the biggest hand in planning and executing the raid.

Another choice prank was to take the cart up to a gate, bring the shafts through the bars and then harness the ass to the other side. This was quite an unusual sight in the morning and very funny – to everyone except the owner of the team.

To turn sense into nonsense, to make us laugh at ourselves was the thrust of Hallowe'en. Sometimes it exceeded the limits. One year, in our village, a horse-cart wheel was taken and rolled down a steep hill that led to the sea. The heavy wheel must have gathered immense speed as it careened to the bottom of the hill, crossed another road and plunged over a cliff face and into the water several hundred yards away. Someone could have been killed. It was a dangerous act, nobody thought it funny and it never happened again.

One of the most amusing spectacles I have ever seen on a November morning was the sight of a flagpole dropped through the chimney of an abandoned house. Adorning the top and fluttering magnificently in the breeze was a pair of long johns stolen from someone's clothesline.

In the next village a farmer well-known for his bad humour kept the whole parish amused for days with his efforts to chase away a 'strange' horse, which was later revealed, after a shower of rain, to be his own horse disguised by a coat of whitewash.

Sometimes we pulled heads of cabbage in the fields and hung them on doors or threw them about the roads, or we hurled turnips at a house where we thought a lively chase might result. It was pointless if there was no danger or if no response could be provoked.

The streets are quiet now and the young people pacified in comfortable living rooms with electronic pastimes. They will never know the magic and wild freedom of nocturnal Hallowe'en raids, when we pillaged and roamed the dark roads and fields with the ghosts and spirits of Samhain for accomplices. Peace, order and harmony, subject to remote control, prevail. I think

I liked the old anarchic holiday a lot better!

In some places turnips or mangels were hollowed out, faces carved on them and a lighted candle put inside. These were left on the porch or carried about. Surreal and ghostly in the dark they were a great amusement for children. Their origins convey deeper meaning. The lamps were an impersonation of the dead and other spirits thought to return on the night. By assuming the character of the departed in the form of spectral lights, people invoked a protection from the power of the otherworld. In Somerset, England and in Wales, these turnip lanterns are hung on gateposts with the specific purpose of deterring evil spirits.

Kevin Danaher in his book *The Year in Ireland* tells us about Hallowe'en customs in other parts of Ireland. In County Waterford Hallowe'en was known as *Oíche na h-Aimleise* ('The Night of Mischief or Con'). It was a custom in the county – it survives still in places – for the boys to assemble in gangs, and, headed by a few hornblowers, who were always selected for their strength of lungs, to visit all the farmers' houses in the district and impose a kind of levy, good-humouredly asked for and just as cheerfully given. The leader of the band chanted a sort of recitative in Gaelic, intoning it with a strong nasal twang to conceal his identity, in which the goodwife was called upon to do honour to Samhain. They afterwards met at some rendezvous, and in merry revelry celebrated the festival of Samhain in their own way.[53]

On the southern coast between Ballycotton and Trabolgan a similar custom was followed except that the visitors there represented themselves as the 'Muck Olla'. They were accompanied by a figure called the *Lár Bhán* (white mare) which was dressed in a white sheet with the head of a horse. The group recited rhymes which were said to savour strongly of paganism, and too crude for the average listener's ear! A horse figure called the *Capall an tSusa* ('blanket horse') was the central figure of a Hallowe'en game played in Limerick. The young people who went around in this way on November eve were called variously, 'guisers', 'vizards', *'hugadais'* or *'buachaillí tuí'* ('strawboys').

Just as at Christmas, treats were anticipated at 'Halloweve'. For the children there was great excitement as the day drew closer. The monotony of a diet of home-baked bread was going to be broken, at least for a little while. Hazelnuts were in plentiful supply in the shops. Even the poorest house had an abundant supply. Those lucky enough to live near hazel groves could pick their own.

There was sure to be apples in the house for ducking games and for eating as well. Orchards were few and far between, and owners must now be particularly vigilant for midnight raiders. There was no amnesty at this or any other time of year for pilferers. The unlucky culprit who got caught was shown no mercy, nor did he expect any.

A raisin cake was the highlight of the evening. Delight lit my mother's face as she squandered her small store of money on nuts, apples and raisins. At other times of the year we might have to count the pennies but at Hallowe'en and Christmas the compulsions of frugality were forgotten for a while. Better an empty purse than a table without a raisin cake. 'Pratie' bread or 'boxty' sizzled on the fire – it wouldn't be Hallowe'en without it! It sputtered and spat in lakes of butter in the cast-iron oven over the hot coals. To understand the excitement about simple delights that we now take for granted we might recall the plain diet described earlier by Mickey McGroarty and Maggie McGowan. Two or three staples provided the entire selection of food. Choice didn't exist. Until the 1960s, shops amounted to a shelf or two. Gourmet belonged to fantasy. Eating was a necessity, not an indulgence.

As night fell on Halloweve there was a fevered rush to get the evening work done and God help the turkey that picked that particular hour to declare its independence. Suppertime couldn't come quickly enough and when darkness eased in around us and the lamp was lit, all was right with the world!

The feast over and the table cleaned off, it was time for games. This was one of the few occasions when even my father, a dour countryman, took an interest in children's pastimes. He watched with amusement as we tried to get a bite out of the apple that weaved back and forth on a string that he had fastened to the 'couplin'', or laughed as we ducked with gasping breath into the water-filled basin for the sixpences or shillings that lay at the bottom. Any treasure hunter lifting a coin with his teeth or lips got to keep it.

These games are very old and were just as popular over two hundred years ago. General Vallencey wrote in 1783 that 'every house abounds in the best viands they can afford: apples and nuts are devoured in abundance: the nutshells are burnt and from the ashes, many strange things are foretold. They dip for apples in a tub of water, and endeavour to bring one up in the mouth; they suspend a cord with a cross stick, with apples at one point, and candles lighted at the other, and endeavour to catch the apple, while it is in a circular motion in the mouth.'

Today, when this game is played, a potato is substituted because of the danger of burning from the candle. The fun is in watching the chagrin of the blindfolded player as he bites into the unsavoury potato instead of a delicious apple. In Scotland, a bannock smeared with treacle is used in the same way; the sticky mess made by the player in his efforts to secure the apple provides great entertainment for the watchers.

Young men often took on more formidable challenges such as spending the night at a haunted house or visiting a cemetery at midnight. Sufferers from toothache could find relief by going to the graveyard that night; all they had to do was find a skull and pull a tooth from it with their own teeth!

The seed of the fern was reputed to have magical properties. Anyone having it was rendered invisible, 'in order that the possessor could, unobserved, enter houses, search rooms, plunder treasures, and indirectly get gold.' Various forms of this folk belief were popular in England and on the Continent. Enrí Ó Muirgheasa observed in 1930 that belief in the potency of the fern seed was firmly held in Farney, County Monaghan:

> The hardy individual who essayed this dangerous task had to repair alone shortly before midnight on Hallow-eve to the solitary place where the ferns grew, with a number of pewter plates – nine or thirteen, I forget which – all regularly laid or imposed over one another, and having a sheet of white paper or linen between the two lower ones. These were held under the fern, and precisely at midnight the seed was dropped, and so great was its enchanted power that it passed through all the plates except the lowermost one, where it got caught on the linen or paper. This was then folded up and carried in the pocket of the adventurer, who thereby could render himself invisible.

As on the Continent, they believed in Monaghan that:

> all the powers of the world of darkness and evil were mustered to frighten off the temerarious individual while in the act of securing the seed. They could not touch him, but yells, screams,

thunders, whirlwinds, lightnings and the actual appearance of fiends, all conspired to shake his nerve. They told of one person who, while waiting for the seed to fall, got such a fright that he became demented, and, though subsequently half-cured by the parish priest, he continued 'simple' or half-witted for the rest of his life.[54]

In all the Celtic countries Hallowe'en night, when the mysterious, unknown underworld opened up, was a time to tell the future. Echoes of earlier magical observances can still be detected in attempts at prediction which, long ago, were taken very seriously indeed. Such customs may well have been used at one time as rites to avert evil or to secure the benefits they now pretend to forecast.

Daithi, High King of Ireland in the fifth century, 'happening to be at the Druid's Hill (Cnoc-an-Draoi) in the county of Sligo one Hallowe'en, ordered his Druid to forecast the future for him that day till the next Hallowe'en should come round. The Druid passed the night on the top of the hill, and next morning made a prediction to the king that came true.'[55]

Nowadays, when foreknowledge is sought these predictions are not taken seriously. They take the nature of games – don't they? Most households in Ireland that get a *báirín breac* (barmbrack) at Hallowe'en know that the finder of the ring will be the first in the house to get married. Of course we don't believe it! But how many have looked at the ring after finding it and wondered if maybe, well, just maybe . . .

Baking a special *báirín breac* is not as common as it used to be. The Schools Manuscript Collection of 1937–8 records that in Sligo a nut, a ring, a button and a penny were mixed with the ingredients. The finder of the nut would remain a bachelor; the ring indicated early marriage; the button meant the finder would become a tailor; a penny, the finder would find riches. In other parts of Ireland additional items were introduced, such as a chip of wood, a rag, a pea, a bean, a religious medal. The fate of the finder of the chip of wood was to be beaten by a spouse, the rag meant poverty, the pea and bean poverty and wealth, the religious medal signified that the finder would join the religious life.

Until recently young people invoked the powers to discover whom they were going to marry. Clareman Brian Merriman in his poem 'Cúirt an Mheán-Oíche' ('The Midnight Court') tried to see into the future:

> No trick of which you'd read or hear
> At dark of moon or when it's clear,
> Crescent, full moon and Harvest moon,
> Whit and All Souls and the First of May.
> Under my pillow I've kept all night
> A stocking stuffed with apples tight,
> I fasted three canonical hours
> To try and come round the heavenly powers.

It was almost exclusively the young women of the family who tried these methods to discover what kind of husband was in their future. Many such procedures were practised in England and Scotland too. Hazelnuts were often used by the seers. In Sligo, two nuts were chosen, one of which was given the name of a boy and the other that of a girl. Both were placed on the *gríosach* (red ashes). If they hopped towards each other, marriage would result. The quicker they moved together the sooner the marriage day. If they moved away from each other, matrimony was out of the question.

Another ruse employed when a girl wished to see her future

husband was to borrow an apple, cut it in two and put it under her pillow when going to bed. During the night the man of her desire would be revealed to her in a dream. In Scotland and Ireland the apple was used to discover the initials of the future mate. Peeled in one long unbroken strip, the skin was thrown over the left shoulder, preferably at midnight. The initials of the gentleman could be read from the form the peel took as it lay on the ground.

At the beginning of this century Mairéad Kerins of Derelehan, County Sligo, recorded that: 'When we are going to bed on Hallowe'en night we place our shoes in the form of a T by the bed and we say this rhyme:

> *I place my shoes in the form of a T,*
> *Hoping tonight my true love to see,*
> *The colour of his hair and the clothes that he'll wear*
> *And the day he'll be married to me.*

She and her friends would obtain a ball of wool and go to a limekiln about twelve o'clock at night. Each one threw the ball into the kiln in turn, holding the end of the thread in their hand. It was then wound back up while the holder repeated, 'Who holds my wool?' They believed the response would be that of the future husband.

Attempting to discover the suitor's voice in a limekiln was one of the more prevalent pastimes carried on at this time of year until quite recently. Many women can still recall unusual experiences they had while trying this as young girls. Some, who left the needles in the wool, deciphered an answer from the echo made as the wool and needles clattered down the stony sides of the kiln.

A woman of Maugherow told me: 'There was a limekiln down at Ballinful quarry and one down at the pump at

Boyle's. There was a hole at the bottom of the kiln where you could climb in; that's where they used to light the fire and take out the lime long ago. This young lad found out that the girls were going down this night and didn't he climb in at the bottom and wait for them. When they came they threw the wool down and shouted "Who am I going to marry?" "Tom the Divil," the voice boomed back up the kiln at them. It frightened the life in them and I'm telling ye, that finished the lime kilns for that night.'

Another true story is told of a man who tried something similar but with a more serious intent. Advanced in years, toothless, and bent over with rheumatism, he had seen better days. Nevertheless, his heart was young and he did not give up on the notion that he would get a young girl to settle down with him. Knowing that a neighbouring girl always went to a limekiln near him on Halloweve, he hit on a plan to hide there and provide the answer to her question. How could she refuse the voice of the limekiln? The evening wore on, darkness fell, and sure enough the girl came and shouted down into the pit, 'Who am I going to marry?' This was just the opportunity for which our friend had been waiting and of course he was ready with an answer, 'Jack K ——,' he shouted back as loudly and convincingly as he could. The young girl froze on hearing the unwelcome answer but as far as we know did not go on to take the proferred advice. Supernatural tip or not, there's a limit to how far a girl will go.

'Cúirt an Mheán-Oíche' mentions the lime kiln:

> Hid my wool in the lime-kiln late
> And my distaff behind the churchyard gate;
> I had flax in the road to halt coach and carriage
> And haycocks stuffed with heads of cabbage,

And night and day on the proper occasions
Invoked Old Nick and all his legions.

Translation by Frank O'Connor

In Sligo, a head of cabbage was hung on the door latch. The first person to come across the threshold afterwards was sure to be the future husband. Heads of cabbage had related uses elsewhere in determining the kind of man in a young girl's future. In County Down, 'girls were blindfolded and sent out in pairs, hand in hand, to the garden or field and told to pull the first cabbage they found. Its size and shape – whether it was big or small, straight or crooked – would indicate the shape and texture of their future spouse. If much earth adhered to the root they would have plenty of money; if there were only a little they would be poor. The taste of the "custock", that is the heart, would tell them his temper and disposition, according to whether it was sweet or bitter. Finally, the "runts" or stems were hung above the door; each was given a number and the name of a boyfriend, for example Barney might be the name given to the third runt. If Barney was the third person to enter the house on the night, this was considered to be a good omen.'[56]

Numerous other methods of marriage divination were used: molten lead was poured through the wards of a key into a container of cold water. The shapes resulting on the bottom of the container indicated the profession of the future husband, e.g. hammer for a carpenter, scissors for a tailor, scythe for a farmer and so on; some girls filled their mouth with water and went outside, 'the first boy's name we hear mentioned will be the name of our future husband'; another plan was to 'eat a salt herring in three bites before going to bed and not speak after eating. Whoever will be your future spouse will come with a drink to you in your dream.' Boys and girls stole a small amount of oats and repeated the following while sowing it in the garden:

> *In the name of God I sow thee*
> *My true love for to show me*
> *The colour of his hair*
> *The clothes that he wears*
> *And the day he'll be married to me.*

Mairead Kerins of Derelehan, County Sligo, recalled that girls tied an ass or horseshoe nail in their stocking. While tying the string they said:

> *I knit this knot, this knot I knit,*
> *To dream of the man I know not yet,*
> *To dream of him in his best array*
> *And the clothes he'll wear on the wedding day.*

The herb yarrow was used too. It was pulled out of the sod while the hopeful maiden repeated:

> *Good morrow fair yarrow, twice good morrow;*
> *Before this time tomorrow*
> *My true love you will show to me.*
> *Bright and balmy may he be*
> *With his face turned to me.*

Darker forces were given a chance to show their power on this night as well. Girls combed their hair in front of a mirror invoking the 'prince of darkness' expecting to see their future husband reflected in the glass.

The following plan was only for the fearless – or the

desperate. Men, and sometimes women, went into the hay-garden with a rake at midnight. They walked around the rick three times in an anticlockwise direction combing the hay as they went in the name of the devil. As they combed they asked for the name of the person they were going to marry. The future spouse was expected to appear beside them and help them rake the rick. It was a brave man or woman who attempted this and many who did got such a fright from things imagined or seen that they never tried it again.

Sometimes good things happened and a marriage resulted from these experiments, a Ballintrillick, County Sligo man told me: 'John C——, an uncle of them that used to live here went out one Halloweve and tried combing the rick. In the middle of the raking, anyway, didn't he see the likeness of a woman. Well, that gave him something to think about! Begod, some time after that didn't he see the same woman on the street when he was at a fair in Manorhamilton. That'd be about 1957. He knew her right away, went up and spoke to her and weren't they married a few months after that!'

A Drumfad, County Sligo, bachelor saw a woman at the end of the rick who had emigrated to America some years before. She came home on holidays some time after, he proposed to her and they got married. Perhaps the marriage would have happened anyway or perhaps the premonition gave him the incentive to make the proposal. Pistroges, fortune, fate or luck, who can question a good result? The answers are in the stars.

Dabbling with the occult brought inherent dangers. A girl from Glencar, County Sligo, set out gaily on Hallowe'en to discover who she would marry. Through a strange turn of events, her gaiety was soon to turn to horror. The dark forces she summoned to her aid on that fateful night ensured that her life would never be the same again. How could anyone know that an innocent childhood game would turn so quickly to tragedy?

On her way home from the limekiln a man fell into step beside her. She was not surprised. The roads were full of young people. Excitement was in the air. Wonderful things could happen on such a special night. They chatted comfortably and as she drew close to her home the stranger asked if he could go in. When the girl put the question to her father, he responded with a hearty welcome and the man sat with them around the fire. As they chatted the girl's father became increasingly uneasy. There was something sinister about this good-looking stranger. Resenting the father's queries the man became aggressive and after a heated exchange was asked to leave. He got up but instead of going out the door he made for the bedroom.

Thoroughly alarmed now the pair rushed into the room and the demon, for that is what it was, seeming to change shape, concealed itself under the bed, out of reach. When it resisted all attempts to expel it from the house the girl's father tried to dislodge it with a pitchfork but this too failed. In the following weeks the family were kept awake at night by loud noises, screams and grunting sounds as if from some wild animal. Furniture was thrown around the house by unseen hands. If the girl was away from home or slept in a neighbour's house, nothing happened. On her return bedlam broke loose again. When all attempts to remove the malicious spirit came to nothing the family, becoming ever more fearful of the evil that had befallen them, sent for the priest.

As the curate read from his book of prayer the screeches and moans of the demon grew louder and louder. Sweat poured from the priest's body. He shook violently from the fierce struggle of spirit against spirit, good against evil. The priest persevered until, with a thunderous sound, the demon or devil, burst from the house 'taking the door jambs with it' as it left. The priest could banish it no further than a culvert near the local cemetery where it then took up residence. The spirit was not done yet and confronted the priest again late one night when he was on his way to answer a sick call. Another fierce struggle ensued and this time the fiend was banished to an island on Glencar Lake, where we may suppose it still resides.

The house where this demonic possession took place still stands, silent and deserted, in the Glencar valley. Those who pass it late at night, who know its dark secret, bless themselves as they hasten their steps and recall the terrible events that took place there long years before. The family's name, although well known locally, is not mentioned here in order to protect their descendants from any further intrusion on their privacy.

There were other things that could be foretold on the night before All Hallows. A coin was put at the backdoor before going to bed at night with the harp side up: 'If it would be turned or shifted from its place in the morning this foretold that the house would have plenty of money for the year.' Others scattered ashes around the fire after it was raked. If footprints were found in the morning then someone in the house would die during the year, if hoofprints then a similar fate would befall one of the farm animals

One of the most popular and widespread games was to put four plates on a table, one of which contained clay, another water, another a ring and salt in the fourth. Each player was then led blindfolded to the table and asked to place their hand on a saucer. The future was determined by which plate the person chose, the saucers being changed each time another person came to the table. The ring signified imminent marriage; the water, a voyage across the sea; the clay, sudden death and the salt, prosperity.

Like so much else, Hallowe'en has been diluted, its supernatural content lost in the frenetic pace of modern living. Omens, portents and ghosts do not appear in busy, crowded places. They haunt our minds instead. Often when the season approaches, in quiet moments, our memories can draw us back to simpler times. A hungry soul transcends distance to watch from the shadows of a country kitchen where no one ages. Two small boys duck for apples there and a small stout woman tends a cast-iron oven hung over an open fire; yellow butter flows in rivulets off hot potato bread. She dishes it out to eager hands while a lean weather-beaten man watches benignly from the chimney corner.

The weather must often have been wet, cold and windy – but I don't remember that. I recall only mellow evenings, soft and warm; night falling gently on fields and farms at peace; gentle breezes wafting smells of perfumed turf smoke, nuts roasting, boxty cooking. I hear only the muted sounds of turkeys gobbling, cows lowing, a murmuring sea. I see black turf-stacks, stubbled fields, golden thatch, purple mountains gathered round.

The Druids and practitioners of the old religions could not have devoted themselves more earnestly to their ritual obser-vances than we did to ours in those Hallowe'ens long ago. Apart from the games and feasting there was another, more serious side, to the seasonal observations – that was to save souls. On the eve of All Souls the Church granted special indulgences to anyone wishing to release souls from Purgatory.

The village turned out en masse then as it always did at times of special religious significance during the year – All Souls, Christmas and the Lenten season. The walkway between the church door and the entrance gates was a bustling thoroughfare as we made our 'visits', said the required prayers, walked outside the gates and back again in a busy rhythm. Each separate visit gained another indulgence. To qualify, we had to go outside the church gates and come back in again. So back and forth we went and back and forth, again and again and again.

For the older ones it was a very solemn occasion, one of the most important religious festivals of the year, equalled only by Christmas and Easter. For the younger ones, sure, wasn't it great fun, and a welcome relief for a short while from the drudgery of farm work – picking potatoes, making pits or feeding cattle. Even the nuns who taught us were more tolerant. If an excess of religious zeal was the excuse for homework left undone they nodded understandingly, and passed on.

In those youthful days, all our geese were swans. Life and death sat easily together as boys and girls, schoolmates, played and laughed on our journeys back and forth between church door and gate. We hardly bothered with the imponderables of how many souls we had released, how many plenary indulgences it took to bring a soul to heaven. There was no way of knowing which or how many of our departed family were still in danger of burning in everlasting flames. But we felt gratified on the way home, believing we had done something of value for those dead friends and relatives.

Peals of laughter came from the girls as they talked animatedly. Shapeless tweed coats hinted at developing breasts, barely cloaking a budding pubescent pulchritude. The changes in the boys were not so apparent, except when they wore the light fabric trousers that came in packages from America. Tommy revelled in showing off the tents he could make. It would take more than this to impress Colm; he had thought about it and come to the conclusion that the height of the tent had more to do with the flimsy material than the size of the tent-pole!

In the schoolyard, unruly contestants engaging in proud displays sent streams of piss arching up the toilet wall. They laid ambushes for the unwary. Painted wooden planks fastened together with a hole in the middle served as a toilet seat. A warm salty jet aimed from atop this platform sprayed the faces

J. McGowan

Encounter with a cutthroat: Jimmy Flynn of Laughy Barr, County Leitrim, living dangerously in 1994

Paul Higgins and Peter McGowan on Cloonerco bog, County Sligo, 1983. Paul is putting a 'crivening' on a crib of turf

Mary Kate and Patrick McGloin, Derryduff, County Leitrim, 'bleeding for St Martin', 1994

'The night was no time in passin' with all the different stories ye'd hear. I learned them all from the oul' people. I learnt it an' I drunk it by heart.'
Mickey McGroarty, Selacis, County Donegal, 1990

Clamping turf in the shadow of Benbulben, c. 1900

Tom Ward: a Sligo tinker practising the old craft, 1994

John Harrison 'scutching' rye straw in preparation for thatching, Cliffoney, County Sligo, 1991

Thatchers at work on J. M. Synge's cottage on Inishmaan, County Galway, 1998

The Christmas Mummers, Sligo, 2001: Finn McCumhaill engages Brian Boru in mortal combat while Dr Brown and the rest of the troupe look on

'What am I bid?' Competition is keen at the Christmas turkey market, Convoy, County Donegal, 1999

'Station' in John Eddie Costello's kitchen, Castlegal, County Sligo, 2000:
a heritage of fugitive Masses in Penal times

Therefore in frights and feares, those holy-dayes we pass
In sorrow and in teares, we spend our Christmass
Luke Waddinge, Bishop of Ferns, 1684
'Penal Times': seventeenth-century woodcut, R. Verstegan,
T. Crud. Haereticorum

And make the most of what we yet may spend
Before we too into the dust descend
Rubaiyat of Omar Khayyam

Mullaghmore, County Sligo, National School, 1898. Anonymous faces from the past: Kellys, Duffys, McGowans, Gonigles, Dowdicans, Rourkes, Conways

Iron Age/early Christian burial site at Knoxspark, County Sligo, 1994. Did this man walk with St. Patrick? Other interments on the site indicate 'ritual burials related to the Celtic cult of the severed head'

of unguarded innocents as they came in the door. Flush hadn't arrived. Under the boards lay a foetid pile of putrefying human waste. Tinkers filled half the village with a foul stench when they took on the loathsome job of cleaning it out with shovel and buckets once a month.

For both sexes there was hair in places where no hair had grown before and for boys erections were uncontrollable and spontaneous. Unbidden they came. We looked and saw and the girls knew that we wanted to know more, and didn't Helen hint at soft delights that her bulky garb could not conceal and was it me she looked at that way, then; and oh, could that be, and wouldn't you like to know her on the way home in the gathering, friendly dusk if you thought it was so.

Primal urges initiated playful tussles. Hands fumbled, exploring the unknown, earnest, fearful, hestitant, reaching for the dewy goal of fevered aspiration.

The girls, paragons of virtue, seemed completely immune to the licentious thoughts occupying male minds. Many of them belonged to the Legion of Mary. Resplendent in blue mantles they had meetings and outings at which they marched in pious ranks of moral rectitude: 'the Queen of Heaven's special soldiers, pledged above all others to her service and defence'. In the 1950s the clergy perceived a growing threat to the morality and innocence of youth. The mission of Mary's special soldiers was 'the preservation of modesty as a powerful bulwark against all attacks upon the sixth comandment'.

Not all the fellows were awed by these pious displays. Some of our more dissolute acquaintances, who liked to brag of their sexual exploits, confided that the journey home from these evangelistic outings 'was the best time to get them'. Rory seemed an astute student of human nature. Although the three Rs were a constant puzzle to him, there was little outside the classroom on which he didn't speak with 'knowledgeable airs'. He declared that with souls gleaming and overcome with spiritual ecstasy was when these young virgins were ripe to partake of a more earthly rapture as well.

> Now I turn
> Away from the ricks, the sheds, the cabbage garden,
> The stones of the street, the thrush song in the tree,
> The potato-pits, the flaggers in the swamp;
> From the country heart that hardly learned to harden,
> From the spotlight of an old-fashioned kitchen lamp
> I go to follow her who winked at me.

> Patrick Kavanagh
> from 'Temptation in Harvest'

In the darkened cinema glamorous screen idols pressed their lips together in mock passion and we watched closely to see how it was done. Into the parish hall we swaggered with awkward feet, mock bravado and sweaty palms to dance and meet. Would tonight be the night to learn, discover or conquer? At Christmas, Easter and Hallowe'en the hopeless as well as the hopeful turned out. Older bachelors confirmed in their celibacy or hindered by lack of confidence, dutiful sons encumbered by aged parents of iron rule, *spailpíns* eager for an opportunity: they all danced with other men's wives or daughters in platitudinous conversation – turkeys, turf, cattle, crops – while their manhood slipped away. The 'pricks that pricked were the pointed pins of harrows', as Kavanagh put it.

From the men's side of the hall we cast furtive, calculating glances at the serried ranks of women lined along the wall on the other side. Chatting away nonchalantly they seemed completely unaware of the sweating hands, shaking hearts and seething testosterone of the pimpled studs on the other side. The desperate and the brave risked refusal's mortification with the enthusiasm of youth. When the dance was called we ran the gauntlet of rejection and a frosty, 'Sorry, I'm ast' or 'Ask me sister, I'm sweatin',' as we charged like lemmings across the floor to the chosen one in the huddled group of girls near the women's toilet. Some had smart answers rehearsed to ease refusal's sting: 'Why didn't ye bring yer knittin'?' or 'Sorry, I forgot about yer wooden leg!' we snarled as disdainfully as our sinking hearts would allow. One rebuff set off a chain reaction as dignity demanded that the girl beside the refuser decline on principle. She didn't want to be seen to be second choice, or maybe she was waiting to be asked by some other heartthrob. It got worse as you begged your way along the row. Better to beat a strategic retreat to another part of the hall, start anew, and hope there was any kind of picking to be had by the time you got there.

We fumbled on the dance floor to make conversation and then over a mineral in Timoney's shop and if we were lucky, later still outside in the corner of Peter Patsy's hayshed: no manuals, a first kiss. I almost strangled on mine. To breathe or not to breathe? Suck or press? What to do with your nose? A taut, perilous adventure.

In the name of the Father! Pubescent arousal that obeys no will imprisoned in stiff corduroy. This is God's plan? Some plan! Much pain! Many questions. Few answers. Guilt. The time is not yet come. Reproduction: another generation must replace those who are gone and we in time must be replaced. Primal desire. Respond to the force. Sin. Three Dark Days. Third Secret of Fatima. Conversion of Russia. Eternal Damnation. Sacrilegehellfirepurgatorylimbo. Confession.

A silent vigil in the gloomy box. Muttered whispered echoes shuffle-flutter from the other cubicle. Waiting, waiting, waiting. The priest turns. The shutter clatters back to the dreaded moment of truth. Purple veil parts. Heart capsizes. Please God, let this cup pass from me. Say something!

'Forgive me, Father, for I have sinned.' Cheeks flushed. Palms sweat. Does he know me?

'How long since your last Confession?'

'Two weeks, Father.' That's easy.

'What are your sins?' ominously.

'I took the name of the Lord in vain.'

'Is that all?'

'I stole?'

'What did you steal?'

'I stole sugar from the bowl when my mother and father were out milking.'

'Is there anything else?'

'Aaah.'

'Talk up, will ye!' Impatiently.

'I commited sins of impurity, Father,' into the vacuum.

'Was it by yourself?'

Not so easy now. Christ! Don't talk so loud, Father! They'll hear you. What does he mean?

Think. Whisper. 'Yes, Father.'

'How many times?'

Oh, shit, I don't know. What's the difference? Quick now. Make something up. Gotta get out of here quick.

Muttered sweaty reply.

'Anything else?'

Relief. 'No, Father.'

'Are you sorry for your sins?'

'Yes, Father.'

'Say ten Our Fathers and ten Hail Marys for your penance.'

'Yes, Father.'

'Make an Act of Perfect Contrition.'

'Yes, Father'.

Contrition was easy, the words embedded by rote from the nuns: 'O my God I am heartily sorry for having offended thee and I detest my sins above every other evil because they displease thee my God who art so deserving of all my love and I firmly resolve by thy Holy Grace never more to offend thee and to amend my life. Amen.' In one breath.

'*Ego te absolvo* . . . ' White vestments. Purple stole. The shadowy figure in the gloomy box raises God's forgiving hand.

It's over. Relief. 'God bless you too, Father'. The veil closes. Shutter bangs home.

Escape! Out the door.

A gauntlet of sidelong glances from queues of waiting penitents. They know; they know! A solitary reflection on the kneeler and then out the path of freedom – to sin again.

Salvation and saving the Holy Souls in Purgatory was simple then; a matter of arithmetic, numbers and rules laid down for us. Don't ask questions. Too stupid to understand the answers. God knows best. Or the priest. So much remission for a plenary indulgence, less for an ordinary indulgence.

Make another visit – remission for another holy soul.

It doesn't seem so clear now; a complicated algebraic equation beyond human knowledge. Luther questioned and he was a heretic. A heretic! The word had a terrible ring to it – like sacrilege or pervert. Who'd want to be a heretic? Well, follow the rules then!

How could we know at which elevation in Purgatory our lost relatives were, how serious their offence, how much compensation must be offered to God for their release?

Better to be sure. So we went back, every year. Year after year. Adolescent longing, laughter, fear; a composite hum of hope and prayer, offered to God on the November air.

8
—

SPIRIT OF CHRISTMAS PAST

A pool of light from the kitchen window shone on the cobbled
street, bright eye of life piercing the gloomy dark of a winter
morning. Inside, standing on tiptoes, a small boy's chin rested
on the flower-printed, knife-scored oilcloth. The covering, its
flowered pattern cracked and faded, concealed the scars of
antiquity marring the planks and sturdy, painted legs of the deal
table underneath. The object of the boy's attention was a raisin
cake sitting on a plate in the centre of the cloth.

Above, a paraffin lamp hung from a nail driven into the
lime-crusted wall. Stones, heavy with a thousand coats of
whitewash and veined with a network of cracks, disclosed
centuries of existence. The lamp's yellow eye lit the boy's curly
hair. The glow from its hairpin-straddled globe illuminated
ancient walls, religious pictures, a holy-water font near the door
and a white-scrubbed flagstone floor. Embracing the burnished,
bog-oak-beamed sod roof overhead, the pale light was lost in
shadowy gloom above the smoke-blackened 'couplin's'. On this
December morning, our kitchen had the character and warm
ambience of an old oil painting.

A red Christmas candle burned in the window, a beacon to lost
souls and a token of welcome to the Holy Family who wandered
without shelter in Bethlehem long ago. Clusters of red berries
peeped from glistening green holly branches arrayed in rows over
the holy pictures. The leafy camouflage gave a festive glow to the

crowded space above the delft-lined dresser concealing my father's small store of tools: builders' level, bicycle pump, pincers, hoof-parer and such. Tucked safely inside were dusty treasures of his seafaring days: charts, dividers, parallel rule, compass. On the opposite wall, a ruby light radiated from the blood-red globe of the Sacred Heart lamp, keeping a constant vigil before the mournful face of Christ. Exposed heart banded with barbed wire, he gazed perpetually skywards, imploring favours from a heavenly father for our sinful humanity. Holy water glistened in a font hung near the door. It safeguarded us from the devil and from lightning; sprinkles from its bowl protected and brought luck on trips away from home by day or night, to fair or field.

Over in the chimney corner, beside the unmade bed, a cut-throat razor glinted as the boy's father, mirror angled to catch the pallid light, rasped the tempered steel across a ravined, wind-beaten face. Sinewy neck tensed, face contorted, he mowed straight furrows, carefully stroking the white lather.

> *I loved to watch him shave, his splayed thumb pressed*
> *on chin upraised, to let the stropped steel skim*
> *the fluffed froth off. I felt I could not rest*
> *till one day I should share this rite with him;*
> *such skill, such peril, such unerring grace.*

John Hewitt
'A Holy Place'

Beside him, her cheeks flushed from the effort, his mother used her apron to fan the sulky fire. The flames she coaxed from the ashes flickered upward from serried rows of turf surrounding the hot coals saved from last night's *gríosach*.

The pungent fragrance of turf smoke pervaded the room;

cheery light and bright flames soon warmed the kitchen. The fire-blackened cast-iron kettle bubbled on the hob but breakfast would have to wait. On Christmas morning, everyone fasted from midnight to receive Holy Communion at Mass. That was the rule. No one questioned it.

The boy continued to gaze intently at the raisin cake in the centre of the table. It dwarfed the everyday items lining the wall: a half-empty saucepan of oatmeal porridge, a box of Fry's cocoa, the heel of a 'Poorman's' loaf, a bottle of the bitter-tasting Irel coffee that we kept for emergencies when tea ran out, a bottle of Sloan's liniment, a half-folded, half-used brown sugar-bag, a salt cellar. The raisin cake stood apart, wondrously superb, an exotic flower blooming among these mundane things. Any kind of sweet cake was a rare sight! It graced country tables only on very special occasions.

This one, the child thought, looked even more tempting than the one his mother had baked at Hallowe'en. At supper the evening before, he had admired it. Finger in mouth, he glanced about him. No one was looking. He reached over, picked one of the plumpest raisins, looked at it and, turning it over in his fingers, felt its soft, juicy sweetness. Mouth-watering temptation overwhelming him, he put the tempting morsel in his mouth, savoured the taste and swallowed it. Heaven! All thought of obligations, sin and Holy Communion vanished now as he reached for another raisin.

'What are y'at there?' His mother swept towards him like an avenging angel.

'N-nothing,' he stuttered.

'Are ye eating the cake?'

His face reddened. 'Aye.'

Conscientious guardian of his soul, she was going to see it was kept free from sin. To do otherwise was to fail in her duties and responsibilities. Her job was to teach respect for laws of God and man. Didn't the catechism state clearly that those receiving Holy Communion 'must be fasting from midnight'? And anyway, wasn't the bloody cake going to be ruined with the raisins picked out of it!

Trembling with wrath, she pulled him away from the table. 'What did ye do that for? Don't ye know you're receiving? My God, ye'll be the laughing stock of the place. Stay in the house, that's what ye'll do!'

He cowered. There was no defence. What had come over him? His mother was right: he was no good. His black soul cringing, he knew what was coming next. She reached for the sally rod and his Christmas morning fell about him in a black whirl of pain and confusion. Angry red welts rose on his vulnerable, short-trousered legs. 'Suffer the little children to come unto me.' How strange it is that this rule of fast, once so rigidly observed, is now only a quaint memory!

'Straighten yerself up,' my father barked later as he teased the shoulders of my coat, his peevishness the tangible expression of deeper concerns. Was I ever going to amount to anything? Would the round shoulders always need padding? What would the neighbours think? 'Isn't it a pity? That son of Petie McGowan's isn't a very strong young fellow, y'know,' he could hear them say. Increase the cod liver oil. Try raw eggs, maybe. Don't spare the rod. Make something of the boy!

My mother tweaked my cheeks to stimulate the blood and bring colour to their natural paleness. Standing back to appraise the effect, her expression betrayed a resigned dissatisfaction, an enduring acceptance. Physically as well as morally, I was a continuing challenge to all the resources available to her.

Hands stuck down in trousers was another unwelcome

indication. It betrayed laziness and was a sure sign of a corner boy. 'Take yer hands out of yer pockets!' my father said irritably as, God's will done, the family crisis over, we walked out into the crisp Christmas-morning air and up the stony road that led to the convent chapel. Columns of smoke drifted towards the sky at drunken angles from rows of whitewashed, thatched houses. Christmas trees had not yet arrived but windows were resplendent with red and green splashes of holly: cheery colours to combat the dull shades of winter.

The meadows and pastures lay peaceful under a light cover of frost that glistened white, pink-tinted by the rising sun. In the tilled fields, the frozen potato pits rose like fossilised memorials to ancient, pagan chieftains: Fomorian, Firbolg or Tuatha dé Danann. Kings and kingmakers walked and worked these acres, their mace a scythe, their sceptre a spade!

Paddy Barry hurried with his loping stride to catch up with us. His carriage betrayed a military background and indeed he had served in the Spanish–American war with the US navy before returning to his home in Mullaghmore. He had settled easily back into the life of a small farmer. 'There'll be a cuttin',' my father remarked to him. 'I never saw it yet but ye'd get it after frost.'

'Aye,' Paddy replied, 'but there'll be a stretch in the days from now on. Every day getting longer by a cock's step in the dunkle.'

> *Mass-going feet*
> *Crunched the wafer-ice on the pot-holes,*
> *Somebody wistfully twisted the bellows wheel.*
>
> *My child poet picked out the letters*
> *On the grey stone,*
> *In silver the wonder of a Christmas townland,*
> *The winking glitter of a frosty dawn.*

Cassiopeia was over
Cassidy's hanging hill,
I looked and three whin bushes rode across
The horizon – the Three Wise Kings.

Patrick Kavanagh
from 'A Christmas Childhood'

Families emerged from their houses up and down our road, prayer books and Rosaries in hand. 'A happy Christmas to ye,' they said as they caught up with us. Every dwelling was home to large families. Soon there was a steady stream of people headed towards the church: Rourkes, Leonards, Kellys, Dowdicans, Gilmartins, Barrys and many others; mostly gone now. For some, not even the trace of a house is left, prey to the decay of country villages, emigration and a changed economy; others, prey to the grim reaper. The older folk chatted amiably as we made our way down the lane and across the close-cropped pasture of the 'farm field' to Mass.

Entering the church, it seemed to us that the crib across from the Confession box was a hushed island of peace. The Christchild in a bed of straw stretched out welcoming arms to us. Plaster statues representing Joseph and Mary, the shepherds, the farm animals that gazed on him – all were bathed in a warm light. It was the simplest and most touching thing we would ever see at Christmas. It remains so to this day: a surprising and welcome constant in a changing world.

Enthralled, we knelt and prayed there to the baby son of God that the nuns had placed with loving care in the manger. When we were finished, we teased out a few straws from Christ's bed to hang up in the cow byre. Other wisps we put behind the picture of the Sacred Heart in the kitchen as a blessing on us and on our stock. A quiet peace pervaded the little chapel. The perpetual light of the red sanctuary lamp flickered and danced as it burned in front of the altar. Time stood still. Eternity dwelt here. As it was, is now, and ever shall be, world without end, amen. Cares would wait for another day. The whole of our year – of our existence – was encompassed in this place. *'Gloria in excelsis Deo'* burst forth from the choir, swelled aloft and echoed around the walls and roof of the little chapel.

As we took our seats, our neighbour Jim's voice resonated sonorously around the little chapel as he recited the Joyful Mysteries. Fingering his beads, he 'let round' the Rosary while we waited for Mass to start. Wearing an air of piety, his deportment on religious occasions indicated a special importance, a privileged level of communion with God. Even when he joined in the responses, his voice always rose an octave or two over everyone else's. This was his delight, and we smiled as we indulged him in one of his idiosyncrasies. It was to Jim people went when death visited their homes. There were no undertakers then and he bustled importantly as he hurried to answer the call. In charge of the 'putting overboard', he shaved the remains, dressed the corpse and generally dispensed advice and help.

As if the Rosary wasn't enough, the Litany of Praises was added:

'Holy Mother of God,' he droned.

'Pray for us,' everyone responded in unison.

'Holy Virgin of Virgins.'

'Pray for us,' they chanted.

It went on and on: 'Spiritual Vessel', 'Mystical Rose', 'Tower of Ivory', 'House of Gold', until at last there was an air of resignation in everyone's voice. 'Pray for us,' they repeated wearily. Nobody ever questioned how it was that any woman could be a Tower of Ivory or a House of Gold. It was just another one of those mysteries of faith which were scattered plentifully throughout our religion. Still, it was nice to conjure up images of ivory towers on Sunday – they seemed so exotic, and made a nice change from the weekday commonplace of turnip fields, warble flies, potato pits and cow-dung!

Sanctuary bells pealed a jangle warning. The celebrant of the Mass, decked in white chasuble and flowing alb, swept to the altar preceded by a retinue of altar boys. Turning to the tabernacle, he raised his eyes to heaven and commenced a practised rote:

'*Introibo ad altare Dei.*'

'*Ad Deum qui laetificat juventutem meum.*'

'*Quia tu es, Deus, fortitudo mea, quare me repulisti? Et quare tristis incedo dum affligit me inimicus?*'

A Druid chant.

The priest on the altar, intermediary between man and God, robed arms outstretched, faced the altar as he intoned the Latin Mass; behind him his congregation segregated as the etiquette of the time demanded. Women knelt on one side with heads covered as a mark of respect in the House of God, obedient to some strange, forgotten dictum; men crouched on the other side, their heads uncovered for the same reason: husbands on one side, wives on the other. Only the important or the rich broke this code and worshipped where the rules forbade. The bulk of the community accepted the idiosyncrasies of the privileged classes with a resigned and quiet acquiescence. Why should such repositories of wealth and importance be restricted by the same rules that bound ordinary mortals?

Some of the congregation prayed out of well-worn, grease-stained missals that displayed the Latin Mass on one side and the English translation on the opposite page. Mass cards and novenas to favourite saints marked important pages. Others silently prayed the Rosary. Lips fluttering, work-worn fingers snaked along the beads as they muttered low the Hail Marys of the Sorrowful, the Joyful or the Glorious Mysteries.

> *A woman said her litany:*
> *That my husband may get his health*
> *. . . We beseech thee hear us*
> *That my daughter Eileen may do well at her music*
> *We beseech thee hear us*
> *That her aunt may remember us in her will*
> *We beseech thee hear us . . .*

Patrick Kavanagh
from 'Lough Derg'

Father Gallagher, a stern man of the old school, led his flock most of the time but had no hesitation in driving them when he felt circumstances demanded it. He favoured the direct approach and there was no waltzing around delicate issues as he teased out God's laws and desires during his sermons:

> *High in front advanced,*
> *The brandished sword of God before them blazed,*
> *Fierce as a comet.*

His flock were left in no doubt as to what was right or wrong as he thundered his disapproval of our indiscretions and failures and apprised us of the generous width of the path that went to hell and the ease with which it could be travelled. He paused and cast dark glances when there was a particularly noisy barrage of coughing or foot-shuffling during one of his dissertations. He let his annoyance at those who were perpetually late for Mass be known, and complained occasionally, but he could tolerate them.

His sermons, when St Patrick's Day came around, were emotional. His homily on our national holiday was invariably about emblems. Over the years, we could recite it word for word, but only he could capture the fire and the passion: Ireland's symbol was the little shamrock, he explained, chosen long ago by Patrick to demonstrate to our pagan ancestors the mystery of three persons in one – the Divine Trinity. The leek, he told us, was the symbol of Wales, and the thistle the chosen insignia of Scotland. For England's badge he reserved special mention. Alone among the nations of the earth, he proclaimed, his voice rising wrathfully, the red rose was England's symbol. And 'well red it might be,' he declared, 'smeared as it is with the blood of generations of martyred Irish men and women.'

If there was one thing that was completely unacceptable to him on any day of the year, and annoyed him above everything else, it was the men's habit of huddling in the porch at the back of the church while the seats at the front remained empty. He tried everything to change this: he wheedled, he cajoled, he threatened, he implored. They stared back at him with shifty eyes. It was no good. With the men at such a safe distance, his entreaties fell on deaf ears.

He even tried psychology. Oppressed and pauperised in the past, we had a lingering inferiority complex, even though those days were gone, he reasoned. Dressed and fed as well as the best of them, we could now take our proud place at the front of any gathering. Still no good. On occasion, some of the weaker souls shuffled sheepishly up the church to a seat, but the hard core remained, immovable and inexorable, in the rear.

It wasn't that they were defying him, it was just that they were comfortable there and felt that God's grace was as abundant at the back of the church as at the front. Standing at the back had the added advantage that you could come in late without being noticed and away like a flash after the last blessing. Sure, they knew it was a mortal sin to miss Mass on Sundays or Holy Days of Obligation, but where was it written that they had to be up at the front of the church? Didn't Christ himself say that the last would be first and the first last? And what about the lesson of the Pharisee and the publican? Anyway, didn't everyone know them oul' craw-thumping hypocrites that was the first at the altar rails would rob the milk out of yer tay once they got outside, given half a chance?

Once or twice, following the biblical example of Christ and the money changers, his temper flared and he charged the defiant back-door mob like an avenging angel. Priestly garments flying, he sped down the aisle in a surprise attack, but it was no good: they fled in every direction except up to the front seats, and the porch was empty by the time he reached it. It was a stalemate, but he never gave up, and the variety and unpredictability of his efforts at filling the front seats made our trips to Mass that much more interesting for many years.

Father Gallagher was convinced that God got it right when he said it was easier for a camel to go through the eye of a needle than for a rich man to enter God's kingdom. 'We must store our riches in heaven,' he thundered, 'where the Bible tells us that neither rust nor moth can consume.' One way of paving the way to paradise was to contribute in generous measure to the various church collections held throughout the year. Of these, the Christmas collection was one of the most important. The congregation, particularly the business people, were expected to give generously.

For years, a contribution of one pound was sufficient guarantee for Mrs Hannon, owner of the local hotel, to head the list and secure a top position in this social order. A pound was a lot of money then: enough to buy groceries for a week for an average-size family. Some gave what they could afford; other contributions varied in size according to the importance, real or imagined, or social aspirations of the donor. Further down the list, the majority of offerings were from the workers and farmers, who usually weighed in with anything from an unpretentious one and sixpence to two shillings.

Contributors were noted and placed on a list according to the size of their donation, the largest, of course, being first. The list was read out on the Sunday after Christmas. Attention peaked as the congregation listened intently to find out if Mrs Hannon had held on to top position or if, maybe, Myles Doyle, the postmaster, or some other aspirant had displaced her. Myles was postmaster, grocer and dictator absolute of the one telephone line in and out of the village. At a time when everyone 'kept a book' at the local shop, Myles frowned on the practice. A sign that he had printed and displayed in a prominent position at the counter provoked comment and knowing smiles: 'In this world of doubt and sorrow,' it read, 'the most doubtful words are, "I'll pay you tomorrow".'

Yes, the collection was sure to be a talking point when Mass was over and we gathered outside the chapel gates for the weekly chat and exchange of the week's news. When the moment of truth arrived, the congregation shuffled, eased into a comfortable position, coughed noisily and fell into an expectant silence. The priest turned around with his list and the show started. 'Mrs Hannon, one pound,' he commenced.

Well, no surprises there. Mrs Hannon, who always arrived late, as befitted important people, and always sat in the front row, a fox fur draped around her neck in the fashion of the time, straightened herself importantly, the tall feather in her hat fluttering triumphantly as, once again, she found herself in the winner's enclosure. Her fox fur was a wonder to me and I always felt sorry for the wee creature as it hung there around her neck, its beady, unseeing little eyes and limp paws dangling helplessly over the undulating curvature of a huge bosom.

The list went on and we lost interest as the priest reached the one and sixpences. But where was Myles Doyle, we wondered idly? His name hadn't featured in its usual place – generally well above the ten-shilling mark, as befitted his status in the community. Then suddenly it came. 'Myles Doyle, one shilling,' the priest read. We were shocked into alertness again by Myles's diminished position on the list.

Father Gallagher read the name once and then, pausing for effect, 'Myles – Doyle – one – shilling!' he repeated again, spacing and emphasising the words, his voice shaking with indignation and contempt as it rose by several decibels. A rustle of disbelief ran through the audience. What moment of misguided misan-thropic folly had allowed Myles to disturb the social equilibrium of our village? What could it be? Both men kept cattle. Myles owned a lot of land; Father Gallagher had very little and often had to resort to the 'long acre' for grazing. Was it true they had fallen out over a piece of land belonging to Martin 'Fat' Gilmartin which was coveted by both? Was Myles sending a subtle and public lesson to the priest in retaliation for what he saw as his unseemly greed? This battle of the gladiators, fought in full public view, was the focal point of conversation in the village for weeks. Savouring the priest's emphasis, we laughed as we mimicked the derision in the priest's voice: 'Did ye hear him? "Myles Doyle, one shilling! Myles – Doyle – one – shilling!"'

The postmaster was a very pompous man and it was no harm to take him down a peg or two, everyone agreed. Father Gallagher hadn't scolded or spoken a single word of reprimand

but, nevertheless, in a master stroke of satirical emphasis, he had
come out of this one a clear winner. Mark Antony couldn't have
done better. Brutus was defeated and a lesson taught to anyone
who dared think they could cross the priest in public and get
away with it. After that, Myles always kept a respectable place
on the Christmas list and in the community, but like the March
blizzard of '47 or the Night of the Big Wind, we always
remembered the Christmas collection of '56.

The night before Christmas had a special magic all its own. A
fast was observed during the day but towards nightfall it was
broken when the candles were lit and supper prepared in the
evening.

Maggie McGowan remembered the evening preparations.
'Me mother made a good sweet cake for us with plenty of raisins
and currants in it. That was baked beforehand and a big feed
of boxty along with it. She'd be the whole day gratin'. Then
she'd put a pan and an oven down on the coals. It was beautiful
– the butter would be running down off that. Ye'd ate a good
feed of it. A good-size bullock wouldn't eat it now, anyway!
When ye'd eat that, the strength was in it.' Food prepared with
strength and muscle in mind was more to the point then than
dainties for delicate palates!

Mairead Kerins of Derelehan, County Sligo, recorded that:
'People kept the twenty-fourth of December as a fast day: very
little dinner was eaten. At night, about six or seven o'clock,
they had a great supper – tea with all nice currant bread, butter
and jam and potato cake. The bottle was opened and a little
taken with the supper; it was then kept to treat the neighbours.
Christmas dinner on the twenty-fifth was a goose or some fowl.

'A currant cake, milk, butter and sometimes a portion of
bacon was given to poorer neighbours. Members of families did

not give presents to one another, although any member out earning might bring presents home. Children usually got something new: a pinafore or dress. Young girls usually got a new hat. People always remained home on Christmas day and night, chatted around the fire and told stories. Christmas cards, Christmas stockings, turkey, plum pudding and shop-bought presents are now becoming more common in this district.'

All that was left of our turkeys when the holiday festivities were over was one lone female retained to provide the basis of next year's flock. Unaware of her great good fortune, she wandered disconsolately outside, missing her companions and trying to adjust to their loss. Bewildered by the speedy turn of events, it was beyond her ken to know what had brought about such devastation. The yard seemed quiet now without her companions' noisy, strutting performances, and in her turkey way she must have grieved for them. She never socialised with the hens before. They spoke a strange language she did not understand. Now her despairing attempts to ingratiate herself with them met with no success and they made great dashes at her. Clucking agitatedly, they chased her, driving her away with their sharp beaks.

A week or so before Christmas, this lone survivor's family had been gathered together and shipped off to the annual market at Kinlough. Rounded up in the early morning, legs tied tightly together, they were suspended one by one, upside down, from the hook of the ouncels. My father held them up while my mother, peering with great intensity at the figures on the brass face of the dial, carefully noted and marked down the weight of each one. A lot of hard work had gone into bringing them this far and she was going to make sure there would be no short weight given by some shady dealer in Kinlough. Prices in the late 1950s ranged from one and tenpence to two shillings per pound for the smaller and lighter hens to one and sixpence and one and eightpence for cocks that could weigh up to twenty-five pounds. Breastbones were checked too. A crooked breast meant an even lower price from the buyer.

As each turkey was probed, tied and weighed, it was deposited in the ass-cart that had been fitted with a 'box' or a slatted 'crib'. I couldn't help feeling sorry for them now. Tightly packed together, they huddled on the floor of the cart like condemned prisoners. But I was glad too: now I didn't have to look after them any more. In addition, there would be money and resulting good humour in the house when the market was over.

It was an important day for the shopkeepers too. A good market meant they could count on a good few pounds to be paid off on the book. In any case, good or bad, they would get something. There were no regular paydays for farmers but it was expected that when produce was sold, a portion would be paid on the account. There was no fixed figure: people paid what they could afford and it was very rarely that the balance could be cleared completely.

The cart moved out of the farmyard onto the rough, stone-paved road. All semblance of dignity gone, the bewildered creatures, heads extended from the slatted sides of the cart, gradually vanished from view as vehicle and cargo disappeared over the brow of the hill at Doherty's brae. Friendless now, they seemed to sense it was all over and they looked back at me through the slats of the cart with pleading eyes. Despite our occasional differences, they had looked on me as a friend and I had to turn my head away as their mournful faces reproached my betrayal.

The close contact that came with rearing turkeys created an emotional bond that wrenched the hearts of some owners. The bustle of activity and gravity of the preparations on this day were always lightened by one of our tender-hearted neighbours, who made no attempt to conceal her grief. Tears rolled down her cheeks as she watched them jolting down the rough road on the iron-shod ass-cart making its way to market. We thought this very funny and laughed ourselves silly as she waved after the turkeys and they looked back disconsolately at her, their long red necks swaying gracefully to the motion of the vehicle.

Our cart was joined by others similarly laden, and soon a long line of the brightly coloured orange vehicles rattled in procession to Kinlough and the market. It was a ten-mile journey, so an early start was essential. Even then, the long queue of vehicles at the point of sale meant a whole day spent in line and sometimes a return journey the next day for those who were unlucky and didn't make it to the weighing point at all. Geese too were brought to market at this time. They were walked from the village to a market at Donlevy's in Cliffoney, three miles away.

Harvest fairs and Christmas markets have now fallen out of fashion. Long ago they were very important dates in the farming calendar and much anticipated. Mairead Kerins of Derelehan related in 1942 that, even where there was no Christmas market, 'In olden times people tried to have something to sell at Christmas, usually a firkin of butter. Some sold hay, turkeys, eggs, geese, vegetables and other farm produce. This was to buy the Christmas things, such as tea, sugar, currants, raisins, big candles, a good piece of bacon, a bag of flour, a few loaves and maybe a bottle of whiskey.'

Even though we raised fat turkeys to sell at the Christmas market at Kinlough, Cliffoney or Grange, no steaming, drum-sticks-in-the-air, well-basted gobbler graced our holiday table. We reared them but we couldn't afford to eat one. Having looked after them all year, they were nothing special to us. Fat duck, goose or hen pleased us well. It was a meal fit for a lord, and we called no man master on that day.

> And our kitchen floor of pot-hole clay
> Was changed as we read
> To a carpeted room on Christmas Day.
> Romance was in every head.
> A brandy-flamed pudding came in on a tray
> Carried high by a well-off dad.

Patrick Kavanagh
from 'The Old Time Christmas Story 1960'

A thousand years ago, when there were plenty of the wild species in the pinewoods, turkey may have been a commoner fare on Irish tables. They weren't turkeys, strictly speaking, but capercaillies – a wild grouse almost as big as a turkey with a blue-green breast similar to that of a peacock. They became extinct in Ireland in the eighteenth century because of overhunting and the destruction of the Irish forests. Aggressive creatures, they would attack humans as well as other birds in defence of their territory.[57]

At Christmas, as well as the rest of the year, the commerce of the countryside depended completely on horse- or ass-drawn carts. That's the way it was in living memory and, for all anyone knew then, that's the way it was always going to be. Anyone remembering iron-shod wheels rattling on stony roads will have only fond memories of these gentle beasts of burden as they went uncomplaining about their work.

In the 1950s, an enterprising neighbour who owned a small van, seeing a business opportunity, tendered for the transportation of the turkeys. His offer was accepted and a carnival atmosphere was lent to the occasion that year as he ferried back and forth all day long with cargoes of doomed turkeys. It was turning out to be a very successful venture, so, in celebration of this, each trip to Kinlough was punctuated by a visit to the pub.

A man of high good humour at any time, his spirit and wit improved even further with each trip. Feathers flew, turkeys gobbled, people laughed and Patrick cheered as the luckless creatures were motored to their fate. It was 'as good as a circus', everyone agreed, and we still remember the technological leap from humble ass to high-class van!

It's interesting to note that, although commonly considered native to Ireland, that favourite beast of burden, the ass or donkey, was not introduced into Europe until the Middle Ages. It made its appearance in Ireland in the late seventeenth century.[58] Clearly defined on every donkey's back is the shape of a Christian cross. Tradition tells us that this is the mark of Christ, bestowed as a special honour in remembrance of when it carried the Virgin Mary into Bethlehem and a triumphant Jesus into Jerusalem on Palm Sunday. In northern France, the 'Flight into Egypt' is celebrated in a Miracle play during the 'Feast of the Ass' in the weeks following Christmas.

For less sacred reasons, I too associate the ass with Christmas. Anyone who ever waited for the delivery of a parcel from America long ago will recall the thrill of the postman reaching into the ass-cart for the brown, twine-wrapped package. What surprises would it hold?

My mother didn't like uncertainty. There was far too much of it about! Occasionally, when her patience expired, or times were especially bad, she peered into the future. When she found some spare time she 'cut the cards', or read the tea leaves. Savouring her cup of tea, she swilled the last drop around and, drinking it, peered intently into the bottom of the cup. Future events were encoded in the designs deposited there. All kinds of things were revealed to her in the mystery of the leaves: births, deaths, marriages, journeys across water, dark handsome strangers for the neighbouring girls who came to call – and parcels from America. She could even unravel whether it was an envelope with money in it that was on its way, or a box.

When I looked over her shoulder, it made no sense at all until she pointed out the pattern in the cup that represented a journey or a letter or a package on the way: then I believed! Part of the magic that marked the season was the sense of excitement and anticipation as we waited on dull, dark days for the prophecy to be fulfilled.

For most of the year, a bicycle, its steel frame mounted over the front wheel, was sufficient to carry the postman and his bag about the countryside. At Christmas, the sheer bulk of mail forced him to abandon his bicycle in favour of the ass and cart. When this happened, our excitement increased, as we knew that it couldn't be long now until out of that mountain of brown packages with hairy string, John Higgins would pull one for us. As it got closer to the holiday, John's load got heavier and he came later and later. We looked anxiously up the road as the short days of winter darkened towards evening. If Christmas has an Advent, this was it. It couldn't be long now until one of those brown parcels with the American stamps had our address on it. Packages that often came from people with strange-sounding names like Snyder or Fanelli, the Irish connection being the maiden name of O'Connor, Gillooly or Murphy.

When John steered his ass-and-cart team to our house, pulled the canvas cover back and carried the long-awaited package to the door, it was joy fulfilled. The delay while the older folk went through the social etiquette of discussing the weather or the price of turkeys or some other topic of local interest with John was unendurable. Before he had drawn his reindeer off the street, we tore at the wrapping. What excitement as we lifted out colouring books, red-striped 'candy-cane' shaped like walking sticks, packs of multi-hued crayons, bright-coloured rock candy and pencil cases decorated with images of Mickey Mouse, Donald Duck and Pluto.

We treated with a great deal of suspicion some of the stranger items these benevolent cousins and aunts had packed for us. The bitter-tasting coffee we just didn't like: it reminded us too much of rationing and the hated Globo coffee of the war years. We were tea people. Nothing else would satisfy our taste buds, so we gave 'Maxwell House' away to an old uncle who had spent some years in America and acquired strange tastes there. The Emergency, ration books and rationing was over, supplies were becoming plentiful again, and we didn't have to drink anything we didn't like any more.

We puzzled over the peculiar-looking little gauze-wrapped bags with tea inside. We hadn't seen anything like this before. They made no sense. Why pack loose tea leaves? It seemed extremely odd to stew the bag the tea came in along with the tea itself. We tore open the strange little pouches and emptied them into the teapot. We were not impressed with the result. So we tried stewing tea, bag and all. But the resulting watery-yellow concoction could not compare with the strong brown draught that was 'drawn' by my mother on the hot coals from loose tea. No doubt about it, we thought, the Yanks still had a lot to learn. Especially when it came to making tea.

Tea bags are now a common sight on supermarket shelves but there are still many, particularly of the older generation, who prefer loose tea. 'A pinch of tea for everyone in the house and one for the pot' was the recipe for the perfect draught. 'It's not tay at all,' Jimmy Flynn complained to me once as he pulled out the red-hot coals and crushed them to set the teapot on. 'Them bloody bags remind me of dead mice in the bottom of the pot, and they taste as bad!'

Then there was the strange-sounding 'chicken noodle soup'. 'Noodle' was the derisory term applied by our teacher at school to students who didn't have their homework done or who generally didn't measure up to her standards. 'Noodle-head' was the last thing a student often heard before they were made to stand shamefaced in a corner of the schoolroom, a tall conical 'dunce cap' on their head – the one with the big 'D' printed on its side, just in case anyone didn't know what it meant. Having a name with such unpleasant associations was a bad start indeed for 'chicken noodle soup'. Not to be wasteful, we drank it, but we were glad when it was finished. Now my mother might kill a hen and we could get back to the real thing!

'Skippy Peanut Butter' the label on the glass jar read. Peanut *butter!* This stuff didn't look like butter and it definitely didn't taste like butter. Butter came from milk and milk came from cows. No, it wasn't likely that the Yanks had learned how to milk peanuts! So we read the label again but could garner no additional information. Nice people, our cousins, but they sure had some strange ways with them. Even our 'uncle who had lived in America' wasn't interested in this one. He often criticised the Americans for their unhealthy eating habits. 'Too much rich, starchy foods,' he said. So we figured, if it wasn't good enough for him, it was no good for anything.

Reluctant to throw something out for which a good use just might be found, it sat on the dresser for a long time. My father, a thrifty man who was loath to let anything go to loss, decided one day, having given the matter much thought, that it might come in useful for greasing the cart. He smeared a good coating of the gooey mixture on the axle but it was a failure here too. Eventually it finished up out on the stone ditch, where even the hens, who would eat almost anything, walked disdainfully around it.

Sometimes it was clothes that came in these Christmas boxes: checked double-breasted suits, heavy woollen shirts, jumpers and strange-looking three-quarter-length pants with elasticated bottoms called 'plus fours'. Nothing could persuade me to wear these odd-looking trousers, as they were exactly like those worn by little Lord Fauntleroy in the comic strips. It was hard enough to hold one's own in the pecking order in the schoolyard without tempting fate and inviting derisory jeers from the school bullies in such a foolish way. The elderly gamekeepers that worked for the local landlords wore a tweed version of these, with long stockings pulled up to their knees. But everyone knew they were different to us anyway. It was one of the things they could get away with, but we couldn't – thank goodness!

My mother had somewhat more success with the fashions than my father had with the peanut butter. She cut the bottoms off the plus fours and made short trousers of them. My protest was ended and I strode out in short-trousered urbanity – to the admiration and envy of my less fortunate peers.

The overwhelming favourites among these gifts were the hooded, wool-lined, heavy lumber-jackets that were impervious to driving snow or biting wind. No encouragement was needed to wear these rugged fur-lined garments that kept me warm as I went about my work feeding calves and milking cows in many a bitter Atlantic gale.

At my mother's insistence, I wrote nice letters to thank my American aunts and cousins for their gifts of clothes, candy and colouring books. It was an exercise in stretching the truth too.

Not to be ungrateful, I applauded the exotic tea bags, peanut butter and plus fours as well.

Opening these wonder-filled boxes is a cherished Christmas memory. It was an excitement that rivalled, but never quite equalled, the thrill of Christmas morning, when we crept from the bedroom in the shadowy half-light to look in the chimney corner beside the slumbering fire. It might only be a simple toy that was there, but that red-costumed, white-whiskered, mysterious midnight voyager that climbed down our chimney on that special morning imparted a magic to its simplicity that can never be equalled.

Nothing could have prepared me for the contrast in lifestyles I encountered when I emigrated to America in 1961. I didn't have a word for it then but it was classical culture shock! The spectacle of my cousin's living room on that first American Christmas morning is something I will never forget. The home I had left behind had a plain flagstone floor. Here there was not just 'wall-to-wall' carpet but wall-to-wall presents too: wrapping paper, boxes and gifts covered the living-room floor. Eyes wide in wonderment and disbelief, I looked on a litter of packages from Santa, presents from Mom and Pop, presents from cousins, aunts and uncles, discarded wrappings everywhere.

My American cousins didn't seem to have any comprehension or appreciation of their privileged lifestyle. They took the hedonistic abundance of their Christmas morning for granted. Never having known any other way of life, they could not have realised their position of superfluous affluence. It has taken a few decades, but today's generation of Irish children enjoy a similarly opulent lifestyle, undreamt of not so long ago.

Who is this improbable Santa Claus? Where did he come from and how did he get to be so popular?

The origins of Santa Claus bring us back to the fourth-century Christian prelate, Saint Nicholas, patron saint of Russia. According to tradition he was Bishop of Myra in Asia Minor (now Turkey) *c.* 304. In addition to his role as patron of Russia, he was also a benefactor of children, scholars and sailors. Legend tells us that St Nicholas began the custom of gift-giving when he secretly provided the three daughters of a poor man with dowries, thus preserving their honour. Otherwise they would have had to seek their fortunes on the street. From this has grown the custom of secret gift-giving on Christmas Eve. In time the legend spread from Russia to neighbouring countries; it was combined in Germany with local folklore to make him the bringer of secret gifts to children.

Nicholas became the patron saint of children when he intervened to rescue three boys. During a famine, a butcher lured three youths to his house. Killing them and cutting up their bodies, he placed them in a barrel to sell as pork. On being told by an angel of the horror, Nicholas ran to the butcher's house and restored the boys to life.

The Dutch were among the first immigrants to settle in the United States. They brought their love of 'San Nicolaas' with them but the pronunciation and spelling became Americanised to Santa Claus and the image grew rounder and merrier. San Nicolaas's feast day, originally celebrated on 6 December, was eventually adopted by English-speaking settlers who incorporated the Dutch tradition as part of their celebrations on 25 December An Irish-Dutch poet who was a professor in a New York seminary, Clement Clarke Moore, helped to popularise the St Nicholas or 'Santa' image when he wrote 'A Visit from St Nicholas' in 1822 for the entertainment of his own children. It became a rapt wonder for children everywhere:

> *'Twas the night before Christmas when all through*
>   *the house*
> *Not a creature was stirring, not even a mouse;*
> *The stockings were hung by the chimney with care*
> *In the hope that St Nicholas soon would be there . . .*
> *He was dressed all in fur, from his head to his foot*
> *And his clothes were all tarnished with ashes and soot;*
> *A bundle of toys he had flung on his back,*
> *And he looked like a pedlar just opening his pack.*
> *His eyes – how they twinkled; his dimples, how merry!*
> *His cheeks were like roses, his nose like a cherry . . .*

The image of Santa in his red fur-trimmed suit was first drawn in 1883 by Thomas Nast, a cartoonist with *Harper's Weekly* – and so the image and legend grew and grew to the jolly, red-suited, white-bearded figure who is credited with bringing presents to children all around the world.

Christmas is celebrated now as Christ's birthday, but for the infant born in Bethlehem the date chosen for celebration of his birthday was not firmly established until early in the fourth century, when Pope Julius I declared 25 December the Nativity. This choice may have been influenced by the fact that the Julian calendar reckoned 25 December as the date of the winter solstice. In addition, the new date had the added advantage of Christianising the old Roman festival of Saturnalia, which fell at this time. For Christians, the decree of Pope Julius diverted to the birth of Jesus the adoration which the Roman 'heathen' had previously given to the sun.

Lasting from 17 to 23 December, the ancient festival of Saturnalia honoured the merry reign of Saturn, the Roman god of sowing and husbandry. During the Roman 'Golden Age', a time of perfect peace and happiness was recreated. Saturnalia was a period of goodwill, devoted to banquets and the exchange of visits and gifts, long before St Nicholas or Santa Claus. A special feature of the festival was the freedom given to slaves. For the duration of the holiday, they had first place at the family table and were served by their masters.

The reign of Cormac Mac Airt is celebrated in poetry and folklore as Ireland's Golden Age. In everyday speech, people still refer to good times as 'the life of Cormac'. When a cow lies down, she always exhales in a great sigh. She is said to be lamenting the good life led by cows during Cormac's reign.

Prior to the establishment of the birth of Christ on 25 December, this event was celebrated at such diverse times as on 6 January, in February, on 25 March, in April, in May and on 17 November. St Augustine exhorted Christians not to celebrate Christmas as pagans did, in honour of the sun, but in honour of the God who made the sun. By the end of the century, the new date was universally acknowledged except in the Greek Orthodox Church, which continued to celebrate on 6 January.

Christianity borrowed many of its practices from the Mithraic faith, which was one of the major religions of the Roman Empire. Mithraism was brought from Persia to Rome c. 68 BC, and became a rival to Christianity for converts in the Roman world. Its followers had beliefs similar to the Christian ideals of humility and brotherly love. Their rites included the taking of Communion and the use of holy water. They believed in the immortality of the soul, the Last Judgement and the Resurrection. They observed Sundays and 25 December (Mithras's birthday) as holy days. It was these similarities that made easy the conversion of many of the followers of the god Mithras to Jesus Christ.[59]

A convergence of many of the above influences was seminal to the establishment of Christianity and the Christmas festival.

The festival's origins and development as a time of celebration and revelry lie too in sacred rites held by pre-Christian Germanic and Celtic peoples to celebrate the winter solstice. Mistletoe, Yule logs, holly and evergreens are of pagan origin, considered sacred and regarded with reverence by Roman and Druid alike.

Mistletoe had special prominence. Pliny the Elder recorded that it was gathered by the Celtic Druids using a golden sickle and carried in a pure white robe to prevent its magical properties draining off into the earth. The Druids believed that, among its many powers, a potion prepared from this plant could fertilise barren women or cattle. In a parallel belief, the Italians held that a piece of mistletoe carried about by a woman would help conceive a child. Other cultures taught that it healed all wounds made with cutting instruments and that it was a powerful deterrent against sorcery or witchcraft. It was firmly believed in many countries, including Ireland, that witches and witchcraft were often employed in the stealing of milk, cream, and butter. In England, if the dairy farm was to thrive, a bunch of mistletoe must be given to the first cow to calve after the New Year. In addition, a sprig of the plant hung inside the home is said to protect against lightning.

A measure of the special significance of this time of year for early man is nowhere more in evidence than in the 5,000-year-old passage tomb at Newgrange in the Boyne valley. Here, for a few days around 21 December, at the height of the winter solstice, a shaft of light strikes through the precisely aligned passage, illuminating the chamber, which at all other times of the year is in darkness.

In addition to its religious significance, the cairn may have been a precision instrument built to allow remote ancestors – to whom the cycles of the seasons were as important as life itself – to monitor the annual turning of the sun. It was a reassurance of the annual renaissance, a time of rejoicing at the imminent reawakening of the season of growth, of lengthening days and the rebirth of the coming Spring. The shaft of light may have been designed to symbolise the male agent entering and impregnating the womblike structure of the passage grave, its light releasing new life and the spirits of the dead into a new existence.

In respect of the significance of folklore and local wisdom to historians and archaeologists, it is important to note that knowledge of the mysterious shaft of light was completely lost up to the 1960s – except in local lore. When archaeologists became increasingly aware of a strong, indigenous belief that the chambers once possessed a much greater significance, this marvel of ancient craftsmanship was reborn. Now there is a ten-year waiting list for persons wishing to observe the phenomenon.

If we view our present celebration of Christmas against this historical background, it becomes apparent that the commemoration of the birth of Jesus on 25 December is serendipitous – that it is only the latest in a long list of celebrations which occurred around this time, even in prehistory. With the increasing consumerism and commercial exploitation which is becoming more and more a part of the modern 'Xmas', it might even be fair to say that we are in the process of returning this religious celebration to an orgy of self-indulgence undreamed of even during the wildest days of the Roman Saturnalia.

In light of this, perhaps it is appropriate that the pine tree, which has no religious significance, is now the symbol most closely identified with the season. There are some conflicting views as to when and where the practice of installing a tree in the home originated. The earliest historical reference to the use of a Christmas tree for this purpose seems to have been in the early sixteenth century and comes from Riga, capital of Latvia in the Baltic. By the seventeenth century, its use had spread as far as Strasbourg and France. From here, the custom spread to Germany and northern Europe. The practice did not extend to Britain or Ireland until the early decades of the nineteenth century, when Prince Albert introduced it there from Germany. Christmas trees were not prevalent in Ireland until well into the 1960s, holly being the preferred option for decoration.

Christmas, for which spiritual preparations were begun one month ahead at the beginning of Advent, has always been the most important festival of the year in Ireland. Even the most hardened cases, who may not have darkened a church door for the rest of the year, showed up on this day. Confession boxes were jammed with penitents for a week before the holiday. The queue for those receiving Holy Communion on Christmas morning seemed endless.

Apart from the business of keeping the soul in order, the house and surroundings were rejuvenated as well at that time. Flagstone floors were scrubbed white and the walls given a fresh coat of whitewash. Everything had to be looking its best. This was the time when members of the family working in the city, or overseas in England or America, returned home for a visit. Neighbours and friends dropped in and, of course, it wouldn't seem like Christmas at all without a visit from the mummers or wrenboys.

Where there were children, it was essential to clean the chimney. Irresponsible was the man who neglected this important duty. Neighbours dropping in for a visit had tongue-in-cheek conversations about the importance of having a clean chimney or of how Santa Claus passed by some houses last year that had dirty chimneys. Eavesdropping on such conversations. I thought it a perfectly reasonable thing for Santa to do. I couldn't understand why the grown-ups thought such discussions so amusing. I didn't think they were funny at all. It was too serious a matter to take lightly, so I inspected the gaping maw of our chimney, where, through the rushing smoke, you could see right up to the starlit sky.

These old fireplaces were huge openings where might have bubbled the mighty container of the Tuatha dé Danann – Dagda's cauldron. The black, cavernous hole that sucked the billowing smoke away was big enough to accommodate even the fat Santa of the Christmas books. Nevertheless, I worried and begged my father to clean the chimney, and fretted when he didn't.

With rain on the way, soot fell down the chimney in chunks, bounced in the fireplace, and out onto the floor. This made my mother very cross, as the remedy was out of her control: it was my father's responsibility to keep the chimney clean. When this affront to her good housekeeping happened, she became more insistent, adding her voice to mine until finally he prepared the spade, hoe and ball of netwire or whitethorn branch needed for the job. He stood up inside the opening and scraped and cleaned and scoured and pulled the bush through until the sides glistened like polished black leather.

We may make a more efficient use of fire and firesides today, but in so doing we have taken away the friendly face of the open, welcoming hearth, where 'warmth and light and laughter came, hurrying after the leaping flame'. The American writer Nathaniel Hawthorne loved it too: 'Beautiful it is to see the strengthening gleam, the deepening light that casts distinct shadows of the human figure, the table and the high-backed chairs upon the opposite wall, and as twilight comes on, replenishes the room with living radiance and makes life all rose colour. Afar the wayfarer discerns the flickering flame as it dances on the windows and hails it as a beacon light of humanity, reminding him in his cold and lonely path that the world is not all snow and solitude and desolation.'

The small fireplaces and centrally heated houses of today are cheaper and more efficient in terms of conserving heat but they extend no warm invitation to fat Santas. 'No, sorry, no room here, I'm busy,' a new house seems to say to him. 'Use the door, please. Mind you don't get the carpet dirty.' Nevertheless, in his kindly, fantastic way he brings more and bigger presents to today's children than he ever carried down the spacious, inviting chimneys of long ago.

Before the Christmas tree became popular, decorations of holly, ivy, mistletoe and other evergreens brought the festive glow. On Christmas Eve children were told that an angel stood on every thorn of the holly leaf, adoring Jesus. Only well-berried holly was picked when it could be found. This was an exercise fraught with peril! Many believed that if the holly leaves brought into the house were prickly, the man would rule the home for the following year; if smooth, then the wife would.

Prickly and smooth, we strung it over the pictures on the wall, over the dresser and on the window sash. The bright green leaves and red berries were a reminder of summer brightness. An abundance of berries on the bough was deemed to be a sign of a severe winter ahead – food for hungry birds. Bushes loaded with berries in late harvest were often disappointingly bare before Christmas.

Winter evergreens were favourites of the pagan Druids and priests of the Roman Saturnalia. The custom of decorating houses with holly at Christmas was frowned on by the early Church. It was expressly forbidden at one Council because of its earlier use by the pagan Romans. Ivy, too, met with similar disapproval from the Church authorities and was prohibited because of its 'heathen' associations. Druids decorated their winter dwelling places with holly and evergreens, thereby providing, as they believed, a refuge for woodland spirits.

Was it because of a remnant of an ancient folk memory of lost rites and rituals that farmers or drovers would never strike an animal with a stick cut from either a holly or boothree (elder) bush? A post from a holly tree would never be used to tie cows in a byre, even though it was straight and quite suitable. 'If a holly trunk was used as a stake, the cow was always restless and it never settled down,' Gene Sheerin of Rossinver in County Leitrim told me.

Basic human inclinations prevail over fashions and prohibitions. It's not surprising that ancient civilisations ascribed a special significance to the holly bough: there is no denying the pervasive spirituality that emanates from the effusive colouring; it proclaims hope, rejuvenation and joy. Entering the third millennium, we continue to 'deck the halls' with this buoyant symbol of cheerfulness, hope and joy.

Christmas decorations were left in place until *Nollaig na mBan* (6 January), 'Women's Christmas', also known as 'Wee Christmas'. In Sligo, when the holly was taken down, it was thrown out, not burned. Holly, it was thought, was the 'Burning Bush' of Moses, so it must never be destroyed by fire. Others considered it disrespectful to throw out the withered greenery, and burned it. Sometimes it was retained until Shrove Tuesday night in order to heat the pan for the making of pancakes.

The custom of kissing associated with the mistletoe has its origins in a Scandanavian legend: Balder, the god of peace, was slain with an arrow made from a twig of mistletoe. Following his restoration to life, the greenery was given into the care of the goddess of love, at the request of the other deities. Ever afterwards, anyone passing under it should receive a kiss in order to show that the plant had become a symbol of love triumphant over hate or death.

In County Armagh, girls hung a sprig over the door as a pretext to kiss the first young fellow that entered. Custom dictated that he then had to buy her a present. In Sligo, the use of mistletoe was confined to the local dance hall, where it was hung for the Christmas social. At least one dance during the night centred around the sprig. When the band stopped playing, the couple caught under it were compelled to kiss. There were blushes and a great show of embarrassment from the couple who found themselves 'on the spot', especially the girl. Round and round we went, afraid of when the music would stop, fearful of the embarrassment of being caught – and perhaps fearful we wouldn't.

A generation ago, Christmas was mainly a religious cele-bration in Ireland. There was none of the hullabaloo and commercialism now associated with the holiday. Despite the modern trappings and Hallmark euphoria, many of the old customs still survive. One of these is the placing of a lighted candle in the window on Christmas Eve. The custom has very ancient origins but is now observed to guide the Holy Family who found no room at the inn in Bethlehem. They wander again on Christmas Eve looking for shelter, as on that first Nativity. The lighted candle is also a token of welcome to deceased members of the family, who are believed to return to their home at this time of year.

The candle had a special significance in Penal times in Ireland, when the price on the head of a Catholic priest was the same as that on a wolf. A Major Morgan addressing the Westminister Parliament on the question of heavy charges for public rewards reminded them that 'We have three beasts to destroy that lay burthen upon us. The first is the wolf, on whom we lay five pounds a head if a dog, and ten pounds if a bitch. The second beast is a priest, on whose head we lay ten pounds . . . if he be eminent, more.' A candle in the window might mean nothing more to a watchful English constabulary than a peasant belief. Unknown to them, it was often a sign to outlawed priests that they would receive shelter and a warm bed for the night.

The most famous Christmas fugitives in Irish history were Red Hugh O'Donnell and Art and Henry O'Neill, sons of the northern chieftains. Imprisoned by the British in 1587, they lowered themselves by rope from the walls of Dublin Castle on Christmas Eve 1591. Aided by Fiach MacHugh O'Byrne, Art Kavanagh and Donal MacSweeney, they travelled through bitter winter weather across the Irish countryside to reach the as-yet-unconquered stronghold of the O'Byrne in Wicklow. Young Art O'Neill died on a snow-covered mountainside. Red Hugh survived with the loss of two toes, which had to be amputated because of frostbite.[60]

Hymns composed by Luke Waddinge, bishop of Ferns, in 1684 are still sung in Kilmore, County Wexford, under the leadership of Jack Devereux. The tradition was encouraged by Father William Devereux when he returned from the Irish college in Salamanca in 1728. As parish priest of Drinagh, according to the Register of Popish Priests of 1731, he said Mass in the corner of a field. The following extract from 'On Christmas Day The Yeare 1678' by Father Luke Waddinge gives us reason to be grateful that we live in better times:

> This is our Christmass day
> The day of Christ's birth
> Yet we are far from Joy
> And far from Christmass mirth.
> On Christmass to have no masse
> Is our great discontent
> That without masse this day should pass
> Doth cause us to lament.

The name of Christmass
Must chang'd and altered be
For since we have noe Masse
No Christmasse have we.
It's therefore we do mourn
With grief our hearts are prest
With tears our Eyes doe Run
Our minds and thoughts want rest.

Good Old times are past
And new bad times are come;
And worser times make hast
And hasten to us soone.
Therefore in frights and feares
Those holy-dayes we pass
In sorrow and in teares
We spend our Christmass.

The Wexford Waddinges lost their homes during the Cromwellian confiscations and were banished to the west of Ireland. Through time, Father Waddinge resumed his duties in Wexford in 1674. He refused the office of bishop, believing this would mean unwanted publicity and certain banishment and exile. When in 1683 it was enquired of him by the church hierarchy why he had not been consecrated bishop of his diocese, he explained that the conditions in Wexford town were atrocious. He alone was responsible for 'ministering to a Catholic population reduced by Cromwell's army from 2,000 to 400.'[61]

'Station' Masses, held to this day in people's homes, had their origins in the penal codes of the seventeenth and early eighteenth centuries, enacted under British law. As a result of these codes, fugitive priests were forced to bring the sacraments by stealth to their parishioners. Mass was said at a rock in a field, in a forest clearing, at a holy well or in a friendly home. These secret meetings were known as the 'stations of confessions' because a celebration of the sacrament of Penance formed part of the ceremony. The dispensation to say Mass in the home is unique to Ireland – a direct consequence of those barbarous times.

Edmund Burke described the Penal code which necessitated such secrecy as 'a machine of wise and elaborate contrivance and as well fitted for the oppression, impoverishment and degradation of a people, and the debasement in them of human nature itself, as ever proceeded from the perverted ingenuity of man.'

The code proscribed the religion of the majority, prevented them from accumulating property and punished industry as a crime; it enforced ignorance by statute law and punished the acquisition of knowledge as a felony. By the time it was relaxed, the bulk of the population had been reduced to a state of the most abject poverty and degradation. 'They ceased to be a nation,' wrote Paul Dubois, 'and became instead an inert mass of exhausted and hopeless humanity.'[62]

When the last penal disability disappeared with the Emancipation Act of 1829, some members of the Catholic hierarchy attempted to discourage the practice of saying Mass in private homes. The Dublin provincial statutes of 1831 strongly recommended that the 'stations' be held only in churches from that time forward.

The recommendation was made obligatory at the Synod of Thurles in the 1850s, causing the custom of the station Mass to fall into disuse in Leinster and many other places. Neither was the practice favoured by certain Irish bishops of the nineteenth century, such as Cardinal Cullen of Dublin or Bishop Murphy of Cloyne. However, these Masses were championed by many others, such as Archbishops McHale of Tuam and Slattery of Cashel. Despite church disapproval, many areas, notably the southern and western dioceses, held on to the old custom, particularly where it was supported by the local priest. Even though the tradition is weakening at the present time, there are 1,811 clearly defined 'Station areas' in the archdiocese of Tuam.

The continuance of this ancient and uniquely Irish tradition, with its roots in the hearts and hearths of the country people, is now both controversial and threatened. Secular and material-istic considerations predominate in a changed and frantic world. To some, the idea of the Masses is quaint, if not bizarre; to others, it is inconvenient.

Nowhere is the feeling of intimacy, neighbourliness and true Christianity more evident than in the friendly and welcoming surroundings of the family home. It is a sacred link with the past. Irish men and women defied hunger and thirst, oppression and death, in order to gather together. The first Mass was not said in a great cathedral but in a modest room in Jerusalem with Jesus and the disciples. In a recent article for *Intercom* magazine, Father Kieran Waldron summed it up: 'That in one corner of the world, over the space of every ten or twelve years, practically every home in a parish has the privilege of having the Eucharist celebrated for the family with their neighbours, must surely be a tradition worth safeguarding and promoting.'

9

'No Witch Hath Power to Charm'

The lighted candle in the window was a special token for family members far away from home. One of the most appealing of all the old customs was the habit of leaving the door on the latch on Christmas Eve as a welcoming invitation to the Holy Family, weary travellers, or absent loved ones to come in and take shelter for the night.

Until recently, emigration was an accepted, if undesirable, fact of Irish family life. In these days of instant communication and a shrinking globe, it is difficult to visualise the vast gulf that, not so long ago, separated emigrants from their familes. Travel was unaffordable well into the second half of the 1900s, so visits were infrequent. Communication was difficult, as there were no phones in the vast majority of houses.[63] An emigrant's ticket to America was one-way: most would never return to see their homes and relations again. The American 'wake' of the departing son or daughter was appropriately named. Just as with a death, this was a crossing over from which there was no return. Hearts went out across the miles at this special time of the year.

In many parts of Ireland, red candles were favoured for the Christmas observance. These were placed in a hollowed-out turnip, lit by the youngest member of the family and placed in a window or sometimes in all three front windows of the house. Here they were allowed to burn until midnight and were then extinguished, for fear of fire. In Cork, as well as a few other areas, three candles, or a three-branched candle, were lit in honour of the Holy Family.

Some believed that bad luck would follow if the candle flickered out without being quenched. In Longford, Kevin Danaher notes in *The Year in Ireland*, 'a large candle is lighted on Christmas night, laid on a table and suffered to burn out. If it should happen by any means to be extinguished, or more particularly if it should (as has sometimes happened) go out without any visible cause, the untoward circumstances would be considered a prognostic of the death of the head of the family.'[64]

In County Armagh it was the practice on Christmas Eve to 'put on a good fire before you go to bed, sweep the floor, put bread on the table and keep a candle lit and the door unbarred.' In Sligo the 'good people' were not forgotten and in some houses 'a plate of currant bread, potato bread and tea was left out for the fairies.' As with the lighted candle, some left food out to provide sustenance for the dead members of the family who might return or pass by during the night.

If death was inevitable, Christmas Eve, or the twelve days following, was deemed a propitious time to die. Heaven was open to all then. Contrary to all other times of the year, to hear the cock crow at midnight then was 'a good sign' and sure to bring good luck. The belief was old even in Shakespeare's time:

> Some say that ever 'gainst that season comes
> Wherein our Saviour's birth is celebrated,
> The bird of dawning singeth all night long.
> And then, they say, no spirit dare stir abroad;
> The nights are wholesome; then no planets strike;
> No fairy takes nor witch hath power to charm,
> So hallow'd and so gracious is the time.

> Hamlet I, i

Jesus was born at midnight on Christmas Eve, my mother told us. In remembrance of that, every year at this time the gift of speech was given to the cows. This belief was firmly held in many parts of Ireland. It was held too that the cows and ass knelt at midnight in memory of Christ's birth. Before going to bed, we always gave them an extra armful of hay on that night and wondered if it was really true that they could converse and, if so, what they might talk about. We thought about it as sleep took us but never went to the byre at midnight to see the miracle or 'talk to the animals'! Well, maybe next year . . .

The *poitín*-makers were busy in the period leading up to the holiday season. They still are. Despite the imposition of heavy penalties for anyone caught with the illegal brew, it is still in plentiful supply. Connoisseurs of the clear sparkling liquid know that Christmas is not a good time to buy. To meet the increased demand, many of the 'distillers' use short cuts in order to produce more whiskey in less time. An inferior product may result.

Stories of the addition of bluestone, car-battery acid, carbide or sulphuric acid to the mix in order to accelerate the process or 'improve' potency have done little to inhibit demand. There are no health or quality-control inspections in mountain caves or hidden barns. An estimated £14,000 worth of *poitín* was seized near Buncrana, County Donegal, on Good Friday, 2 April 1999. Gardaí found two dead rats floating on top of one of the barrels of wash! 'What probably happened was that the rats were running across the top of the barrel and fell through the sugar bags that covered the opening,' a garda spokesman told reporters.[65] Maybe. Perhaps if the rats had stayed sober, they might not have fallen!

Poitín-makers have been outside the law since the imposition, by the British Parliament, of an excise tax on whiskey in the 1640s. The small distiller had choices: pay up, go out of business or go underground. Most chose the last. Providers of the brew had no lack of customers. Having no overheads, their product could be made and sold much cheaper than shop-bought whiskey. In the early 1800s, a twenty-four-stone barrel of oats costing fourteen shillings yielded eight gallons of *poitín*. Retailed at seven to eight shillings per gallon, this yielded a handsome profit for the entrepreneur. There were few patrons who could resist the thrill of partaking of the fruit of the honest, if forbidden, labour of local 'businessmen'. The secrecy and mystique of the process, as well as the danger of capture, served to add to the aura and excitement of the enticing liquid.

One of the tasks of the 'Revenue Police' was to control the trade. In the middle of the last century, 240 such men garrisoned six separate barracks in County Sligo, which was rated only the sixth-highest county in Ireland in terms of the making of *poitín*. In 1848, forty-nine offenders were confined in Sligo Gaol, convicted of illicit distilling. The capture of eighty-five stills and eighty-three worms (the spiral pipe of a still) in one year about this time gives an indication of the numbers that evaded arrest.[66]

If I was a monarch in state,
Like Romulus or Julius Caesar,
With the best of fine victuals to eat,
And drink like Nebuchadnezzar,
A rasher of bacon I'd have,
And potatoes the finest was seen, sir;
And for drink, it's no claret I'd crave,
But a keg of oul' Mullen's poitín, sir,
With the smell of the smoke on it still.

Charles Lever

Inishmurray Island, off the Sligo coast, was one of the remote and lonely places where the industry thrived. The quality and quantity of *poitín* made there is as legendary as the stories and adventures of distillers, suppliers and raiders having to do with the trade. The island, three miles offshore, had a commanding view of the sea and coast from where the law launched sudden invasions.

Maggie McGowan knew all the shebeens in her area that carried stocks of the island brew: 'Patsy Donlevy, Broges, Pat McGowan, Paddy over at the bog, Paddy Feeney at Carrigans, they were all shebeen houses. You'd go in an' sit down an' have someone watching the road. When the islanders came into Cloonagh with the *poitín*, every man was there waiting with his five-naggin or pint bottle or whatever he wanted. Others that was reselling it had crockery jars an' they'd get the full of that, maybe a gallon in each one. They'd sell it out then in naggins and pints, an' there was great demand for it. I used to see the boats coming out of the island with the *poitín* – they lived on it there, ye know. An' was very well reared, an' grand houses, an' good scholars, every one o' them.'

Anne Maloney, whose people had been evicted during the clearances of the Seven Cartrons,[67] eked out a living by running one of these shebeens out of a little house in Lissadell. 'She sold matches, paraffin oil and tobacco for an excuse,' Maggie told me. 'As well as the *poitín*, my father, Lord have mercy on him, used to bring her two-gallon jars of whiskey out from Sligo when he was carting. She had a big wide frieze dress with two big pockets on the inside where she always carried a quart of it. People went to her if they wanted a pint of whiskey for making a rick or for a wake or a drop at Christmas. She used to keep it buried in the garden too.

'The old women that time used to take a half-one on the QT.

One day when I was a young girl, my father sent me to the shop for tobacco. Old Eliza Barber from Munianeane was having a drop when who arrived but Sergeant Glendenning from the barracks. Eliza threw the whiskey behind the fire and stuck the glass down her breast.

'"What were they at when I came in," the sergeant said to me. "I smelled whiskey."

'But I was cute enough for him. "I'm only up here for tobacco for my father," says I. "I saw no whiskey" – an' me knowin' well. They'd all help her out: they were all agin the oul' police.

'But that wasn't all! She had a trap laid for them this time. She had "whiskey" buried in the garden a few days before. They found it and arrested her. When they brought it to the barracks and opened it, they were glad to go out and empty it. It might have been the colour of straw but it wasn't whiskey was in it!'

Such raids were always unpopular, but a raid on Foran's pub in Lissadell, which took place during the festive season, was especially so. The gathering at Foran's was traditional for the twelve nights of Christmas. Musicians came from all over. The noted fiddler Peter Mullaney, travelling ten miles on foot from his home in Mullaghmore, 'never missed a night'. One of those caught was Mick Herrity, who became a garda sergeant himself in later years. The whole affair had a sequel in court when Mrs Foran pleaded in defence that Our Lord had wine at the last supper. Judge Flattery agreed and fined her half a crown – the least amount allowed by law. The event was immortalised in song by James Currid of Raughley:

> Sergeant Kelly marched on, he was out on parade;
> Said he, 'Try Ballyconnell,' but he was afraid.
> He came to the barracks and gazed all around
> Saying, 'Lislarry is quiet, I think I'll go down.'

'Promotion,' he whispered, 'we'll try for down here.
It's a woman that runs it so there's nothing to fear.'
He arrived at the pub as he oft did before
And roared in the keyhole to open the door.

Now the famed twelve apostles were clustered inside;
They knew they were captured and not bona fide.
They thought they were safer to stay where they were,
So they off with their hats and assembled in prayer.

Peter the apostle looked quiet, no doubt
With his head bended over a large pint of stout.
Kitty Meehan was singin' 'The Night of the Wind'
When the famous Red Robber he chanced to come in.

She thought it was 'Suggart' till she turned in her chair
But she puckered her brow when she saw the red hair.
He took out his notebook, the names to take down
While the boys that were with him kept smelling around.

The writing was bad and the spelling was slow
But sure what could you expect from a man from Mayo!

Again Kitty Meehan got out of her shell
Saying, 'I wish you were roasted and toasted in hell.
You infamous red robber, you might stay away
And give us a chance as it is Christmas Day.'

The trial came on and it stood half a day
Dolly swore she invited them all down for tay,
And to give them a drink, it was no crime at all
She could swear there was wine at the Feast of St Paul.

> The judge he looked down with a frown on his face
> Saying, 'Kelly, you should never have brought up this
>   case.
> These twelve pious men you have caused them to
>   mourn,
> This case I dismiss, you are free, Dolly Foran.'

Despite the advantageous position of the islanders, the long arm of the law had its successes on Inishmurray too. The gardaí were particularly vigilant at Christmastime, in the knowledge that hundreds of gallons of the stuff was on the move, making its way to the parched throats of anxious customers. The *Sligo Independent* reported on 24 December 1897 the discovery and destruction of 195 gallons of wash on Inishmurray by a party of police under Sergeants Morrain and Finnegan. So much for Christmas spirit! Gardaí had substantially more success in 1924, when they captured three stills, eight kegs of finished product and a thousand gallons of wash, as well as several containers of raw materials.

Constable Jeremiah Mee, stationed at Grange, recalled in his memoirs a raid on Inishmurray in 1918. Before setting out on their journey, he and another constable were equipped with 'long, pointed steel rods which were to be used for probing hay and corn stacks, and shingle along the strand, in our search for illicit stills,' he recalled. He describes boarding a boat at Streedagh Point manned by 'two hefty Mullaghmore fishermen'. The boat was anchored a distance from shore, as there was no proper harbour. 'With their pants folded well above their knees, the two fishermen advanced from the boat to meet us,' he said. 'On reaching the strand, after a peremptory greeting, they turned their backs on the sergeant and Clarke, who got up on the fishermen's backs and were carried high and dry to the little boat. The two RIC men took this as a matter of course and the sergeant did not even smile as I sat on the shore laughing at the unusual sight. One of the boatmen returned, when I, too, got up on his back, and never in my life did I feel less like a policeman.'

On their arrival, they distributed a number of parcels which they had brought with them, and received a friendly welcome from the islanders. The RIC were accustomed to delivering packages and letters on these visits. Mee learned sometime later that these innocent-looking parcels, unknown to the police, often contained supplies of treacle, yeast and barm used in the manufacture of *poitín*. The innocent-looking letters often contained orders for *poitín* from customers on the mainland!

Having engaged in a fruitless search of the fields and shore, Constable Mee and the other stalwarts of the law retired, as was the custom on these visits, to the home of Mrs Harte for tea. According to Mee, the whole affair was very civilised, after an Irish fashion: 'Believe it or not, at the end of our meal we were treated to a few glasses of *poitín!*'

The return voyage of the police raiding party to the mainland was very rough, 'the sea a mass of angry water and foam'. Mee made no secret of the fact that he was scared out of his wits when the boat started to take on water. To console him, 'one of the boatmen took out a bottle of *poitín*, which was passed around, and all had a drink.' As the drink permeated his veins, his mood changed, and 'between the buffeting of the waves and the strong *poitín*, I did not care whether the boat went up or down.' Eventually, they reached the mainland two miles away from their intended landing place, and so ended in ignominy one assault on an island industry.

Later transferred to Kerry, Mee travelled there by train with two other officers in the troubled year of 1919. On leaving

Grange, he was presented with a bottle of 'good Inishmurray *poitín* and by way of turning our thoughts from sordid shootings I produced my bottle and we impartially drank toasts to the king and the republic on Irish whiskey for which neither king nor republic had received duty.' Becoming disenchanted with the activities of the RIC as the War of Independence progressed, he later resigned from the force to join the IRA.

Christmas Day was a quiet family affair spent at home. We went to Mass and Holy Communion in the morning, or to Midnight Mass at twelve o'clock the night before. On all other Sundays of the year, we changed back into working clothes on arriving home. Cattle took no holiday, and required milking, feeding and watering every day. On Christmas Day, however, an exception was made. Work was kept to a minimum and we kept our Sunday clothes on for most of the day.

In some of the northern counties of Ireland, where the descendants of the Scottish Puritans lived, Christmas was no different from any other day: 'the dissenters, not considering it a holiday, follow their usual occupations.' Among Presbyterians, it was a day of family gatherings, although it was not regarded primarily as such.

The power of the Puritans in England grew in the early seventeenth century. Largely due to the influence of Oliver Cromwell, Christmas celebrations shortly came under censure of law. Such festivities, which went contrary to the Puritan philosophy of simplicity of worship, were banned. Severe penalties were imposed on those who celebrated or who stayed home from work.

When the Puritan Pilgrim Fathers sailed to the New England states in America, they brought their stern beliefs with them. Christmas there was not celebrated as a legal holiday until 1856. Ireland did not escape unscathed: in the mid-seventeenth century any observance of the holiday was forbidden by public order.

Hunting hares and foxes with dog and gun was a favourite Christmas-day pastime in many districts. In Monaghan and other northern counties, shooting matches were held. Reports from some counties – Donegal and Limerick among them – relate that after Mass the men and boys of neighbouring villages played against each other in hurling and football or went hunting. Such activities were probably another remnant of early man's celebration of the winter solstice.

Along the seashore, if no other venue was available, beaches were used as a pitch to play *camánacht* or hurling. It was a favourite game among the Irish from the earliest ages and is often mentioned in old sagas. Cúchulainn, when a boy, going to Emhain to visit his uncle, King Conchobhair, took with him 'his hurley of bronze and his ball of silver'. Hurling is still a popular game in many Irish counties and is one of the most exciting and skilful of sports. According to Jeanne Cooper Foster in *Ulster Folklore*, in 1951 '*camán* was played within living memory on the beaches of Magilligan, Portrush and Bush Bay . . . ' The teams were usually from neighbouring townlands, which meant they were natural rivals. There appears to have been no idea of selecting a team, and as many men as wished could play. There was no limit to the numbers: 'If one side happened to have more than the other, well, that was unfortunate for their opponents.' It was a very rough sport, she said, that had waned in popularity in later years.

Hurling was popular in many places, including Sligo, into the early years of the twentieth century. Matches took place on Sundays and during holidays along the seashore prior to permission being given by Lord Ashley to play on the 'Flat' or 'Strand' near Cliffoney village. The Strand derives its name from ancient times, when the village of Mullaghmore was an island and the tide washed between there and Cliffoney twice a day.

Rules regarding team size were vague and were determined by the numbers that showed up. Squads of twenty or twenty-five a side were not uncommon. The game was played in working clothes: there were no uniforms, shorts or special shoes. The ball was round, made of a hard wood, 'slightly bigger than a duck egg and covered over with leather,' Cliffoney man Pat Whyte told me. Hurling sticks called *camáns* were cut from growing bushes with a turn at the end, or roughly fashioned by the local wheelwright. Some looked like a walking stick, except that the butt-end was wider and stronger. Two branches of trees were stuck in the ground fifteen feet apart for goalposts. There was no crossbar.

Matches were frequently played between Carns and Cliffoney. The Carns team included players from the townlands of Carns, Edenreagh and Cloyspar. In addition to players from the village itself, Cliffoney drew additional members from Cartron, Carnduff and Creevykeel. An account of a great match played on Bunduff beach between Sligo and Leitrim during Land League times in 1880 was often brought to mind by Pat Whyte.

'The captain of the Sligo team was Hudy McGloin from near the bridge of Bunduff,' he recalled. 'Two mighty players I remember were Thomas McGarrigle from Creevykeel and Thomas McGowan from Bunduff. On the Leitrim side there was Paddy Gethins from Finner and a traitor from Grellagh called Pat Mick McGloin. You see, Grellagh is in Sligo, so they should have been playing with us; you might say it was Leitrim and Grellagh versus the rest of Sligo,' he said, a glint of rancour sharpening his eyes, even though the match had taken place sixty years before.

'When the Leitrim men arrived,' he continued, 'Gethins showed up in a uniform wearing a sword. That might have been to show his authority. The Sligo leader, McGloin, had a similar attire.

'Gethins walked over to McGloin. "Take off your hat and salute me," he says. McGloin, naturally enough, refused, and then the challenge took place. The agreement was that the losing side had to salute the winners and then clear off the playing ground.

'They started to play but before long the row got up and developed into a regular mêlée, both sides whacking each other. The Leitrim side won in the end and the other side had to leave the field as agreed.'

That wasn't the end of it. There was a sequel a month later during a rematch at the annual 'Pattern' in the Leitrim village of Tullaghan. This time there was bad blood on both sides. Fights broke out again during the game; these fights resulted in severe injuries for some of the players and a term in jail for several others. The parish priest denounced the practice and, according to Pat, this put an end to the sport in this area for a long time afterwardes.

Hurling took place on the Great Blasket too. Tomas Ó Criomhthain in *The Islandman* described a match played on the White Strand, 'without shoes or stockings, and we went in up to our necks whenever the ball went into the sea. Throughout the twelve days of Christmastime, there wasn't a man able to drive his cow to the hill for the stiffness of his back and bones; a pair or so would have a bruised foot and another would be limping on one leg for a month.'

Tea – that great favourite for holiday repasts – was unknown on the Blaskets until around the turn of the twentieth century. When eventually it arrived, it was used sparingly, 'and the remainder saved up till the next Christmas'. Strong drink was a part of the celebrations too, 'for however much or little drink comes to the island, it is put aside for Christmas Eve. Maybe an old man would be singing who hadn't lifted his voice for a year. As for the old women, they're always lilting away':

> 'Tis the best of the doctor's prescriptions
> If whiskey and porther are cheap,
> For it cures us of all our afflictions
> And puts all men's sorrows to sleep.
> And the old woman wheezing and groaning,
> A-bed for a year in despair,
> When she sups her half-pint, stops her moaning,
> And kicks the bedclothes in the air.

Charles Lever

The day after Christmas was another favourite time for sporting pastimes, particularly in the north-western counties of Sligo, Cavan and Leitrim. Peadar Mac Giolla Chonaigh of County Leitrim told the Irish Folklore Commission in 1942 that this day was always kept for hunting and fowling. Young men went out in batches with hounds and guns after hares, foxes and birds. He also related that no meat of any description was allowed to be eaten on that day. Nevertheless, there were some who believed, 'You could take meat in another's house but not in your own!'

Pat Healy, *seanchaí* and raconteur from Mullaghmore in County Sligo, related in 1947 that this fast was kept even more strictly than on Good Friday. All sickness, fevers and disorders were kept from people and animals for the ensuing twelve months in any house where the abstinence was observed.

According to Pat, hunting with hounds for rabbits or hares was a favourite pastime with the people of Mullaghmore and surrounding areas on that day. He recalled that the young lads kept up the chase for hours when the hare was 'ris' (started).

The day often ended in a party fight. 'The dogs started it and the lads finished it,' was how he put it.

Faction fighting was a way of life in Ireland at one time. Fracas involving fists and sticks took place between opposing families or between opposing groups from different townlands during 'Patterns' and on fair days. Old, undecided party or faction fights were brought to a conclusion either on Candlemas Day or on St Patrick's Day.

The twelve days following Christmas had a special significance in former times. A church meeting in Tours in 567 ordained that the twelve days following Christmas should be kept holy by prayer and by refraining from work. As the years, progressed this requirement was reduced to three days. Although continuing to be recognised as part of the season, the twelve days are not kept in any meaningful way any more.

Formerly, witches, wizards and evil spirits were thought to be particularly active on the twelve days from Christmas to Twelfth Night. Even in Christian Europe, people carried on with the old pagan practice of expelling evil powers at such times. This allowed the purging of evil and a fresh start free from evil influences. Relics of those earlier customs are still practised on Twelfth Night in the Piazza Navona in Rome. Here a crowd assembles and, after raising a huge roar, marches through the streets carrying cardboard cut-outs and making a loud din. The ceremony, ostensibly in honour of Bethana, is probably of pre-Christian origin – a relic of earlier, pagan times, when witches were driven out, and yet another example of the amalgamation of Christian and pagan beliefs.

Evil spirits were a concern to many diverse cultures. Chinese New Year (*Yuan Tan*) starts on the day of the second new moon after the winter solstice. On the eve of *Yuan Tan*, evil spirits are prevented from entering the house simply by sealing all the doors and windows with paper strips. No one is allowed to break the seals by leaving or entering until they are ceremonially broken on the following morning before dawn.

In the western world, there were days of special importance during the twelve days of the Christian Christmas. One of these was the feast day of the Holy Innocents, celebrated on 28 December. This is not remembered so much now but was once commemorated as the day of the massacre of the children by King Herod. It was thought to be an unfavourable time to start any job of work or to take on any new project. If something unavoidable had to be undertaken, such as digging a grave, the bad luck could be avoided by starting the first sod before midnight the previous evening.

This was one of the 'cross' days, meaning an unlucky day. On whichever day it fell, bad luck would follow on that day of the week for the rest of the year. If, say, the feast fell on a Monday, then no new work would be undertaken or business transacted, graves dug or marriages undertaken on any Monday throughout the year. It is said that Dean Swift kept Friday and what he called Childermas Day as 'two cross days in the week, and it is impossible to have good luck in either of them.'[68]

With the exception of the Chinese, Muslims and Jews, the acceptance of 1 January as the first day of the New Year is universal. It wasn't always so! Down through the centuries New Year began at various times: on 1 January, 1 March, 25 March, 25 December; sometimes it coincided with Easter. In the early years of the Roman Republic, March was fixed as the first month of the New Year because the newly elected officials of the Roman Senate took up office then. After 153 BC, the inauguration of the consuls was changed to 1 January. As a consequence, New Year's Day was moved to that date as well.

In France, prior to AD 800, New Year's Day was on 1 March. It was changed to 25 March and in 996 changed again to coincide with Easter before finally reverting to 1 January. Before the Norman conquest of England, the New Year was celebrated there on Christmas Day. Following the defeat of the Anglo-Saxons at the Battle of Hastings in 1066, the Normans introduced the Roman practice of starting the New Year on 1 January. A century later, the New Year was changed once more, to begin on Lady Day, 25 March, where it stayed until 1851. Lady Day, known as Annunciation Day, was celebrated in the Christian calendar as the occasion on which it was revealed to Mary that she would give birth to the son of God.

The Julian calendar instituted by Julius Caesar in 46 BC was adjusted by Pope Gregory XIII in 1582. This became necessary in order to correct an accumulated error caused by previous faulty calculations of the length of a year. At this time, New Year's Day was again fixed on 1 January. This new date and the revamped calendar, called the Gregorian calendar, was greeted with suspicion and hostility in a number of countries. Although it was accepted in Scotland in 1600 and in Germany, Denmark and Sweden a hundred years later, it was not accepted in England until 1752. The reorganised calendar was regarded there as part of a 'Popish' plot. Change was inevitable, as England and Ireland were out of step with everyone else in Europe, whose year began on 1 January. The British Act, eventually passed in March 1751, dictated that the correction should take place between 2 and 14 September 1752. In that year, 2 September was followed on the next day by 14 September. Even after this alignment with world time, many official business transactions continued to date from Lady Day. April Fool's Day is said to have originated when some people continued to celebrate New Year's Day on 1 April, refusing to recognise the new date prescribed by law. The fools celebrated on the old date. Should 25 March be March Fool's Day?

Calendars meant little to country people managing crops and land. They reckoned their working year from 1 February, regardless of official diktats. The time of lengthening days, a warmer sun and improving weather could not be influenced by either Julius Caesar or Pope Gregory. The first of February was the old Celtic festival of Imbolc, the first day of spring: St Brigid's Day.

Although some countries, notably Scotland, treat New Year's Day as a major holiday, Christmas was the more important festive time of year in Ireland. Traditionally observed as a religious feast, New Year's Eve, once known as St Sylvester's Eve, has become in modern times a night for celebration and bacchanalia. It is time to shed the disappointments and frustrated hopes of the Old Year and to welcome the bright and promising New Year – a fresh start, where everything is possible!

In former times, it was a very lucky thing if the first person to enter the house on the first day of the New Year was black-haired or, even better, a dark-haired man. Trouble was in store for the rest of the year if the first person through the door was a red-haired woman! 'First footing' was carried out by people with the desired characteristics who, by virtue of being the first to cross their neighbours' thresholds, brought good luck. The tradition in Ireland is confined to the northern counties, where many of the inhabitants are of Scottish origin or influence.

This was the time of year when the Scots visited their byres. Napier's *Folk-Lore* recorded in 1779 that 'a block of wood was put on the fire about ten o'clock so that it would be burning briskly before the household retired to bed. The last thing done by those who possessed a cow or horse was to visit the byre or stable, and I have been told that it was the practice with some, twenty years before my recollection, to say the Lord's Prayer during this visit.'

Some of the practices associated with Samhain, such as attempting to foretell the future, were observed then too. On New Year's Eve, a young woman wishing to discover the name of a future husband put holly and ivy leaves or mistletoe under her pillow before going to bed while reciting the words: 'Oh, ivy green and holly red, tell me, tell me whom I shall wed.' The man she would marry was then sure to appear in a dream.

Young men didn't have any facility for determining what lay ahead, so their lot was to travel artlessly into the future, to be waylaid by these wise young women, who knew exactly what and whom to look for! That is, except in some fishing villages in England, where on St Agnes' Eve, 21 January, the men too were given a vision of their future bride if they ate a raw herring!

New Year's Eve was a good time to determine the weather for the coming year. Two other dates in January were also advantageous in this regard: 25 January, the feast of the conversion of St Paul, and 22 January, the Feast of St Vincent:

> Remember on St Vincent's Day,
> That if the sun his beams display,
> Be sure to mark his transient beam,
> Which through the casement sheds a gleam;
> For 'tis a token bright and clear
> Of prosperous weather all the year.

One of the names by which New Year's Eve was known was *Oíche na Coda Móire* ('the night of the big portion'). Those who wished to ensure a plentiful supply of food for the coming year ate heartily at suppertime. The old custom of 'battering away hunger', observed by some at Hallowe'en, was also carried out at New Year's Eve, or alternatively on the eve of Twelfth Night. Crofton Croker related that in Munster the head of the house threw a loaf of bread against the outside door 'on the last night of the year' to ward off hunger in the coming twelve months.

In Kilkenny this was done on the eve of the Twelfth Day. Kevin Danaher in *The Year in Ireland* notes the following extract from 'The Transactions of the Kilkenny Archaeological Society' for 1849–55:

> There is one custom which I found practised by a family moving in a very respectable sphere, and which I am informed was not long ago, probably still is, practised in the County of Kilkenny, and to which I wish to call to your attention, because it appears to me to savour of paganism of the rankest kind. On the eve of the Twelfth Day, a large loaf called the 'Christmas Loaf', which is usually baked some days previously, is laid with great solemnity on the table; the doors and windows are closed and strongly bolted; and one of the family, generally the housewife, then takes the loaf, and pounding it against the closed doors, etc, repeats three times in Irish the following *rann*:

> > *Fógramuid an Ghorta,*
> > *Amach go tír na d-Turcach;*
> > *Ó nocht go bliadhain ó nocht,*
> > *Agus ó nocht féin amach.*

> > *(We warn famine to retire*
> > *To the country of the Turks;*
> > *From this night to this night twelvemonth,*
> > *And even this very night.)*

In County Limerick, the Holy Trinity was invoked during a similar ceremony – yet another example of the Christianising of what was possibly an old, pre-Christian custom. In other places, the ceremony was repeated at the byre door, thus ensuring a plentiful supply of food for the cattle also. There was a reluctance in some areas, as on May Eve, to give away or to allow foodstuffs out of the house on New Year's Eve.

Epiphany, also called *Nollaig na mBan* ('Women's Christmas'), the twelfth day after 25 December, fell on 6 January. Formerly a festival of the highest rank celebrated as early as AD 194, it was once accorded much more importance than it is now. The festival, also known as 'wee Christmas', was 'old Christmas' prior to the changeover to the Gregorian calendar. Contributing to the significance of the day may be the fact that, up to then, Christmas Day fell on the day we now designate 6 January.

The significance of 6 January as a Church holy day originated as a celebration of the anniversary of the baptism of Christ. Epiphany now commemorates the revelation of Jesus Christ as Saviour occasioned by the arrival of the Three Wise Men, as described in Matthew 2.1–12.

The explanation for the link between this day and women seems to be that, while strong fare like turkey, beef and whiskey was partaken at Christmas, daintier fare such as confectioneries, wine, etc. were more likely to be on offer at *Nollaig na mBan*. Following the celebration, all decorations were taken down and the holly and ivy stored to start the fire on which pancakes would be made on Shrove Tuesday.

It was not only in Ireland that Twelfth Night was celebrated as a night of special importance. The custom of electing a King and Queen of the Bean was observed in Germany, Belgium, England and France until recently. On the eve of the festival, families mixed a cake into which they put two beans. After being baked, it was divided among the members of the family with three extra portions: one for God, one for the Blessed Virgin and one for the poor. The people who got the portions with the beans were elected King and Queen of the Bean. Upon election, the King of the Bean was enthroned, saluted by all present and lifted up in the air three times, each time making crosses with chalk on the beams and rafters of the ceiling. These crosses were credited with the power to protect the house and family against all kinds of evil and against 'all injuryes and harmes, of cursed devils, sprites and bugges, of conjuringes and charmes,' as Sir James George Frazer notes in *The Golden Bough*.

The twelve days have probably had special significance from prehistoric times: 'an ancient intercalary period inserted for the purpose of equating the lunar to the solar year'.[69] In former times, such an interval was a space when the ordinary rules of conduct did not apply. The practitioners of such magic, like the King and Queen of the Bean, taking advantage of this, could take on special powers too and ward off evil.

In the Christian world, Epiphany also commemorates the marriage feast at Cana, where Christ performed his first miracle of turning water into wine. It is held by some that this still happens on the eve of the Twelfth Day in honour of that first miracle. However, the fact that it is deemed unlucky to spy on the transformation acts as a deterrent to thirsty voyeurs. Proof of the unfortunate consequences of beholding the mutation is to be seen at a holy well dedicated to St Brendan in Cill a' Ruith, near Ventry in County Kerry. Here can be found three boulders – all that remains of three inebriates who sat up, expecting to take advantage of this wondrous occurrence. On witnessing the miracle, they were instantly petrified and remain as an example to anyone daring to spy or take advantage of this unique happening.

In parts of France, people dance around bonfires lit on Twelfth Night singing, 'Good year, come back, bread and wine come back,' in order to bring good luck to the crops. In Herefordshire, England, twelve fires are lit, plus one large fire to burn the old witch, in order that the people may have good crops. The fires represent the twelve days of Christmas and the twelve months of the year.

Long ago in Ireland, twelve candles were lit on Twelfth Night in honour of the twelve apostles. Sometimes this was used to determine future events. Patrick McHugh of Cliffoney, County Sligo, recorded that in the parish of Ahamlish, most families bought twelve candles and lit them in honour of the apostles, naming one candle for each member of the family. If there were not enough people in the family, then neighbours' names were used to make up the twelve. The candles were then allowed to burn out, the belief being that this indicated which person would be the first to die. We can imagine that it must have been a pretty traumatic experience to watch a candle with your name flicker and die!

This curious custom was not confined to County Sligo, although the lighting was often done without any attempt at death-divination. In parts of Leinster, Connacht and south Ulster, 'A round cake of sufficient size was made of dough, or of ashes or clay, or even of dried cow-dung, and in it were put standing a small number of candles, rushlights or bog-deal splinters, one for each member of the family, and each named for a particular individual. In the evening, when the whole household was assembled, these were lighted and then carefully observed and the order in which they burned out or quenched was regarded as an indication of the order in which the persons represented by them would die. This was usually a solemn occasion, and no levity was permitted. Indeed, more than one informant told that the ceremony was accompanied by prayer or performed during the normal family evening prayers.'[70]

The use of dried cow-dung as a candle-holder in the description above may seem bizarre to us now, but it did happen – and within living memory in north Sligo. Cow manure was a basic and vital element in the fertilisation and revitalisation of the soil. Its use as a candleholder belongs to a time, now beyond the comprehension of a privileged society, when people were far closer, in understanding and practice, to the raw and the elemental than we can ever imagine.

10

Cois na Tine

My mother mixed the dough for our Christmas cake on the kitchen table. Then and Hallowe'en were the only times of the year when we were sure to have raisin bread. Watching in mouth-watering anticipation, I hoped she wouldn't put in any of the caraway seeds that were a favourite of my father but which I hated.

Beside the fire, my father sat in the chimney corner fixing the burning coals expertly as he added more turf. Chatting as he worked, he swapped stories with ramblers Dan Kelly, Kevin McGrath, Jimmy McGowan and Mary Dowdican. Gathered close to the dancing flames, weather-beaten faces ruddy in the reflected firelight, they sat around in a friendly circle. Even with a good blaze, the heat that radiated from the burning turf fought a constant battle with draughts of cold air for dominance of the kitchen. Memories of roasting shins and cold backs linger. Prior to thermal glazing and attic insulation, a warm coat was essential for a night spent in these draughty, stone-flagged kitchens with their high, vaulted sod roofs.

The fire made its mark on the lazy by stamping its revealing imprint on exposed shins. As trousers were rarely worn by women before the 1960s, repeated exposure to the heat branded a thick, brownish-red network pattern on bare legs. It was a dead give-away: if a woman had 'brockety' shins, she spent too much time at the hearth. Coatings of 'Calamine' lotion helped camouflage the tell-tale marks but never fooled the village gossips. In a quarrel, the epithet of 'brockety shins' spoke volumes and was an irredeemable insult!

Chatting away, the men spoke of daily events, of cattle, crops, weather and the other things that affected their everyday existence. The fireside acted as a people's courthouse too: the forum where opinion was formulated, codes of behaviour discussed, approved or rejected. It was the final and deciding place of arbitration, independent of priest or judge. Poaching, rebellion, smuggling – these were not crimes here but rights.

Ernie O'Malley wrote of long nights spent with such people during his time on the run during the War of Independence. 'Here was their paper,' he commented, 'a living warp and weft spun of their own thoughts, fancies and doings. Now and again a biting turn of phrase, for in their nature was the old Gaelic satire . . . there was a love of discussion and argument that would take up a subject casually without belief and in a searching way develop it . . . Deferential to a stranger, they evoked in themselves a sympathetic mood, changing gears in conversation to suit his beliefs and half-believing then through sympathy whilst he was present. Afterwards when they checked up on themselves it might be different; they would laugh at the strangers' outlandish opinions when their mood hardened.'

Nothing has changed. Country people will yet agree with the stranger for fear of giving offence. The visitor will go away confirmed in his beliefs; the local will smile and take his own counsel.

Sometimes the fireside conversation turned to things that happened long ago or to a discussion of remarkable people in Irish history. It was in gatherings like this that the quiet longing, the burning desire for freedom was nurtured in troubled times. Hope and despair were their constant companions during the dark centuries when O'Neill and O'Donnell, Teeling and Parnell strove to make Ireland a free nation. They spoke in admiration and affection of the exploits of local heroes of indomitable courage: Ned Bofin or Billy Pilkington, Linda Kearns or Constance Markievicz.

A gesture of the hand, a facial expression drew pictures from words. The listeners looked into the flames and saw there the clamour and conflict, the fire of ancient battles. Fionn's pursuit of Diarmuid and Grainne; the great cattle raid of Maugherow that took place a thousand years before; the 'Moneygold ambush' that happened during Ireland's War of Independence: all were told around the fireside, year after year, by men like John Gilbride of Carrigans. Handed on from one generation to another, they passed from living memory into legend. There was no timescale; past and present were all tangled up. Jimmy McGowan had heard John tell the story of the cattle raid at a fair in Grange, and often repeated it.

Conall was a chieftain who lived in the townland now known as Ballyconnell. His community earning a living by sea and shore. Herds of cattle grazed their lands. Once, when Conall was out fishing in Sligo Bay, Costello, a rival chieftain from the other side of Sligo town, arrived in the area with a strong force of men. Rounding up all the cattle, they started to drive them off to their own territory. Hurrying to the shore, Conall's herdsmen lit fires as a signal to the boats that they should return imediately. They set sail at once and landed at Cloonagh. Hearing the bad news, Conall immediately set about organising and arming his men. When they caught up to the enemy, they were to infiltrate them; each man was to select an opponent. At a given signal, each man was to draw his blade and stab his opposite number.

Costello and his raiders had reached the townland of Ballinfull when Conall's men caught up with them. They moved in according to plan. Jimmy recalled that when the signal was given, a fierce battle took place. This battle lasted 'until the sun went down in the Western sea'. Conall and his men won the day. The cattle were recovered and driven back to Ballyconnell.'

Ballyconnell, Conall's townland, still bears his name. Ballinfull, or *Baile na Fola*, literally 'the town of the blood', retains its title to this day as a reminder of that gory encounter of long ago.

Talk of Ballinfull brought to mind the neighbouring townland of Lissadell, birthplace of Constance Markievicz. An accomplished horsewoman, locals admired her when she galloped across Moffit's Burra from Lissadell to visit the Ashleys at Classiebawn Castle. Lord Shaftesbury and the Leslies of Glaslough, guests of the Mullaghmore landlords, were her friends too. They wondered how she, a lady of the landlord classes born to privilege and power, had turned her back on the aristocratic lifestyle to champion Ireland's poor.

As a child, when she walked outside the demesne walls she found it strange that she had so much while the children of her father's tenants had nothing. In later years, when a workers' strike was in progress on the estate, she wrote to her brother, Josslyn, urging him to be generous and reminding him that they came from a family of 'tyrants and usurpers'. The family disapproved of Constance and, except for her sister Eva, her mother and her daughter Maeve, they ostracised her. Meetings with her mother were held in secret at Mespil House, the home of Sarah Purser, and at her mother's home in Ardeevin, County Sligo.

A year before she died, among Dublin's poor, she wrote that her daughter Maeve and Eva were the 'only relations' she had left; she understood how 'embarrassing' it was for Sir Josslyn and the others to have a member of the family fight in a revolution to which they were opposed. She recalled that it was 'the heroic spirits, in her own desolate county, that generation after generation fought and died with arms in their hands' who inspired her. It was they, she said, who took her heart and imagination.

The Maugherow people often spoke of her rebellious nature: overcome by the impoverished condition of her father's tenants and unhappy with the way they were treated and the high rents they paid, she asked her father, Sir Henry, for an explanation. Dissatisfied with his answer, she ran off into the woods around Lissadell House. Two days later, when she was found, she was unrepentant. Insisting on better treatment for her friends, she promised that one day she would wipe out the shame of her family's deeds.

She rode with her father, Sir Henry Gore-Booth, through Cliffoney village during a Land League meeting. Stopping the carriage to see what the excitement was about, she heard Parnell's secretary, a man named Sexton, addressing the crowd in front of Cummin's Hotel. Reputed to be one of the most eloquent speakers who ever came to Sligo, he spoke of how her grandfather, Sir Robert Gore-Booth, 'banished the people of the Seven Cartrons and sent them to sea on a rotten boat.'[71] His speech was said to 'entirely transform her', making her from that moment a committed supporter of tenants' rights. The journey that started in Sligo on that day eventually led her to march into Dublin, with Pearse and Connolly, on a fateful Easter Monday morning in 1916.

Tommy Devins had pulled a chair up to join the ramblers. He was down from Raughley with a load of kelp to ship out of the harbour and had been listening intently to the conversation. 'We don't have to be afraid of anyone now. We're living!' he said. 'Miss Penelope from the big house was coming down the road by my place one day. "Oh, Toamy, you used to work in our gawden, didn't you," says she with that fancy accent.

'"I did," says I.

'She started to blame McCaffrey and Father Ward and Alfie Lang for the ruination of the estates. "How could it ever be" she says, "that I'd turn a Catholic and that to happen?"

'Says I in me own mind, "What's this one getting up to?"

'"Well now," says I, "Miss Penelope, you know what you'll do. On your life," says I, "don't turn a Catholic! I'm a Catholic, but don't you! And ye know why? Because around here, as far as I can see, the Catholics got nothing but hard times."

'She blazed up in the face and looked down at the ground. "You worked in the big house," she said.

'"I did," says I. "I was fifteen years in it. Ye had three thousand acres over there and I always considered ye had too much. The simple reason is, there's people around here – an' I'm sure you know them as well as I do – and they haven't the place of a hundred of cabbage on top of the bare rocks, an' ye havin' three thousand acres of the best of land." They lived on our bones in them times. I was nearly quoting a verse of the song about the *Pomano* but I said to meself: to hell with it, I won't bother. I thank God I seen the day I could stand on my own two feet on my own land and I'm afraid of no one.

'When she settled down, anyway, I says to her, "I'll put one question to you, and I hope," says I, "ye'll answer it. Who did that place belong to before the Gores took it over? Who did it belong to?"

'She wasn't fit to answer me. She turned on her foot an' away with her as quick as she could down the road!'

Funny stories brought gusts of laughter from the gathering, as one or another told of amusing incidents or encounters with locals. Dan was 'a great one' for the yarns but everyone knew you couldn't believe half of what he said. With neither radio nor television to amuse, storytelling – lies or truth – was a favourite way of passing the time. Accounts of the doings of neighbours with unconventional ways always made good telling. Having an intimate knowledge of the individuals and their eccentricities added to the enjoyment of the story.

'Did ye hear about the trick Paddy Newman played on Jimmy with the sandwiches?' Dan enquired.

'What was that about?' Jimmy McGowan said. 'I might have heard something about it, I'm not sure.'

Of course they had heard it before. But it was a good story and worth telling again. Everyone knew Jimmy was a good neighbour, a hard worker and a great man to enjoy a practical joke or to 'take a hand' at someone. He could sing 'The Auction of Parkes' Meadow' when called on or he could write a song if he took the notion. He could pick up the 'melojin' and enchant the listener with the haunting strains of 'The Hills of Glenswilly' or he could make your feet dance with lively reels, 'The Longford Collector' or 'The Swallow's Tail'.

Stories of his exploits and sense of humour abounded. He had a great grasp of the ridiculous; like the time he was at a football match in Sligo. As the match progressed, his annoyance with the referee increased. Jimmy was convinced he was making a lot of bad decisions – and most of these against Grange, the home team. He showered insults on him. Hopping mad when he felt there was yet another bad call, Jimmy, who was as bald as an egg himself, roared at the top of his voice at the referee, who was even balder, 'God blast ye t' hell, will ye get the hair out of yer eyes!'

A joke at Jimmy's expense was rare, and all the more appreciated for that. 'Well,' said Dan, 'ye know yerself, Jimmy couldn't go into a house where there was a cake on the table or a plate of buns but he'd eat as much as he could and put the rest in his pocket. It was as much for the devilment of it as anything else!'

This brought a smile. That was Jimmy all right! 'One day last summer, Paddy Newman had a few fellas helping him with the hay,' Dan continued. 'Around the middle of the day, he went down to the shop, bought a lok of cheese and ham, came up to the house and made a plate of sandwiches for the fellas was helping him. He went back out to the field and after a while everyone went in for a bite to eat.

'It was one of the best days came that summer and Newman had the front and back doors open. When he went into the house, who was sittin' in the corner but Jimmy. Paddy looked over at the table. The plate was there but no sandwiches.

'"What happened to the sandwiches?" he says, looking at Jimmy, knowing full well what happened.

'"Oh, what happened the sandwiches," says Jimmy. "When I was coming into the house here, there was this big brute of a dog up on the table. He nearly knocked me down making out the door when he saw me and away with him down the lane. That must be what happened to your sandwiches. They're gone."

'"The bastard," says Paddy. "Well it's good enough for him, he'll not go far. I'm plagued with rats about the house. That was bread I made up with rat poison to try and kill them. I suppose I'll have to make another batch now. Did ye see whose dog it was?"

'"Naw," says Jimmy, an' th' eyes as big as saucers.

'He said nothing but cut out of the house as quick as he could. Down with him to Miss Clancy at the post office. "Quick," says he, "call Chrissie Coyne, I have to get into Sligo in a hurry." He went into the hospital in Sligo and got his stomach pumped out. That put manners on Jimmy: he didn't have so much oul' chat out of him for a long time after that!'

Shouts of laughter rang around the gathering at the way the tables had been turned on Jimmy. Bent over from laughing, my mother rested her hands on the table and laughed till the tears came into her eyes.

'Well, Jasus, that's the best I ever heard,' said Johnny Cummins, when the laughter subsided. 'He was in England for a while too, ye know.'

'That's right, my father said, 'but I don't think he stuck it long. The Land Commission was going to take the land off him an' he had to come back or lose it. It was a bad law too!'

'I worked at the buildings with him there for a while,' Johnny went on. 'This day he was down in a trench laying pipes. He didn't like the job and there was bad hair on him. There was a fella going around the building site organising for the unions and it was pouring rain and blowing a gale. He shouted down to Jimmy in the trench, "Say there, Paddy, do you belong to the union?"

'Over there, you know the Englishman called everyone from Ireland "Paddy", no matter what his name was. Anyway, Jimmy was a bit deaf and he mustn't have heard him. He shouted louder this time and tried a different name. "Hey there, Jack," he said, "are you in the union?"

'Jimmy heard him this time and he looked up. "What's that yer saying?" Jimmy shouted. "I can't hear ye."

'The union man was getting exasperated, an' he shouted louder this time. "Are ye in the union, Jack?"

'"Arrah, who d'ye think ye're talking to," says Jimmy. "Fuck the Union Jack, an' fuck you," says he, jumping up out of the trench. "Up th' IRA an' to hell with you and the Union Jack, I'm going home."

When Dan was going to tell a story, he'd spit a stream of glistening yellow tobacco juice into the hot *gríosach* heaped at the side of the fire.

Spitting is now a lost art. Years ago, men took pride in their skill at aiming a spit with deadly accuracy from a distance of ten feet into a cat's eye, or in the eye of some cheeky young fellow. There is nothing so harmful to the pride or demoralising to the spirit as wiping someone else's spit out of your eye, especially if it has the burning sting of tobacco. This time I watched it erupt harmlessly in a little Vesuvius of powdery ash, hissing and spluttering indignantly.

Wedging the cud of tobacco well back into his cheek and pushing the cap to the back of his head, a slow grin spreading across his face, Dan teetered back on the hind legs of the chair and began. 'Did ye hear about Pat Healy when he got the parcel from America last Christmas?'

'No,' they affirmed, looking at each other. No, they hadn't heard a thing about it, but Pat was well known to be 'fit for anything' and there was sure to be a good story in it.

'Well,' Johnny began, 'he got a parcel from one of his cousins in America a few days before Christmas. It was too heavy for John Higgins to deliver on the bike, so he left a note with Pat a couple of times to collect it at Doyle's. Pat was an aisygoing kind of a buck and he let it go, hoping that John'd deliver it – but he didn't! Eventually, anyway, he had to walk over to the post office himself to collect it. The next thing was Mylie the postmaster an' himself had an argument about why the parcel wasn't delivered – an' if that wasn't bad enough, he was dancin' altogether when Mylie wouldn't let him open it.

'"What's wrong now?" says Pat.

'"There's one pound ten shillings revenue tax to be paid on it, otherwise ye can't open it," says Mylie.

'Well, ye know yerself, thirty bob was a lot of money to pay for something ye hadn't even seen, but anyway curiosity got the better of him an' Pat paid up. When he opened the package, what was in it but a big crucifix! Well, ye should have seen the gob on him, after paying his money. He didn't know whether to laugh or cry!

'Feeling the loss of his thirty bob, his face was a picture as he took the crucifix out of the paper. Sayin' how grand it was and takin' the cap off, he knelt down and blessed himself. Looking at Mylie first, with a lonesome air about him, an' then the cross, he says, "God knows, little Jesus, you went through a lot – the Agony in the Garden, falling three times, the Jews crucifying you on Calvary, an' after all that . . . after all that, ye had to come to Mullaghmore to be taxed!"'

Johnny could hardly get the last words out of him with the dint of laughing as he let the chair forward with a bang onto its four legs and slapped his thigh while everyone went into gusts of laughter. Every time they repeated the last bit – 'Ye had to come to Mullaghmore to be taxed' – they looked at each other and burst into fits of laughter again and again at the idea of our little village inflicting this final indignity on poor Jesus.

'C'mon, give us a song. What about that one "I'll Forgive and I'll Try to Forget",' Jimmy said to Mary Dowdican when things had gone quiet again.

'Ahh, I only know bits of it,' Mary replied. 'I don't have it all.'

'Go on, go on, what's the difference,' everyone said. 'Sure it might come back to you while you're singing it.'

Mary lived next door and had a beautiful voice. It was she that took me by the hand and brought me to school on my first day. It was then I fell in love with her. She was very pretty and I have an old photograph to prove it. I was over this, my first infatuation by the time I was ten. By that time, I sensed she was too old for me – and I knew she went out with other men because my mother often covered for her when she stole out of her own house at night. Next day they laughed as they chatted about some liaison of the night before.

I can still hear her sweet voice singing an old sad ballad of unrequited passion around our fireside, all about a boy and girl who fell in love but eventually drifted apart. I was only nine but some instinct told me that men didn't cry. Blinking back the tears that welled in my eyes, I looked fiercely into the fire as Mary sang:

> Oh, don't you remember the evening,
> When the moon through the trees it did shine;
> With a smile and a kiss as a token,
> You promised to me you'd be mine.

> I'll give back every fond little token,
> First the ring and the lock of your hair;
> And the card with your picture upon it,
> Of a face that's as false as it's fair.

Everyone knew my father as a man who had his feet on the ground, a man who would listen to the ghost and fairy stories good-humouredly but didn't believe them. Now and again he would reluctantly admit that there were things out there that didn't make sense, that defied explanation. Because of his scepticism, people listened when, very rarely, he told about an encounter he had had with the fairies many years before. His cynicism regarding the supernatural gave him a credibility not afforded those thought to be more credulous – individuals who were too ready to swallow and pass on any tall story told to them.

'It was when me father was cartin' for the lodges years ago,' he began. 'He came home late one evening after delivering a load of groceries to Classiebawn that he brought from Sligo. He was taking the horse out of the cart, round the back of the house there, when he realised that he left the cart-cover after him. "Away up with you," he says to me, "an' get it, will ye. It'll not take ye a minute." It was gettin' dusk in the evening but I was quick on me feet that time, an' away with me anyway. When I was goin' across the Burra and getting close to Classiebawn, I heard this music and clatter of talk and dancin' and I thought to meself there must be a party on at the castle.

'When I got as far as the place, anyway, Kate Murtagh, the housekeeper, opened the door, and when I says to her, "There must be a party going on there with the Ashleys this evening", she looked at me kinda strange. "Ah, there's no party here," she says, "but pay no attention to that, I hear that often." She says to me then that she often heard noises like that comin' from the fairy rock just down under Classiebawn. Well I'll tell ye, it put me thinkin'. I couldn't believe it, I was full sure I heard the music and still I couldn't believe her.

'I went round the back anyway, got the cart-cover and started to head home again across the Burra. I was halfway across when I heard this loud whistle, ye know, rale loud like ye had yer two fingers in yer mouth – a piercing whistle. I looked back an' damme t' Jasus if I didn't see these two wee small fellas down under the fairy rock and them comin' towards me. I often heard people talkin' about the hair standing on your head with fright and I didn't believe there was such a thing. I haven't much hair on me now,' says he, 'but I had that time, and I'm tellin' ye every hair that I had stood straight up on me head. I turned round and cut for home and I don't think me feet touched the ground until I burst in the back door there.'

When he was finished, there was an appreciative silence as the listeners savoured the story, turning it over in their minds.

They had heard of such things before; this was nothing new, but further proof that, indeed, the fairy rock, or *Doras na Bríonna* ('the Portal of Dreams'), as it was called by some, was aptly named. Was there such a thing as fairies? Was the fairy rock one of the refuges of the enchanted race of Tuatha dé Danann defeated by the Milesians and driven underground long ago?

As the talk flowed, the house was battered by one of the fierce gales that swept in off the Atlantic with great regularity. In its exposed position, on a hill overlooking the ocean, it was the first obstacle the raging wind met on leaving the vast expanse of ocean. Venting all its fury, it seemed hell-bent on levelling the walls and scattering the fragile straw roof. The rumbling chimney was a sound to which the ramblers were well accustomed. Like some huge wind instrument conversing with the elements, the noise rose and fell according to the intensity of the gusts. Its reverberating crescendos filled the occasional silences in the conversation. It seemed all the louder now for the ruminative stillness that had fallen on the little group.

A sudden loud banging on the front door and a shout shocked the gathering back from stories of fairies, unwelcome crucifixes and lost love. They turned, startled, to the sudden noise. Shock showing on her face, my mother turned to the door too, her mouth open.

'Any room for mummers?' a rough, loud voice outside the door demanded.

My mother dropped her floured hands when she heard this, relief showing on her face. 'Aah, it's only the mummers,' she said. 'Come in,' she smiled, facing to the door, *'Tá fáilte romhaimh!'* ('You're welcome!')

The visitors accepted the invitation, the door burst open and a strange-looking masked figure dressed in rags decorated with

ribbons and papers and wearing a tall, conical straw hat leaped
with a few mad bounds into the kitchen. A draught of air
whirling through the open door sent the flame of the oil lamp
dancing wildly. The disturbed light sent grotesque shadows
pirouetting along the whitewashed wall from the prancing figure
in the middle of the floor. I ran terrified from the table to hide
behind my father in the corner and watched as the menacing
figure, like some mad hobgoblin of the dark, paced across the
flagstones. Following him was a motley array of creatures with
strange names: Captain, Green Knight, Oliver Cromwell,
Beelzebub and Devil Doubt paraded in quick succession, each
one reciting a weird gibberish of words. Turning in sharp and
crazy circles, the first caller gestured and shouted:

> *Room, room, gallant room, give us room to rhyme,*
> *Until we show our actitude upon this Christmas time.*
> *Christmas comes but once a year*
> *And when it comes it brings good cheer.*
> *And if you don't believe these words I say,*
> *Enter Captain. Clear the way.*

A tall masked figure, his coat turned inside out, straw bandoliers
across his shoulders and a peaked cap jammed on his head,
strode arrogantly into the kitchen in response to this, paced up
and down the floor and rhymed:

> *Here comes I, the Captain,*
> *The captain of this noble crew,*
> *The same I will relate to you.*
> *Active young and active age,*
> *The like of this was never acted on a stage.*
> *If you have patience to abide,*

None of our activities we will hide.
If you don't believe these words I say,
Enter Oliver Cromwell. Clear the way.

Oliver Cromwell jumped in the door carrying a sword. Sporting an imitation metal nose attached to a cloth mask, he shouted and threatened:

Here comes I, Oliver Cromwell as you may suppose,
I've conquered many nations with my long copper nose.
I've made my foes to tremble and my enemies to quake
And I massacred a gander coming home from
　　Paddy's wake.
And if you don't believe these words I say,
Enter in Beelzebub and clear the way.

Enter an evil-looking hunchback wearing a torn cloak and carrying a club on his shoulder:

Here comes I, Beelzebub,
Over my shoulder I carry my club,
In my hand a frying pan,
And I think myself a jolly wee man.
And if you don't believe these words I say,
Enter in the Wren, clear the way.

The Wren, dressed in feathers and cap and with an imitation beak over his mouth, gestured and postured and claimed:

I am the Wren, the Wren, the king of all birds,
On St Stephen's Night I was caught in the flood.
Although I am small, my family is great,

So rise up landlady and give us a thrate.
If your thrate be of the best
I hope in heaven your soul will rest,
But if your thrate be of the small
It won't agree with the boys at all.
And if you don't believe these words I say,
Enter in Wee Devil Doubt, clear the way.

Wee Devil Doubt barged in the door dressed in old clothes, horns and long red streamers:

Here comes I, Wee Devil Doubt,
If ye don't give me money I'll sweep ye all out.
Money I want and money I crave,
And if ye don't give me money, I'll sweep ye all to
    the grave.
Up with the kettle and down with the pan,
Give us the money and let us be gone.
Five shillings, no less, bad money won't pass,
All silver and no brass.
And if you don't believe these words I say,
Enter in Jack Straw, clear the way.

Jack Straw rustled in, dressed in straw hat, coat and leggings:

Here comes I, Jack Straw,
Such a man you never saw.
My father was straw, my mother was straw,
We live in straw and we'll die in straw.
And if you don't believe these words I say,
Enter in Prince George, and clear the way.

A foppish-looking dandy dressed in a tall hat minced in the door and said:

> Here comes I, Prince George,
> From England I have sprung.
> Noble deeds I've done
> And valour I have won.
> If you don't believe these words I say,
> Enter in Green Knight, clear the way.

Dressed in green with a leather hat and carrying a wooden sword, a figure marched through the door, military style:

> Here comes I, Green Knight,
> With my bayonet for to fight.
> With sword and buckle by my side
> I hope to gain the day.
> Ireland's right and England's treason
> For which I draw my bloody weapon.
> If you don't believe these words I say,
> Enter in St Patrick, clear the way.

St Patrick entered, dressed in a long green robe and white beard, carrying a *camán* instead of a crozier. He strode to the middle of the floor and said:

> Here comes I, St Patrick,
> In shining armour bright.
> I am a worthy champion,
> I am a famous knight.

Prince George then rushed to the middle of the floor, confronted St Patrick and said:

> *What are you but Prince George's stable boy?*
> *For seven years you fed my horse on oats and hay, sir!*

St Patrick: *You lie, sir.*
Prince George (drawing his sword): *Take out your sword and try, sir.*
St Patrick: *Take out your purse and pay, sir.*

Prince George attacked St Patrick with his sword, saying:

> *I'll run my rapier through your heart*
> *And make you die away, sir.*

I watched wide-eyed as over in the corner a fight broke out between Prince George and St Patrick. After a fierce struggle, St Patrick dropped to the floor, mortally wounded. The Captain strode to the middle of the floor, stood over St Patrick and shouted:

> *Oh, horrible, terrible, was the sight ever seen?*
> *A man with seven senses knocked into seventeen.*
> *By a buck, by a bear, by the devil's own aunt*
> *That cures all diseases by pistroges and cant.*
> *A doctor, a doctor! Is there any doctor to be found*
> *To cure this man of his deep and mortal wound?'*

In response to the Captain's call, a crazy doctor in outlandish dress carrying a bag and cane rushed in, shouting:

> *Here comes I, the Doctor, most pure and good.*
> *With my broad sword I'll staunch his blood*

>   And take the poison all away,
>   But forty gold guineas you'll have to pay.

Captain: *What can you cure, Doctor?*
Doctor: *I can kill or cure!*
Captain: *But what can you cure?*
Doctor: *I can cure the plague within, the plague without,*
>   *The palsy, ague and the gout.*
>   *If there was nine devils within,*
>   *I could drive eleven out.*
>   *If there was an old woman on critches,*
>   *I could have her jumping stone ditches.*

Feigning uncertainty, the Captain asked: *What medicine do you use, Doctor?* Like an African witch doctor, the strange medicine man pranced and gyrated and claimed that he cured with:

>   *The foo of the fee and the hillis the bee,*
>   *Nine pills, nine drills, nine fortnights before day,*
>   *And if that doesn't cure, I'll ask no pay.*
>   *Moreover, I've a little bottle here on top of my cane*
>   *Called hocus-pocus ellecampane.*
>   *Rise up dead man and fight again.*

As the dead man rose up from the floor, Tom Fool dashed in dressed like a circus clown, prancing and shouting:

>   *Here comes I that didn't come yet,*
>   *Big head and little wit.*
>   *Though my head is big and my wit is small*
>   *I'll do my best to please ye all.*

And if you don't believe these words I say,
Enter the Lady, clear the way.

A man dressed as a woman came in silently. Without saying a word, she took hold of Tom Fool and danced a lively reel with him. The Captain then called on different members of the party to dance, sing or play an instrument according to their abilities. The strange company played and danced around the floor, taking the fireside ramblers with them. While this was going on, Devil Doubt went around with an old tin box, collecting a few coins from everyone. Shillings and two-shilling pieces jangled into the box. The performance over, the mummers skipped out into the darkness, thanking the household for their contribution and singing together:

We are the neighbours' childer
Who have come from far and near.
We thank you all and wish you well
And hope to meet next year.

The ramblers settled back around the fire. My mother continued with the cake and everyone chatted and laughed about the strange interruption. 'It wouldn't be Christmas without a visit from the mummers,' everyone agreed. That first visit of the mummers has etched itself on my memory as in a photograph; I can see it as clearly today as I did then through a child's eyes. The rhymes have been remembered in part from that first visit and learned from repeated Christmas visits of the mummers each year in the days before the holiday.

Some years later, we formed our own group. Faces covered and dressed in rags and costumes, we learned the rhymes and went from house to house in the towns and villages of north

Sligo and north Leitrim. It was a great pastime for us and most houses gave us a warm welcome. Through the slits in our masks, we could see the delight in the faces of the household. Many of the houses had members of the family home for Christmas who seemed to enjoy the interruption more than anyone.

A young band of mummers went out from house to house in the 1980s in the traditional way – but Mullaghmore had changed over the years. Now there was an influx of strangers who, knowing nothing of the tradition, mocked it. The young mummers came home from their last outing convinced their play was nonsense: they had been told they should be singing Christmas carols instead of saying silly rhymes. Peer pressure is everything at that age, so that finished the new mummers.

Despite such criticism and competition from television, video and the Internet, at least three groups of mummers can still be seen on the roads of Leitrim and Sligo during the dark days of the Christmas season. One of these is the *Sidhe Gaoithe*, a group of dancers, musicians and singers comprised of individuals from towns all over Sligo. A 'fairy wind' that obeys no mortal law, we gather in 'gentle' places. From there we travel out to storm gatherings and bring high spirits and revelry to people all over the north-west, as mummers have always done.

Rhymes quoted on previous pages, used in north Leitrim and north Sligo, have much in common with, and may even have been influenced by, those popular in Derry, Antrim and Fermanagh. Alan Gailey records a comprehensive list of these in his book *Irish Folk Drama*. The versions we used in north Sligo were much briefer. There is a tendency now to cut these rhymes even shorter or, during certain appearances, to eliminate them altogether. Wandering groups of mummers, when they go from pub to pub, often entertain now with music, song and dance only. The words of the ancient characters were composed for quieter places!

Mummer rhymes have changed over the centuries; characters have been added, and others have been dropped. The verses vary in content between, say, Antrim and Wexford, yet the basic tradition is the same. In the context of Irish history, the addition of Oliver Cromwell, probably in the seventeenth century, is something of a surprise.

An example of the diversity of the play and the dramatic changes that have taken place is nowhere more evident than in Wexford. Here you will find characters, such as Daniel O'Connell and Napoleon Bonaparte, who do not exist in the northern tradition:

Here I am Napoleon Bonaparte, a conqueror of renown.
It's with my skill and mighty deeds great nations I
    cut down.
France and Spain I did obtain, Russia and Prussia too,
I crossed the Alps and Pyrenees great nations to subdue.

The Sligo mummers too have evolved over the years. New rhymes and characters have been introduced while others, such as Dr Brown, remain. The essential mummer ritual of death and revival has been retained, integrating the basic elements of an ancient tradition with innovation. A pantheon of historical and mythological figures spring to life as they prance across the floor, rhyming, playing or dancing. At one point St Patrick enters with a long green cassock, bishop's hat and crosier:

A Bishop called Patrick am I
For whose help all the Irish did cry.
A flame I did light
That is still burning bright
On lowlands and grand mountains high.

Theology, 'twas my strong suit
Although I've been known to boot
Shrivelled serpents and snakes
Into rivers and lakes
As I played the Dead March on my flute.
If you don't believe these words I say
Enter Queen Maeve, clear the way!

Enter Queen Maeve with crown, cape and long gown:

I'm Maeve, famed warrior Queen.
To the Red Hand of Ulster I've been,
Where I stole the Brown Bull
And cracked every skull
Of Ulstermen – Orange and Green.
But I never enjoyed the great spoil,
In spite of my labour and toil,
For Cuchulain bold
Stretched Ferdia out cold
And caused the rest of my men to recoil.
If you don't believe these words I say
Enter Willie Yeats, clear the way!

Enter William Butler Yeats wearing a rough imitation of the dress of that time:

Now Eliot, Auden and Pound
In my time they all were around.
All three were acclaimed
And their verses were famed
In literary circles renowned.
But despite all their wonderful feats

In scholarly and poetic conceits,
There was none could compare
To the talent so rare
Of myself – Sligo's own Willie Yeats.
If you don't believe these words I say,
Enter Granuaile, clear the way!'

And so the entertainment continued through the night.

What's the difference between mummers and wrenboys? Where does the custom come from? Do they have their origins in Ireland or elsewhere? How did they originate?

Christmas plays or folk dramas marked a very early part of folk culture in Ireland. As well as that, they are well known in many countries throughout Europe and further afield too. Here, although influenced by colonisations such as those of the seventeenth century, they retain many elements that are uniquely Irish.

Some regard the mummers' play as a surviving remnant in Ireland of medieval miracle plays. Once popular in England, the miracle plays are thought to have been introduced to Ireland during the British plantations. There is no doubt that many of the mummers' rhymes were influenced by the arrival of the colonists, but it is also clear that, as Alan Gailey points out, 'When these earlier plays were introduced into Ireland, they did not come into a folk culture without comparable customs. They had to compete with ceremonies already well known to Irish people in the areas where the British planters settled.'[72]

Further evidence for indigenous foundations is found in the symbolism inherent in the resurrection of the dead hero and the mimed human life cycle in other Irish folk ceremonies. This is not found in British counterparts. In his book *Irish Folk Drama*,

Alan Gailey observes that the use of straw in many Irish folk plays marks these plays out as separate, stating that, 'In preserving this lively tradition of the use of straw disguise, Ireland clearly evokes an original feature of the folk drama, one deeply rooted in rural, agricultural society.' The wearing of straw is seen as a way of stimulating regrowth in nature. The uniformity of this idea of encouraging nature is almost without parallel in British folk drama.[73] Conversely, Gailey tells us that, while the use of greenery in similar folk drama has been recorded in England, it is hardly known at all in Ireland.

Some scholars believe mumming represents a survival of an agricultural fertility ceremony of pagan times which has been displaced from its proper season of spring to the more powerful and popular Christmas period. Perhaps the origin of the tradition is rooted in all of these factors. Whichever is the case, we are lucky that from the remote antiquity of these origins, time has woven the various strands of the play into an intricate and wonderful pattern that is sure to survive and give pleasure to countless future generations.

Any quest for origins must bring us to the importance to our ancestors of Newgrange in the Boyne Valley over five thousand years ago. Every year at the winter solstice, it seemed to them the waning sun was in imminent danger of disappearing. Something must be done that would please the gods and encourage the light and longer days to return. The result, as we have already seen, was the life-giving symbolism represented by the sun as a male agent entering and impregnating the womblike structure of the passage grave. The light releases the spirits of the dead into a new existence. From that moment, the light revives and the days grow longer.

Did the death and revival aspects of the mummers' play have its earliest manifestation in a kind of sympathetic magic designed to encourage the rebirth of the dying sun? Was the play an ancient ritual which may have had its origins in old pagan religious ceremonies? The annual rebirth of sun and life in midwinter is symbolised in the mummers' play by the resurrection of the dead hero by Doctor Brown. It is a comical transaction but it has a serious intent and a much deeper significance than is readily apparent.

Its roots embedded in pagan rituals, when sacrifice was deemed necessary to appease the gods, the tradition is ancient and timeless. There is evidence of such human sacrifice even in the Christian period: in the early years of the first millennium, Timothy, the first Bishop of Ephesus, was sacrificed at a ceremony in a survival of the ritual human sacrifices of the old religions.

Denouncing these religions over the centuries, the Church did everything it could to discourage such practices. It reserved special condemnation for the custom of wearing masks, which it felt represented the releasing of demons from the spirit underworld. Despite such condemnation, mummers and wrenboys have evolved, survived and prospered.

Folk drama using vegetation and other readily available materials as disguise is not confined to these islands but is also well known throughout Europe. An Irish viewer would feel at home watching similar presentations in the Balkans. Here the theme, pageant and disguises used are very like our own. They too have a sword dance and mock revival performed by a doctor following a combat in which one of the participants is killed.

Early in the twentieth century, a traveller described a group, similar to our mummers, travelling from house to house in Greece at Epiphany. Again, the similarity to the Irish play is striking. A scene is acted out where a character called the 'Groom' is killed by the 'Arab' defending the 'Bride's' honour; at the end, the Groom is revived by a doctor.

Traditionally, women did not go out with mummers or wrenboys. Only men or boys participated. In past times, it would not have been seemly for young women to travel out at night in mixed company. In addition, women may not have wanted to take part in the horseplay which was sometimes part of the high spirits of the evening. Also, the company of women would have inhibited the freedom and antics of the boys.

In the 1950s, the 'new woman' arrived and began to join mummer groups. Some of the men who went out then say that, prior to that time, no woman had expressed a desire to join. When they first joined the troupe, there would be 'a fellow giving out about it here and there', but it was generally accepted.

Although common in most counties of Ulster, notably Antrim, Derry, Fermanagh and Donegal, the mumming tradition is not universal in Ireland. No study of the observance would be complete without a mention of Wexford, where the tradition is strong. It survives, too, in parts of County Dublin.

The wrenboy tradition has been strong in Clare, Cavan, Galway, Tipperary, Leitrim and north Sligo, and in some of the southern counties, notably Kerry. Wrenboys were also prevalent in south Sligo. In parts of Mayo there was great rivalry between groups of mummers and wrenboys where they existed side by side.

The earliest written reference to these practices is found in the chronicles of early Irish historians. They referred to *Na Drútha Ríoga* ('the Royal Jesters') that performed during the great gatherings at Tara at the time of the High Kings. At a later point, there is reference to strolling players at the great gatherings at Tailteann in Meath and Carman in Wexford. These groups may well have been precursors of the early mumming tradition.

Evidence for the mummers' early existence in Ireland is provided also by Hanmer's *Chronicle*, which describes the festivities taking place during King Henry's celebration of Christmas in Dublin in 1172. It tells of 'the pastime, the sport and the mirth, and the continual music, the masking, mumming and strange shows, the gold, the silver and plate, the precious ornaments, the dainty dishes . . . '[74] The fact that this mumming performance took place at Christmas indicates that the description refers to an early mummers' play.

A description of such a play, showing some evidence of modern trappings, comes from Cork city in 1685. A visitor there described the scene:

> Last evening there was presented the drollest piece of mummery I ever saw in or out of Ireland. There was St George and St Denis and St Patrick in their buff coats, and the Turk was there likewise and a doctor and Oliver Cromwell, and an old woman who made rare sport, till Beelzebub came in with a frying pan upon his shoulder and a great flail in his hand thrashing about him on friends and foes, and at last running away with the bold usurper, Cromwell, whom he tweaked by his gilded nose – and there came a little devil with a broom to gather up the money that was thrown to the mummers for their sport. It is an ancient pastime, they tell me, of the citizens.

Mumming fell into disfavour in medieval times. Statutes enacted in 1383, at a provincial synod held at that time by John Colton, Archbishop of Armagh, banned the activity. The archbishop, in agreement with his predecessor, declared that this sort of frivolity was contrary to the common good when he renewed 'the statute or statutes of his predecessors Richard (Fitzralph) and David (Magheraghty) against mimes, jugglers, poets, drummers or harpers, and especially against *kernarii* and importunate and wicked seekers, or rather extorters, of gifts.'

Things had not improved much even by the 1920s. In Bannow, County Wexford, the parish priest denounced the custom in a sermon. 'It has come to my notice,' he declared, 'that a blackguard mummering set has risen in our midst, contrary to the laws of our church, with a variety of foolish tricks and manoeuvrings, in order to obtain food, drink and money by false purposes . . . '

As late as 1947, the local constabulary were vigilant in their prosecution of the provisions of the Dance Hall Act. Sergeant McEvoy prosecuted Patrick Fanning of Raheen, Taghmon, for violating the law. Seventy people were found watching mummers in a loft; of these, fifty-three had paid two shillings to play cards for chickens. Even though Patrick pleaded precedence, in that his grandfather allowed mumming in the loft in days gone by, the justice showed his disregard for tradition by fining him a pound!

No doubt all this banning was a great boost to the early mummers. Nothing will popularise an activity so much as its prohibition. Mimers, musicians and 'seekers or extorters after gifts' are all part and parcel of lively performances that are still a familiar sight at Christmas in many places.

Previously they went out before Christmas Day. Now most go out in the period between Christmas and New Year. In changed times, this provides the best opportunity to play to large gatherings. In the 1950s, after several nights on the road, groups were well pleased to make seventeen shillings and sixpence (eighty-seven pence in today's money) for the season. Now a night out can reap as much as £500, of which most is distributed to charities.

The wrenboys ritual seems to be a remnant of more elaborate performances of exclusively native origin. The inclusion of the wren as a mumming character indicates an overlap of two traditions. Although there may sometimes be an interchange of rhymes, the two groups differ in that mummers have many parts which require rhyming players, whereas wrenboys have just one. Unlike the mummers, the central theme of the wrenboy visit is the wren. Another defining characteristic of wrenboys is that they go out exclusively on St Stephen's Day.

Why, of all birds, is the inoffensive little wren chosen as the martyr for display by groups who take their name from it? Because of its treachery, some claim! When the Irish forces were about to catch Cromwell's troops by surprise, a wren perched on the drum of one of the soldiers, making a noise that woke the sleeping sentries just in time, thereby saving the camp.

Another explanation is that the wren betrayed St Stephen, the first Christian martyr, by flapping its wings to attract his pursuers when he was hiding. More say the hostility towards this most harmless of creatures results from the efforts of clerics in the Middle Ages to undermine vestiges of Druidic reverence and practices regarding the bird. Medieval texts say that the word *'dreolín'*, the Irish for 'wren', is derived from *'dreán'* or *'draoi éan'*, which means 'Druid bird'.

One of the most interesting legends relating to the wren is that Cliona, a woman of the otherworld, seduced young men to follow her to the seashore. Here they drowned in the ocean, into which she had enticed them. Eventually a charm was discovered that not only protected against her wiles but could also bring about her destruction. Her only method of escape was to turn herself into a wren. As a punishment for her crimes, she was forced to take the shape of the little bird on every succeeding Christmas Day and was fated to die by human hand: hence the seemingly barbarous practice of hunting the wren.

Groups who went out in the Sligo–Leitrim area could only

say, by way of explanation, that 'she betrayed Our Lord'. In what way, nobody knew, but because of this 'it was good to hunt and kill her around Christmas.' Long ago, bands of youths knocked ditches and scoured hedges in order to capture and kill the bird to have it for display. 'The Boys of Barr na Sraide' immortalises in ballad form the young men 'who roamed about with cudgels stout, a-searching for the wran.' Pursuit of the bird persisted, with the wrenboys of County Kildare, into the early years of the twentieth century. Accounts relate that, for a day or two before the holiday, it was 'hunted and knocked over with stick or stone. Two or three of them are tied to a branch torn from a holly bush, which is decorated with coloured ribbons. On St Stephen's Day, small parties of young boys carry one of these bushes about the country and visit the houses along the road, soliciting coin or eatables. At each house they come to, they repeat a version of a "song", which varies in different localities. All versions seem disjointed and in no way refer to St Stephen's Day nor to the object of killing the wren.'

Some groups settled for a cork with feathers attached to take the place of the wren, thereby allowing the creature spend the holiday undisturbed. They 'carry around little toy birds on a decorated bier, and they themselves have ribbons and coloured pieces of cloth tied to their clothes. If they receive no welcome at a house and are told to "be off out of that", there is the danger of them burying one of the wrens opposite the hall door, through which no luck would then enter for a twelvemonth. Eventually, at the end of the day, each wren is buried with a penny.'[75]

Wrenboy ceremonies, with forms of verse different from those used in Ireland, were popular in France, England and the Isle of Man. There were cultural differences too, in that the wren was hunted in England but not in Scotland. In France, the first person to kill the bird was king! Except for the ritual killing on St Stephen's Day, it was universally regarded as unlucky to injure the wren at any other time or to rob its nest. Where the tradition survives today, a fake bird is always used.

In Munster, particularly in County Kerry, the wrenboys ritual is almost as elaborate as that relating to the mummers. The associated drama, performed in Dingle, at one time incorporated ceremonial group combat. The play was thought to be very ancient, 'possibly dating back to the second millenium BC,' according to Alan Gailey. Here, a Captain is dressed in a sort of uniform carrying a sword. There is another character called the *amadán* ('fool') and an *óinseach* ('female jester'). A wooden frame resembling a horse, called a *láir bhán* ('white mare'), is carried on the shoulders. In some places, names are given to the characters, as in the mummers, and a mock battle held between one group with wooden swords and another with large bladders tied to sticks.

Accounts survive of two different sets of wrenboys who went out in Ballinamore, County Leitrim, in the early 1900s. One group consisted of five- to fifteen-year-olds. The other was composed of grown-ups. The younger people went out dressed in women's clothes, with false faces made of calico painted with shoe polish or black paint. Holes were cut for the nose and eyes. They went along the road, knocking on doors collecting money. When someone answered their knock, they would say:

> *Up with the kettle and down with the pan,*
> *Give us a penny to bury the wran.*

The grown-ups were more professional. They went out in batches of ten or twelve dressed in old trousers made of calico or curtain cloth. Coats were made of the same material. Hats with feathers or red handkerchiefs were worn on the head.

Masks similar to those worn by the younger wrenboys concealed their identity. Sometimes horsehair was worn on the hat or attached to the false face to look like whiskers. Eyewitnesses wrote that 'there was a great splash of colour about them.' In compliance with laws in force at the time, the man with the money box always went unmasked.

The group pretended to have a wren concealed in a starch box nailed on top of a stick and decorated with ribbons, but in reality there was no bird there. 'Sometimes it might be a mouse and sometimes, sorry to say, a robin. Usually it was only a bunch of hay or moss. The group that could boast a real wren were out on their own because the wren was the most difficult of birds to catch. The lad carrying the standard would stand well back because the young lassies in the house would try to capture it to see if it was a real wren. If you were caught with a substitute for the real thing, you lost face and came in for some banter and humbugging.'

Dancers and musicians, fiddle, flute, melodeon, *bodhrán* and at least one good singer went along. Cycling to neighbouring towns, they sang, danced and played as they travelled from house to house. When lorries came along, they journeyed further, to Longford and Boyle. Collecting money as they went, sixpence to a shilling was the usual contribution in a house; they got more in a pub or place where a few were gathered to play cards or ramble. The wrenboys rhyme, which was recited before the collection, varied from place to place but was generally a variation on the following:

> *The wran, the wran, the king of all birds,*
> *On St Stephen's day was caught in the furze.*
> *His body is little but his family is great,*
> *So rise up landlady and give us a trate.*

And if your trate be of the best,
Your soul in heaven can find its rest.
And if your trate be of the small,
It's on yer children it shall fall.
A glass of whiskey and a bottle of beer,
Merry Christmas and a glad New Year.
So up with the kettle and down with the pan,
And give us a penny to bury the wran.

Sometimes these lines were included:

We chased him from bush to bush and from tree to tree,
And in Donnelly's Hollow we cracked his knee.

The proceeds of the collection was spent on a party called a 'join'. Picking a house for the shindig, a barrel of porter was bought for the men and wine for the ladies. Jam, currant cake, bread, sugar and lemonade was provided for everyone. A 'great night of sport and fun, dancing and music' followed that lasted until morning.

A man from Tullaghan, County Leitrim, who went out with a mummer band in west Fermanagh in 1911, recalled that they were generally made welcome. However, 'in a few places dogs were set on us and in one place we were fired on,' he recalled. They were required to have 'a line' (written permission) from the local Justice of the Peace. RIC patrols often challenged them to produce this as evidence of their 'authority'.

Over three nights, they travelled a distance of thirty miles, during which they accumulated ten pounds. This they spent on stout and minerals for their mummers' dance. They had two pounds left over, which they gave to a poor woman in the locality with no means.

Mummers and wrenboys still collect money at the end of their visit; they still hold a 'join' or 'mummers' ball' after the holidays. Most groups do not go from house to house any more but to pubs and other places where large crowds gather. This transition has been forced by migrations in rural populations almost as great as those during the Great Famine. Lifestyles too have changed dramatically.

For mummers doing the rounds in the 1950s, it was a short walk from house to house, each home filled with young and old. Now, silence pervades the lonely roads; the step of carefree feet, the ring of laughing voices, the joyous faces that filled the welcoming kitchens are gone. Derelict ruins, vacant holiday homes, devoid of life or light, gauntly silhouette the night sky. Briars thrive, rats scurry in the rotten roof sods and fallen thatch that heap the kitchen floor. Street lights, unprofitably bright, illuminate the abandoned roads and sepulchral abodes of summer visitors. No ramblers' footstep wending its way to a neighbour's house breaks the interminable silence of a once-populous countryside.

Yet the mummers survive. Pub or house – wherever people gather, we follow. Nursing and retirement homes are entertained at least once over the holiday season. Especially important is a visit to houses where there are young children, so they can experience the magic of the mummers and, remembering the merriment, carry on this oldest of traditions.

Mummers receive a particularly enthusiastic welcome in rural areas. Perhaps atavistic resonances survive here of ancient death and revival ceremonies – rituals that were as important as life itself to men and women who lived by the soil and the whims of unseen gods. Do country dwellers harbour ancestral memories of deities that in a dark past required not just ceremony but human sacrifice as well?

Now the mummer tale is nothing more than a diversion, an exhibition of outrageous fantasy, common sense turned on its head to relieve the gloom of short, dark days. Who can resist a festive invitation to dress in absurd costumes, don ridiculous masks and headdress, and go about from place to place unrecognised; free spirits of the otherworld, or any world, bursting upon an unsuspecting audience with song, music and dance.

This lively custom is sprung from the hearts and hearths of country people. Remarkably, it has withstood the challenge of packaged entertainment. The mummers are reborn each year. Like the mythical phoenix, they burst forth from the fireplaces and spark the ancient revels. Dressed in bizarre and colourful garb, they storm houses and meeting places, bringing a whirlwind of high spirits for a short while to the lucky occupants. Don't miss the mummers or wrenboys next year when they call forth the shades of Christmas past!

11

A Winter's Tale

Great age held something for me that was awesome.
I was much fonder of the old people in the
darkness than I was of the young people in the
daytime. It's at night that you're able to get the
value of old people. And it was listening to the old
people that I got my idea of Irish nationality.

Michael Collins

'Video Killed the Radio Star' go the words of a pop song of the
eighties. It pronounced the wrong victim! Radio stars have
survived and are doing well. It is to the storyteller or *seanchaí*
of the Irish countryside that television and video have brought
an end.

As wraiths of mist vanish before the morning sun, so the old
ways evaporated before the onslaught of new technology. In
rural areas the storyteller's art was secure until black poles with
their miles of invading wire stretched across the hills, valleys
and open plains in the electrification schemes of the 1950s.
Before this there was radio – for the few who could afford it –
but the complicated and expensive system of 'wet' and 'dry'
batteries that powered the early 'wireless' ensured it was played
sparingly.

Much has been said and much has been written about television's negative cultural impact. Another influence, equally disruptive but little noticed, that has changed entirely the community's mobility patterns is the family car. Wider roads and faster transportation now bring people far beyond the boundaries of their own townlands for diversion and entertainment. Sophistication demands greater thrills.

'Rambling', or '*ceilidh*-ing' to a neighbour's house throughout the winter months was the custom until the middle of the twentieth century. In every town and village there were storytellers born with the gift to enthral. Clay-pipe smoking was a fashionable virtue then and an integral part of storytelling. It was a social ritual that bonded friendships, relaxed the audience and mellowed the atmosphere. The Native American may have had his peace pipe, but the Irish had their friendship pipe. Memories sharpened and visions danced in the blue haze and spiralling smoke rings. The world outside ceased to exist; fact and fantasy merged and followed the pungent fumes in ethereal flight. Mickey McGroarty captured for me the ambience of a night-time fireside in the heartland of County Donegal, beloved of the great storyteller Seamus MacManus.

'There might be seven or eight people in a rambling house,' Mickey recalled. ''Twas all clay pipes was goin' that time. They'd fill the pipe and when one man had a good smoke on it, he'd pull his fingers on the shank and pass it on to the man beside him. When he'd have a smoke, he'd pull his fingers on it an' pass it on to the next man, an' so on till every man had a good smoke. All ye had to do was fill one pipe in the night because every man took a turn filling his pipe an' passing it on. When the seven or eight pipes was filled, ye had a big night's smoking done – the one pipe gave every man a smoke. The 'baccy that's goin' today, it's not 'baccy at all. Ye haven't it lit till it's gone!

'The night was no time in passin' with all the different stories ye'd hear. I learned them all from the oul' people. I learnt it an' I drunk it by heart. When I was goin' home on a dark winter's night, I was going over the story in me mind the same way the oul' people told it. Even when I went to bed, before the sleep took me, I'd be trying to remember what I heard from the oul' men. The next day I had it off be heart!'

Storytelling may be universally applauded but not everyone shared Mickey's approval of smoking. One far-sighted nineteenth-century observer was confounded by the phenomenon. 'It is difficult to account for even ordinary human taste or acquirement of habit,' he wrote. 'Tobacco in itself is a somewhat disgusting weed and no doubt its narcotic properties have more or less evil influence on the human system unless smoking is moderately indulged in.

'As for chewing, that vile habit should be considered outside the pale of civilisation. No human being with any pretensions to decency would think of revealing the coarseness of his appetites – in public, at least. But if people will smoke, it is only proper that smoking tools should be provided for them.

'The cigar is not popular in Ireland and neither, except among the city dudes, is the cigarette. The meerschaum is too costly for the ordinary smoker and therefore there has to be on sale something that the poorest can purchase.

'The clay pipe meets this requirement. In general the shank is curtailed by the rural purchaser until the bowl almost touches the lips and then it is called in the Irish vernacular the "dudeen". Nothing so consoles the labouring Irishman as "a blast of the pipe" before and after meals and more particularly at bedtime. His dreams follow the smoke heavenwards and behind the dudeen his hopes revive.'

The pipe was a vital part of the night-time ritual in County

Sligo too. Maggie McGowan recalled how her father would 'fill his pipe with tobacco. He'd light it, take a pull, wipe the shank on a corner of his coat and pass it on to the next man. He'd clean it the same way till all had a pull. 'Twas a grand old custom,' she declared.

So it was with the last of these fireside storytellers. Clay pipe in hand, they drew a rapt audience. Moulded in the tradition of the *filí*, their skill was honed to a fine edge during the long nights between Samhain and Bealtaine. Imbedded in a Druid past, their art was an oral one – the last living remnant of a time when nothing was written down and long apprenticeships served to commit the ancient legends and knowledge to memory.

The ancient bards were respected and highly valued. Their verses and tales were told in Tara's halls; their memories the repositories of great deeds of the Irish race and treasured epics like 'The Song of Amergin' or the *Táin Bó Cuailnge*. They cherished the ancient sagas passed on from generation to generation through the mists of prehistory until the sagas were written down by the early Christian monks. Sometimes it was almost too late. The chief *file*, Senchan Torpeist, endeavoured to gather together the elements of the *Táin* in the reign of Guaire Aidne, the seventh-century King of Connacht. Together with his son, Muirgen, he had to call up the spirit of the dead hero Fergus to help them with their task.

Many of the fireside *seanchaithe*, survivors of a crucible of conquest and colonisation, were men who had little or no formal education. Yet, in the manner of the bards of long ago, they could commit to memory endless anecdotes, stories, riddles and legends. Their minds were a treasure house of lore and tradition, inspiring a unique and natural-born talent that could never be acquired. They possessed a simplicity and authenticity, a cadence, rhythm and sense of timing that formal education would have destroyed.

Chiefs and kings feared the bards; they curried favour with them for fear of their sharp tongues. If someone displeased them, a quickly composed satirical verse could hold the subject up to ridicule, particularly in small communities. The power of their modern successor was no less fearful. The following excerpt from a lengthy composition criticises harsh foremen on a Sligo landlord's estate; the sting of the overseer's lash has faded but the verse is indelible:

> There's another Scotchman, Pat, that has two
> crooked feet,
> You know the lad that sets the bulbs way down at
> Carter's Seat.
> He wears a pair of knickers brown, vest and dark
> grey coat.
> You could know him on the avenues for he always
> walks by note . . .

Henry Conway of Carns, County Sligo, would dismiss any accolades or tributes to his talent. Yet his contribution to our knowledge of things past is as great as the men who memorised the *Táin*, his mind a repository of tales and verse, comic and sad, of the glories of the Gael. His was no bardic school but a modest fireside where he pitted his intelligence against Roger Moore of Drumfad in verse and storytelling feats. Their knowledge, tempered by their own experience, was handed down to them by men and women of another generation. Out of the treasure chest of his mind Henry drew for me 'The Ballad of Pat Donlevy',[76] a song and story of treachery and deceit remembered from Land League times over a hundred years before. Without his scholarship and interest, the story of this hero of another age would have been consigned to that vast black hole, with so much else that has already been lost.

Other yarns had no purpose other than to pass the long dark hours till bedtime. 'I'd be all right only I'm kilt with this oul' arthritis on me knee,' Mickey McGroarty complained to me one evening when he and Johnny Monahan and Peter Quinn came over for a ramble. The three were neighbours and long-time friends. Johnny was one of nature's gentlemen: a great storyteller and a fine accordion player. Peter was an elegant fiddler who, undervaluing his skill, never promoted his natural gift.

'I was with the doctor the other day,' Mickey continued, 'and I got no sympathy from him. "What d'ye expect for a man of your age?" he says to me. "There's not a thing I can do for that knee."

'"What d'ye mane," says I to him. "Why wouldn't ye? Isn't the other knee the same age as this one an' there's not a hate wrong with it?" That stopped him! He had no answer for that!'

Mickey was a man of many skills. His talents were more than adequate to tackle most trades required in the running of a house and farm. When a visiting relative stayed months instead of days, Mickey became embarrassed at his meagre furnishings. Deciding to build a chair for his guest, he set to and built a seat out of blocks of wood, sally-rods and whatever other materials came to hand. It was a fine chair when he was finished and, as a neighbour, Sean Ward, commented, 'You could sit in it, anyway.'

Country people rarely went to a barber. In every townland there was a man who was handy with a hair clippers and that was enough. They got no pay, except maybe an ounce of tobacco now and again or the loan of a wheelbarrow or a spade when they needed it. It was a social occasion too and the work always relaxed into easy chat, local gossip or the state of the cattle trade or country. After a haircut, very few country 'barbers' ever burned hair, for fear the spirits of the dead might come looking for it. It was rolled up tightly and put in a hole in the ditch.

Mickey's kitchen was one such place where these customs were observed and where neighbours came, mostly on Sunday afternoons, for a haircut.

Shortly after the chair was built, a local tradesman and small contractor, George Gallagher, came in to get his hair trimmed. Mickey sat him on a chair in the middle of the kitchen floor as usual. Flushed with his recent success at furniture-making, he explained about building the chair. 'It's there in the corner. What d'ye think of it?' he asked finally.

'It's all right,' George replied. 'It's a fine chair.' He paused for a while and then added, 'Ye know, Mickey, it takes a hatter to make a hat.'

'Oh, is that so?' replied Mickey, leaving the scissors and comb on the table. 'Well, I have news for you. It takes a barber to cut hair!'

He stamped out to his work in the meadow in a flaming temper at the insult. George's hair was only half cut, so he had to wait around until Mickey cooled down. This he did in his own good time and after some persuasion from the chastened George came back in to the kitchen to finish the haircut.

Playing the mouth organ was another one of Mickey's accomplishments. He'd play contentedly for hours if there was anyone to listen. On visits to his home he'd fix me with a level gaze over the top of the instrument between tunes and catch me out with a question after playing one of his favourites.

'Did ye know the name of that one?' he'd ask.

'No,' I'd have to admit.

'That was "Maurice Making Pandies",' he'd say with satisfaction, and I should have known because he always caught me on that tune. It was a strange name and I had a vague notion that Maurice's skill had something to do with going to the toilet until I found out that 'pandies' were what we called 'ponjers' in Sligo.

They were oversize mugs made by the tinkers out of tin, so Maurice must have been a tinker – but maybe I'm wrong about that too.

In between tunes on the accordion and the mouth organ, stories were told in turn by the men.

'Did I tell ye about these two brothers that lived in Kilcar one time?' Mickey would ask.

'No, Mickey, I don't remember hearing that one.'

I could tell by the twinkle in his eyes and the half-smile playing on his lips that this was going to be a funny one.

'Well, one of the men was called Mick an' they called th' other fella John. Mick was a great fella for dalin' in cattle. He attended all the fairs roun' Donegal and Mountcharles and Glenties up as far as Ballyshannon and even up about your country in Sligo. Any time he went to a fair he never came home that he wouldn't have tobacco or sweets or something home to his brother.

'Times got bad, fairs went down a bit, cattle was a fierce bad price an' things wasn't so good. "Now," says Mick to John one day, "I think," says he, "when we get the lock o' spuds dug, I think I'll go over to Scotland an' see if I can make fifty or sixty pound for the winter."

'"All right," says John. "I'll try and watch things at home while you're away. I'll look after the lock o' sheep that's up on the mountain and the cattle, and that's all I'll have to do."

'So anyway, when the time came, Mick started off for Scotland, an' when he landed he got a job with the Cowcaddens. He was workin' there an' he never wrote home to John, and John had no word from him for the six months and he was annoyed.

'"Begod," says John to himself one day, "Mick must be dead and only for he is surely there'd be some word from him. I'll have to see for meself," says he, and off with him for Scotland.

'The night before he left he made an oat scone an' next morning he tied it in a cloth, put it on a stick across his shoulder and he made off for Derry. There was no cars nor buses nor nothing that time so he had to walk it all the way. He paid his passage on the boat there – I think it was about four and ninepence across. When he landed over in Scotland he had no address, of course, an' he didn't know where Mick was working. He was walking up from the pier anyway, an' there was a nice gentleman comin' down, an Englishman with a wee small dog behind him. John was hungry an' he was eating a bit of the oatbread, an' the gentleman says to him, "Throw the dog a bit."

"'I will indeed," says John, "but how far I'll be fit to throw him I'm not fit to tell ye."

'He stooped down an' he caught the dog an' he wasn't yet far from the boat, an' he fired the dog and he put him so far that he knocked his brains out on the boat.

'Of course the gentleman then shouted for the police an' John was arrested an' next day he was taken before a magistrate.

"'What did ye do, my good man," says the judge, "that has ye in court today?"

"'Well" says John, "I did nothing only what I was asked, Yer Honour," telling the judge he was just off the boat over from Ireland and looking for his brother.

"'I was kind of hungry an' I was chewing a bit of bread and this man came an' asked me to throw his dog a bit. Yer Honour," says he, "I threw the dog as far as I could an' if ye gave me five pound I couldn't throw it a bit further."

"'Oh," says the magistrate, "ye done what ye were told! I dismiss this case, so."

"'Thank ye, Yer Honour," says John. "That ye may live long an' die happy."

'John left the court and away down the road but the gentleman was annoyed an' wanted satisfaction on John by hook or by crook. He spotted a hawker coming up the road with an ass-and-cart selling delft. The gentleman went over to the hawker, told him the story, an', says he, "If ye play a trick on John I'll trate ye very dacent."

"'Oh! Lave that to me," says the old hawker. "Don't worry."

'John came on down and the hawker spoke to him. "Hello, Paddy from Ireland," says he, "an' how are ye getting on?"

"'Hello," says John. "I'm not Paddy, I'm John, an' I'm lookin' for my brother Mick. Did ye see him?"

"I did," says the hawker. "Come over here an' I'll show him to ye."

"'Where is he or where is he working?" says John.

"'There he is there," says the old man, pointing to the donkey in the cart.

"'Be God then," says John, "if that's him there grew a lot of hair on him since he left Kilcar, but let it be him or not, I must talk to him."

'John was a great chewer of tobacco. He had a big chew in his mouth an' when he went over an' started speaking into the donkey's ear he fired in a big spit as far as he could. The ass went away mad up the street at a gallop an' there wasn't a bowl or a plate on the cart but went east and west an' the old hawker away after him. He shouted for the police and John was arrested again. The next morning he found himself before the same magistrate as before.

"'My God," says the magistrate, "are ye here the day again?"

"'I am," says John, "an' it's not me own fault today either."

"'Well," says the judge, "what did ye do or what's yer crime this time?"

'John told him the story about looking for his brother and the hawker pointing out the ass to him and him thinking he was very hairy to be his brother.

"'I went over to give the donkey a kiss an' as soon as I did he went away mad. Whether he knew I was a stranger or not I couldn't tell ye."

"'Oh, is that so," says the judge. "Get out of my court right away and don't come back here again, for you're far too smart for the boys 'round these parts!"

'John was getting upset at this time that he wasn't finding his brother. He was walking the streets this day and he got taken kinda short an' couldn't find a toilet. He decided to knock on a door and ask permission, an' when he did this woman answered. Thinking he was the milkman, didn't she hand him out a jug right away. John thought they had some strange customs in Scotland but he did what he had to do anyway an' handed her in the jug again.

'Between one thing and another word started to get around about this man just off the boat lookin' for his brother. Mick heard about it soon enough and says to himself, "If that's anyone it's our John that's in it!" They met up eventually and Mick said he had fifty pounds saved an' says he to John, "Now here's this money an' you go home again an' watch the things at home an' about Patrick's Day I'll be back to put in the crops and I might have another fifty pounds saved by that time if all goes well."

'He got a new suit of clothes for John, left him down at the boat and said goodbye. He went back to his digs very glad to have seen John and happy that he was on his way back to look after the old home again.

'During the time that John was over in Scotland, he heard about a great arguer an', thinking about this, he asked the sea captain when he was sailing.

"'Well," says the captain, "I won't be sailing till eight o'clock, till everyone is aboard."

"'D'ye know where this great arguer of scripture lives?" says John.

"'I do rightly," says the captain. "Go up there to that corner, take a left and go to the second house; the number two is on the door," he says, "an' if ye knock there ye'll get in but if ye take my advice ye won't go next nor near him, for if ye have any money he'll take it off ye. There's nobody in the world able to beat him at arguing scripture."

"'Well," says John, "nothing beats a try. I'll go up till I see."

'Up goes John anyway and knocks on the door. This girl answered the knock and "What can I do for ye?" she says.

"'Is this where the famous arguer is?" says John.

"'This is the very place," says she.

"'Well," says John, "I want to see him."

'She showed him into the room and sitting by the fire was a fine big gentleman.

"'Did ye come to argue scripture?" says he.

"'I did," says John. "That's the very thing I came to do!"

"'Well," says the arguer, "you know that I argue for big stakes only."

"'I heard tell of that all right," says John.

"'How much money do you have on you?

"'Oh," John replied, "I have fifty pound!"

"'Well," says the arguer, looking John up and down, "that's not very much, but put it down there on the table, an' seeing that that's all ye have I'll back it up with a hundred."

"'Good enough," says John. "Damn but ye're a dacent sort of a man!"

"'Well now," says the arguer, "we'll cut the cards for the first call."

"'Right y'are," John said. "No bother."

'They got the cards, John cut the ten of diamonds and the

arguer cut the four of spades.

'"Well now," says the arguer, "that's it. I get the first call."

'"Fair enough," says John. "Rattle away, me good man."

'"This is my question then," said the man. "Who was God's father?"

'John hadn't the catechism learned too well when he was going to school. The only curse ever he had when he was stuck or annoyed was "God Almighty!". He was just about to say, "God Almighty! I have no idea," but he only got as far as "God Almighty" when, "Right," says the arguer, "that's the correct answer."

'"Now," says he to John, "it's your turn."

'"Well, me good man, since ye did start to talk about fathers and mothers an' all that," says he, "can ye tell me who was my father?"

'"How could I do that?" was the reply. "I could not, my good man, for in the first place I didn't ask you your name!"

'"Is that so?" says John. "Well you can't blame me for that. Thank ye and good luck to ye, the hundred and fifty is mine."

'Sweeping the hundred and fifty off the table, he bade the famous man goodbye, caught the boat to Derry and walked all the way home to Kilcar. The neighbours all gathered into the house, delighted to see him an' asking him about what kind of a country Scotland was. John ordered a couple of bottles of whiskey and sent word for Johnny Doherty the famous fiddle player to come and play for the people. There was two days and nights of dancing and singing. John was the centre of attention as he told everyone about his adventures, and ye can be sure if he added nothing to the story he took nothing away. I never heard nothing about the two men since but that was a long time ago an' ye can be sure the two of them are long dead since, the Lord have mercy on their souls.'

Mickey and Johnny Monahan often pondered on the reasons for the disappearance of the fairies and ghosts; they didn't seem as plentiful now as when the men were young. It was a prayer the priest said after Mass for years that banished them, Johnny thought. Mickey blamed it on the electric light. Other times they thought they might still be there. Neighbours rambled from house to house no more along the secret places and paths, nor did they pass by the fairy rath. Sweeping from place to place now in a blaze of headlights on broad highways, how can we know what spirits wander in fields and lonely ways?

Maggie McGowan wondered about the dearth of fairies and spirits too. She recalled that when she was a young woman, three 'Hail Marys', one 'Our Father' and a 'Hail Holy Queen' was offered after Mass, 'for the souls that wandered through the world.' Perhaps the prayers are answered now and all the souls at rest, she thought.

Ramblers went on foot to their destinations along the darkened roads of long ago. Haunted houses, encounters with banshees, headless death coaches, ghosts of the departed and nocturnal apparitions of frightening black dogs were common-place. Around the winter fires where these stories were told, there were few who had not a tale to recount of a strange or frightening encounter with things that were not part of the human world.

Outside of the camaraderie of that comforting circle, in the murky, dim-lit corners of the kitchen, phantasmal ancestors long passed away listened unseen in the shadows. Spirits who once had a place by the firelit circle of mortals loitered where the dancing flames of the burning turf fire and pallid glow of the oil lamp faded into gloom. Overhead, where the light strove to penetrate the dim-lit recesses around the smoke-blackened purlins, were concealed creatures that crept away only with the dawn light. Flickering flame-thrown shadows of the fireside company danced with phantom visitors on the whitewashed wall, bringing our two worlds into a shadowy unison. Stories of banshees that wailed to foretell a death, desperate struggles with ghosts on lonely paths – anything became possible as we flirted with the spirit-peopled otherworld that from time to time crossed over darkly to ours.

Those fortunate enough to have sat as children in such ghost-filled rooms will remember the power and presence of forces that took on a new life when darkness covered the earth. Even the bravest felt a tremulous fear.

Creeping to bed in the pitch black of the 'upper room', grim possibilities lurked in every shadow that leered and leaped as we walked reluctantly along the path of light thrown through the bedroom door. We lingered here long as at the entrance to some foreboding cave, and then a cry of 'Get away to bed out o' that with ye' precipitated a reluctant dash through the eyes and claws of threatening dark to comforting blankets. Hearts frighted with grotesque images, our eyes held a lifeline: the comforting crack of light around the door. Ghoulish shapes formed, changed, shimmered and threatened in the darkling room. Familiar objects moved, became menacing fiends. Boyce's chimneys through the murky window were two shadowy heads bent towards each other, conspiring in the moiling darkness. Advancing malevolently on the bedroom window, they threatened, shifted, crept slowly closer. Sleep overcoming terror drew us to the morning light.

In later years when I listened to these stories in a neighbour's house, bravado was a façade that disintegrated as soon as the closing door shut off the comforting glow. Enveloped in shrouding dark, some whistled away the danger on their way home. It didn't work for me. Bushes, paling posts, the half-seen starlit shadow of an inquisitive ass – was it ghost or demon?

I walked past Donlevy's field, where Danny Cummins fought the ghost. He and James and Frank Donlevy were walking from Cliffoney late at night. About a mile from home, near the end of the Burra road, they saw 'this thing up agin the ditch lying across the wall'.

'Me bully fella,' Cummins shouted out, 'why don't you come away with us?' They were young men in high good spirits, afraid of nothing, kings of their world.

At Donlevy's the friends parted. Here Danny had to make his way home alone across the fields. An uneasy feeling had come over the group about the encounter on the Burra road. They knew they should never answer 'Come in' to a knock on the door at night. The old people warned against it. You either got up and opened it or enquired 'Who's there?' before extending an invitation.

What kind of creature had the comrades now invited to join their company? They thought they were being followed but couldn't be sure. Concerned about his friend's safety, old James Christie offered to leave Cummins part of the way home. 'No!' said he. 'What would I be afraid of?'

He didn't know it at that moment but his life was shortly to change forever. As he made his way across the fields, the shadowy creature came before him and launched a savage attack. Defending himself as best he could, he was no match for the ferocious onslaught. The ghost 'kicked him and rowlt him' across the fields until he was put crashing through Anthony Rogers' door. He did not know or recognise the person or thing he fought; later he could not say for sure if it was man or demon. Exhausted and badly shaken from the encounter, he was unable to leave Rogers' until morning. Neighbours said he was never the same man again. Emigrating to America shortly afterwards with his wife, he was never heard from more.

When word of the affray went out through the village, many speculated that the spectre was a Protestant man who had died some time before – and with whom Cummins had had a fight. The man was from outside the area and often rambled at Anthony Rogers', an ill-reputed house and favourite meeting place for those associated with Palmerston's lodges. 'Poor fella,' Bernie Kelly recalled, 'My father remembered when he went away, the crickets left his house and came over here. They were still here when I was a-growing up.'

It was unwise to make an offer to something half seen, half heard. When a capricious breeze blew open the door of a house in a small village in County Fermanagh, just across the border, the owners made a joke of it, shouting, 'Come in, ye boy ye!' It was no joke! From that day forward the occupants were terrified with strange noises, footsteps where there was no person, rapping on the walls, screams, loud cavernous noises as if from deep underground, bedclothes snatched off sleeping members of the family. The house sold cheap and changed hands several times but the ghost or poltergeist remained. When Father Coyle from Maguiresbridge was called on for help, he witnessed the clothes on an empty bed rising and falling in rhythm as if to a person breathing. A cold presence filled the room as pots and pans flew through the air. Father Smith came to support Father Coyle. All was silent as the priests prayed. Suddenly it seemed the spirit could take no more. A loud crash was heard from upstairs, following which a tremendous rush of air passed between the two men.

The priests were powerless in the face of the evil presence. The family had had enough. They locked the door, left the house and booked passage on a ship for America. As the coast of Ireland receded behind them, they were sad but hopeful that their nightmare was over. It wasn't! Halfway through the voyage, the evil spirit reasserted itself with the same antics as before. On reaching New York, they were forced to move house several times until eventually, inexplicably, after several torturous years, the poltergeist left for good.

John Feeney of Aughagad was born in 1827. When he was an old man, he told his son Michael about a similar encounter that happened during Penal times. The story began with a fierce fight between McMorrough of Drumcliffe and a landlord's agent. The agent was on horseback and armed with a sword. Mc-Morrough defended himself with a blackthorn stick. He was losing the fight when, in a last desperate bid, he threw the stick, knocking the man off the horse. The agent died in the fall but before he passed to the next world he vowed that vengeance would be his. 'Dead or alive, I will have my revenge on you,' he swore.

Forced to leave home and go on the run, McMorrough became a hunted man. Yeomen scoured the countryside, forcing him to sleep in safe houses and move about only at night. A year or so later, when his nocturnal wanderings took him past Drumcliffe cemetery at the dead hour, Feeney recalled, the vengeful spirit appeared before McMurrough, 'riding on the same horse he rode at the fight and dressed in the same way.' Seizing the reins of the mule that McMurrough rode, the demented shade attempted to force him through the cemetery gate. A desperate struggle followed. Several times the dead man almost succeeded in forcing McMorrough through, and each time he struggled free. Blow for blow the fierce contest carried on through the night, until dawn streaked the weary sky and the loud call of a cock from a neighbouring farm shrilled across fields and churchyard.

> *I have heard*
> *The cock that is the trumpet to the morn,*
> *Doth with his lofty and shrill-sounding throat*
> *Awake the god of day, and at his warning,*
> *Whether in sea or fire, in earth or air*
> *The extravagant spirit hies*
> *To his confine . . .*

> Hamlet I, i

Ceasing the struggle at once, the ghostly horse and rider melted with a despairing cry into the deep shadows that lurched across the slanting headstones in the graveyard. McMurrough fell exhausted; the cock's call had saved him – but he never again ventured to pass Drumcliffe churchyard by day or night.

There are some who scorn the existence of any experience outside the natural world. They pity the credulous fools who relate paranormal experiences of banshees, ghosts or fairies. They have never seen such things! But what does that prove? Does the absence of an encounter with unnatural beings prove they don't exist? Can it be that some have a perception, an ability to perceive the spirit world which is not given to all? Men discover underground springs with a forked hazel rod. Pointing to unseen streams, the rod quivers, twists and contorts in their grip like a living thing. In the hands of those less gifted, it is nothing more than a piece of lifeless wood.

Broader minds will admit to forces beyond our understanding, to unquiet spirits of the departed that visit familiar places, to phantoms doomed to walk the earth completing mortal business left undone. They will agree with Shakespeare, who conceded, through the voice of Hamlet, that 'There are more things in heaven and earth, Horatio, than are dreamt of in your philosophy.'

During a conversation with Robin Flower, Peig Sayers confided that she had never seen a ghost. She accepted, though, that such things could be. 'There are many strange things beyond our knowledge,' she admitted, 'and maybe there are ghosts too.' She found it difficult to understand why they would want to come back here after leaving. 'It would be better for them to rest in their graves and not be bothering us,' was her opinion.

'When ye die sudden, ye'll be seen,' Thomas Boyce told me. Others believed that the departed spirit returned to take care of unfinished business. Or to settle a debt left unpaid. The fate of the person who died owing money was to remain in purgatory until the bill was discharged for them by a living being. John Sheridan of Glangevlin, County Cavan, knew a man who, on several occasions, met a person on his way home from 'ceilidh-ing'. He recognised him as a neighbour who had died several months before. Following advice from the priest, he plucked up courage one night and addressed the apparition.

'In the name of God, what is wrong with you?' he said.

'I'm glad you spoke to me, because until you did I couldn't talk to you. I left a bill of seven pounds ten shillings in the shop. Will you tell my people about it and ask them to pay it?'

The man took the message as he was bid, the debt was paid, and the ghostly figure was never seen again.

Sean McColgan of Ballyharry on the Inishowen peninsula in County Donegal was seen by neighbours at night after he had been waked and buried. They were sure there was something troubling him but didn't know what to do about it. On a Sunday afternoon Sean's wife sat alone in the kitchen. Sensing something strange, she looked up and saw her dead husband standing outside the door. He put his finger to his lips, indicating that he could not speak. With his other hand he pointed at an old cupboard and stared hard at it. Casting another glance at his wife, he passed out of sight. When she had recovered from the shock of her experience, she searched the cupboard. There she found an unpaid bill for shoes Sean had bought some time before. Next day she went into Moville and paid off the account. From that day her husband was never seen again.

James McGovern and his wife lived long ago in a mud hut beside Big John Callery's at the end of the Green Road in Mullaghmore, County Sligo. Following a long illness, James lay dying. Two neighbours went to visit and offer help to his wife. On their way to the house, near Pat Charlie's, they were surprised to meet the sick man on the road. It was a moonlit night, so his features were clearly visible. They thought it strange when he passed by without responding to their greeting. Pleased to see he had recovered, they decided to continue to the house anyway. On arriving, they were astonished to discover that James had passed away shortly before. The remains lay before them on what had been his sickbed a short time previously.

Following the wake and funeral, James's wife lived on her own. As time went on, neighbours' visits became less frequent, so she was delighted one night to hear a knock on the door. Opening it, she froze in terror at the sight of her dead husband standing there. She stood for an instant and, not knowing what else to do, slammed the door shut. A few nights later, the same thing happened again. This time, she went to Father Malachai Brennan in nearby Cliffoney to have her husband prayed for and to ask the priest what she should do. He advised her to keep a bottle of holy water on the dresser. When the spirit returned, she should invite him in and ask if there was any way she could help him.

A few days later, the knock came to the door again but this

time, even though she was deadly afraid, she was prepared. Knowing the holy water was in the house, she felt secure. When she opened the door, it was her dead husband again. This time it was different: he seemed disturbed. She addressed him anyway, as the priest had advised.

'James,' she said, 'won't you come in!'

'How can I come in,' he responded angrily, 'when you have holy water in the house!'

Losing her courage, the woman slammed the door, shutting out the terrifying vision. The appearances happened repeatedly until the distracted woman could take it no longer and moved to the neighbouring townland of Carnduff. She was aghast when the visits continued there. She never did any good after that, Annie Callery, who remembered the events, said. Even though the neighbours were kind and sympathetic to the troubled woman, there was nothing they could do.

The story has no happy ending; James's widow could not placate his tormented spirit or discover why he kept returning. Her health deteriorated from the strain and she joined her husband in death soon after.

Not all ghosts are so troublesome. There is the story of a man who returned to his wife following an early death brought about by a lifetime of torment at her hands. He appeared silently at the foot of the bed one night with a pleading look on his face. Belligerent as ever, she glared at him and snarled, 'I thought you had enough?' upon which he fled into the darkness, never to return!

Priests, too, were bound by obligations relating to the spirit world. They returned in order to fulfil commitments made while on earth. Often their obligation was to say a Mass in return for an offering of money which had been given.

In the north Leitrim townland of Lecklasser, a light was

often seen at dead of night in an old church situated where Drummons National School now stands. Mary McGovern went there to pray after her day's work was over. One night, while she knelt in front of the altar, wearied from her labours, sleep overcame her. Startled awake in the small hours by a light that suddenly flamed on the altar, she looked around. There was a pale moon that night that limned the green meadows and purple mountains of north Leitrim, draining them of colour. A shaft of light beaming through the small window formed a white pool on the floor of the church, dimly illuminating the interior.

To her amazement, the sacristy door opened and a priest in full vestments silently emerged and climbed the steps to the altar. Turning around, he stared down the chapel as if expecting something or someone. Waiting there a while, he turned, descended the steps again and returned to the sacristy. The lights went out and darkness descended on the church, leaving Mary wondering if she was dreaming.

Curious now, she returned the following night to see if it would happen again. This time, wide awake, she hid in the back and, sure enough, shortly after 12 o'clock the lights came on, the priest ascended the altar as before, waited, and then retraced his steps to the sacristy. Next day, not sure if she was going to be ridiculed, Mary described to the local priest what she had witnessed. The priest listened attentively and, when she was finished, advised her to go back another night. When the ghostly priest turned around again on the altar, she should ask him in the name of God if she could do something for him.

Mary returned and waited until the scene was repeated as before. She was frightened but, thinking of the priest's advice, plucked up courage. She was ready. 'Can I help you, Father?' The sound of her own voice echoing through the silent church startled her still further. The priest looked straight at her.

'Thank God!' he replied. 'For years I have been trying to say a Mass for someone who gave me money.' He explained that he couldn't offer the Holy Sacrifice without a server. Neither could his soul go to rest until he had fulfilled his earthly obligation. Although Mary had never served Mass before, she attended the priest anyway and was surprised when it came as easily to her as if she had being doing it all her life. When the Mass was over, the apparition disappeared from view, and even though Mary often went back to the church after that, she never again saw anything out of the ordinary. She was ill for some time after the experience but when she recovered people said she could ever afterwards serve Mass with any of the best-trained young boys in the parish.

Card-playing was more than a game at McGowan's in Lecklasser – it was a passion. Gambling went on all night until morning's rays dimmed the oil lamp's gleam. Weary from a night spent playing and smoking around the kitchen table, James Gallagher stretched and parted the blinds. It was just breaking day and he was astonished to discern the figure of a woman looking in at the house. She raised her hand in a gesture meaning that he should say nothing.

Fear compelled him to hold his silence that morning but he couldn't keep the secret for long. Eventually he revealed what he had seen to his companions. They were not surprised. They had heard that a figure called 'the white woman of Lios' was often seen on the old road. It frequently entered a byre in Lios townland at night while a woman there was milking her cows. On one such visit the spirit asked for milk and, receiving it, promised the woman that it would never harm her or anyone belonging to her. They believed this was the person or spirit Gallagher had seen. That finished the card-playing at Mc-Gowan's. The owners made wooden shutters and installed them on the windows in fear of the spectre.

Shortly afterwards two men – McGee of Carnduff and McCormack of Tawley – were returning home from Manor-hamilton by Lecklasser. They knew nothing of the white woman of Lios so they were unconcerned when they saw a person dressed in white at the side of the road. 'Come away for a jaunt,' McCormack shouted jokingly at her. Immediately she started to follow them. She never spoke, so after a while the two men became uneasy, as they sensed that this was no ordinary creature.

When they came to Brocky Bridge, she disappeared and the two men heaved a sigh of relief to be rid of her. Spirits cannot cross water, so they reckoned she was thwarted in her pursuit by the stream that ran there. They were soon disappointed, however, for when they re-crossed the stream at O'Beirne's bridge, she reappeared.

She continued to follow the two men until they reached home. Unharnessing the pony in feverish haste, they tied it in the stable, went into the house as fast as they could and bolted the doors. When a great knocking was heard on the doors and windows, they knelt down and prayed. They heard the pony break its tying in the outhouse, so one of the men, plucking up his courage, took the tongs in his hand and went out into the yard. People believed that iron had power over the supernatural. He called on the ghost to come forward in the name of God. He commanded her that, if she had any nearer friends than him, to go to them or to some other place where she would stay forever.[77]

When McCormack looked for his pony in the morning, he found it drowned in a nearby stream. It was conjectured that the spirit had entered the body of the pony. When the animal died, so too was the spirit destroyed. Whatever happened on that night we can only guess, but it is certain that the white woman of Lios was never seen in Lecklasser again.

The castles of Ireland speak of a colonial, battle-scarred past. They are occupied now by phantoms of a class of people who once held the power of life and death over those who served under them. 'Speaking monuments of the troubled and insecure state of the country' was how George Burrow, author of *Lavengro*, described them. Kilkea Castle is one such place, now a hotel, where 'stories have been whispered of strange apparitions in the castle and neighbourhood, the eerie clash of steel upon steel on the lofty battlements, of phantom warriors re-enacting old skirmishes on history-soaked ground.'[78]

The building was originally built by the Normans, possibly by Hugh de Lacy, in the twelfth century. It became associated with the Fitzgeralds in 1244. History's pages are filled with the exploits of this great family that became, as did many of the Norman invaders, 'more Irish than the Irish themselves'. The castle had close links with Silken Thomas, one-time Lord Deputy of Ireland, who was imprisoned in the Tower of London and hanged, drawn and quartered at Tyburn, along with his five uncles, for supporting the Irish cause.

It has associations too with other players on Ireland's troubled stage: Cardinal Rinuccini and Thomas Reynolds, who betrayed the United Irishmen in 1798, and the patriot Lord Edward Fitzgerald. The mysterious Gearoid Óg Fitzgerald practised black magic in a room in this enchanted castle. It is he who now sleeps, under a spell, in the nearby Rath of Mullaghmast, 'from which he rides out sometimes at dead of night to gallop across the windswept plains of the Curragh on a magnificent white horse shod with silver shoes.'

The best-known haunting in Ireland is that of a room in Maynooth College, County Kildare. The building is erected on

the same ground as an earlier college built by Gearóid Óg
Fitzgerald in 1515 close to Maynooth Castle, ancient seat of the
Fitzgeralds. The later college was erected by the English
government in 1795 for the education of Catholic priests, who,
because of the operation of the Penal Laws, went to France for
education and ordination. The British, at war with France,
feared the introduction of revolutionary ideas to Ireland with
the returning priests. Students at Maynooth were required to
take an oath of allegiance to the crown and to use their 'utmost
endeavour to disclose and make known to His Majesty and heirs
all treasons and traitorous conspiracies.'

The haunted room is No. 2 on the top corridor of Rhetoric
House, the upper two floors of which are used exclusively as a
dormitory for students. The bizarre series of events are said to
have taken place there sometime between 1842 and 1848. A
student assigned to the room was found on the following
morning, an apparent suicide, having used a razor to end his life.
The apartment was cleaned up and after a time assigned to
another student. He died in exactly the same way. Some
accounts say that his friends got to him before he passed away.
He whispered that he was attacked by a creature that was half-
human and half-animal. A spiritualist who visited the room
afterwards sensed something similar that drew her inexorably
towards the window. Another youth who slept there awoke
during the night to see his clothes being thrown about the room.

The college authorities, attributing the two apparent suicides
to nothing more than an unfortunate coincidence, eventually
assigned the room to another student. This man almost suffered
a similar fate when he was overcome with a compulsion during
the night to end his life with a razor. He described afterwards
a struggle with overwhelming unseen forces that drew him to
the window, threatening to kill him. In a desperate struggle, he

escaped by jumping out of the window to the Rhetoric yard two storeys below, thinking himself fortunate to have survived at the expense of nothing more than some broken bones.

Following this, no student could be found to occupy the room. The college governors were at a loss to know what to do. A priest volunteered to spend a night there in an effort to discover what was going on. We have no account of what harrowing experiences he underwent during his lonely vigil, but in the morning the priest's hair had turned white.

From that time forth, the college authorities never again invited anyone to stay in Room No. 2. Official proof that strange things happened there is found in the college trustees' resolution dated 23 October 1860 which reads: 'That the President be authorised to convert Room No. 2 on the top corridor of Rhetoric House into an oratory of St Joseph, and to fit up an oratory of St Aloysius in the prayer hall of the junior students.'

The corridor wall of Room No. 2 was pulled away, the window bricked up and the oratory of St Joseph installed. It can be seen to this day. The mystery continues. There have been stories of footprints burned into the wooden floor, of bloodstains that could not be washed out. A crucifix hung on the wall near the oratory repeatedly fell off, no matter how many times it was replaced nor how securely it was fastened.

Father John Walsh of Maugherow, County Sligo, spent many years there studying for the priesthood. He knew of the room and slept next door to it, against the advice of other seminarians. Nothing untoward happened to him, nor did he hear anything unusual. He often went into the haunted room. 'Ye can still see the blood on the floor,' he told me. 'They planed it and sanded it several times and you can still see it!'

Some say the evil force is the tortured spirit of the young

student assigned to this room who discovered he had no vocation. Not wanting to continue his studies, he feared even more to return home bearing the stigma of a failed priest. When he was found underneath the window, an apparent suicide, he was buried in unconsecrated ground, according to the practice of the day.

Whatever occurred there over 150 years ago inspires awe and speculation to this day. No one denies that something remarkable – something outside our understanding of the normal – happened there. Father Denis Meehan in his book *Window on Maynooth* ventures the cautious assertion that 'The basic details of the story have doubtless some foundation in fact, and it is safe to assume that something very unpleasant did occur.' No simple explanation can be offered but surely even the most incredulous must conclude that there are indeed more things that inhabit this earth than we can understand.

The changing tides of history and fortune forced the once-powerful landed gentry to abandon their palatial holdings. Their ghosts and the ghosts of their retainers often remained in the crumbling 'big houses' and deserted mansions. Behind the vacant windows and lifeless walls, troubled shadows flitted; a palpable air of mystery and menace remained. 'Beyond here be dragons,' wrote the ancient mapmakers across the frontiers of the uncharted world. Across the alien boundary of what is real and what is not, we may claim, 'Here be ghosts.'

Tom William Higgins, Palmerston's bailiff, lived in Cliffoney village. His was a reign of terror as he impounded cattle for late rent payments or, at the head of the infamous 'crowbar brigade', tore down the homes of tenants who were unable to pay. Death lays its icy hand on bailiff and king alike; they 'are equal made with the poor, crooked scythe and spade.' When Higgins's turn came to meet his maker, neighbours were not surprised to hear 'terrible noises' in the house every night following his death.

To this day, locals will insist on repeating accounts prevalent at the time of a 'rat wearing glasses' seen near the house. The first time the story is told it seems so bizarre and unbelievable as to bring a smile. Surely it's a joke! When unrelated witnesses insist on its truth and tell you that Higgins wore glasses when he was alive, you know it's no jest. Surely such a spectre could only be the figment of fevered imaginations; but doesn't the Bible tell of demons expelled from the human body entering that of a pig? There's poetic justice in the image: a rat in life condemned to live out eternity in a rat's body! Perhaps that is what people wanted to believe.

Disturbed by the upheaval in the home, the family sent for the parish priest. An exorcism was performed; this brought an end to the haunting. Afterwards a sealed upstairs room was all that remained to show that something strange had happened there at one time.

Was the list of unexplainable deaths and misfortune associated with Classiebawn Castle curse or coincidence? Did the woman in white seen standing, mysterious and enigmatic, in the middle window know things beyond human reason? Did the gatekeeper, long passed to his eternal reward, return to sit by the familiar fire through the dead hours, as claimed by the servants, Brigid and Mary Kate Duffy? No matter how much fuel was stacked by the hearth in the evening or how well raked the fire was at bedtime, morning revealed only a heap of warm ashes in the grate and no trace of the firewood that had been carefully stored the previous night. When they told their employer about this, she expressed no surprise. Nothing unusual about that, she said. Telling them there was nothing to be afraid of, she confided eventually that it was the spirit of her dead husband Alfie.

W. B. Yeats, a disciple of Swedenborg, the eighteenth-century scientist and mystic, believed that 'the soul lives a life so like that of the world that it may not even believe that it has died.' Could this explain the return of the gatekeeper, whose name I cannot tell, to his familiar place?

Perhaps there is a different explanation. In many parts of Ireland there was a belief in the *marbh bheo* or *neamhmharbh*, the living dead. This phenomenon was embodied in the actual corpse, which returned after death. Was Abhartach, one-time chieftain in Glenullin, north Derry, the first Count Dracula? It seems clear from the evidence that this pernicious overlord gave the Irish writer Bram Stoker the idea for his classic horror tale of bats and vampires set in Transylvania. Indeed it requires no great feat of imagination to infer the name Dracula from *dearg-díulaí*, meaning bloodsucker.

Driven to despair at Abhartach's harsh and cruel treatment, his tenants in Glenullin begged a neighbouring chieftain, Cathán, to kill him. Cathán slew Abhartach in time, but to everyone's horror the tyrant returned shortly after, evil as ever, and now demanding a bowl of blood from the veins of his subjects to sustain his undead body. At the request of the people, Cathán slew and buried him again – and again he returned. Seeking the advice of a holy man, Cathán was advised to go out again, but this time he was to kill the tyrant with a sword made of yew wood, bury him upside down in the earth and scatter thorns all about the grave. Cathán carried out the instructions exactly as he was told and this time Abhartach returned no more. His grave may still be seen in a spot known as the 'Giant's Grave' in a lonely field in the townland of Slaughtaverty in north Derry.

Another progenitor of Dracula, recorded by Jeremiah Curtin, came from Drimoleague parish in County Cork. This charmer, identified as Michael Derrihy in 'The Blood-drawing Ghost', forced a young girl to 'carry him on her shoulders all through the countryside whilst he slit the throats of sleepers with an open razor'.[79] Similar incidents were well known in many other counties.

Douglas Hyde was well aware of the phenomenon when he recorded it in a story called 'Teig O'Kane and the Corpse'. Teig is carrying a corpse on his back to bury it when the dead man speaks.

'What's that?' said Teig, startled, the cold sweat running from his forehead. 'Who spoke to me?'

'It's I, the corpse, that spoke to you,' said the voice.

'Can you talk?' said Teig, the hair standing on his head.

'Now and again,' said the cadaver. And so the conversation went . . .

Some *marbh bheo* are much more akin to living people who have returned with some specific beneficial purpose in mind or who are reluctant to leave the 'land of the living'. Anticipating such a visit, some families were known to leave food on the table during the night for deceased family members. When an old person died in Dingle, County Kerry, the custom was to leave a space for him in the bed as well as to place a pipeful of tobacco along with a light for them in the cubbyhole. This was done for a full month after the death.[80]

An old man in north Cavan remembered, when he was a small boy, his grandfather returning from the nearby graveyard even though he was three months dead. He sat at the fire and smoked his pipe – his greatest pleasure when he was alive. The family was not afraid of him, although he never spoke to them. The old man recalled climbing on the corpse's knee and noticing that, when he touched his skin, it was very cold.

Until the late nineteenth century, it was deemed that the corpse had rights to property. The Brehon Laws, recognising the claim, stated that 'every dead body has in its own right a cow and a horse and a garment, and the furniture of his bed; nor shall any of these be paid in satisfaction of his debts; because they are, as it were, the property of his body.'

Ruined walls are all that now remain of the house in Bunduff where Owen Daly lived with his wife and family. Here too the fire is the central part of the tale. Neighbours recalled that when Owen raked the fire prior to retiring at night, 'it was all scattered away in the morning'. Believing that there was a message in the mischief and respecting the unknown forces at work, he started to put down a good fire before going to bed. After that, when a fire was lit at night it still blazed heartily in the morning; when it was raked, it was 'all thrown away'.

Yeats chastised the Scots for ill-treating their ghosts and fairies. In Ireland he discerned a kind of 'timid affection' between men and spirits. 'They only ill-treat each other within reason,' he said. 'Each admits the other to have feelings.' We had learned to live with them. Owen Daly was a wise man. If he had ever met the great poet, they would have found much to talk about. Yeats learned a great deal from such men when he visited their homes in the Irish countryside.[81]

Jimmy McGettrick told me of a Catholic priest who was approached by a gang of men when out walking one day near Ballymote. 'You'll not leave this spot alive,' they said, 'unless you tell us will we get back to heaven again.'

They were fallen spirits, Jimmy thought. The priest wasn't sure what was the best thing to do but, thinking as quick as he could, came up with a reply. 'If ye can find one drop of blood among ye, ye're safe,' he said. They tried their best, and Jimmy recalled that when they couldn't find any they went away through the air 'with a loud wailing in a gush of wind'.

The priest's answer, Jimmy believed, was inspired by God.

Yeats held that, when priests had to make such a judgement, it was often done 'more in sadness than in anger'. The Catholic Church, he maintained, liked to keep on good terms with its neighbours, both dead and alive.

Local workers employed at the gamekeeper's lodge in Mullaghmore feared to be left there alone. It was haunted, they said, by the ghost of a caretaker who lived there years ago. When he died, the old people said, they couldn't get his hands into the coffin. They chanced to look out the window and saw him there with his hands held up over his shoulders. He was often seen afterwards, a shadowy figure walking past the window keeping a lonely vigil. Sometimes a heavy step was heard inside the house making its way across the upstairs floor and down the stairs, 'every step like a ton weight,' neighbours said. A search of the house revealed nothing.

A door leading to the kitchen could never be closed. Thomas Boyce rambled there in the evenings with the gamekeepers. On a stormy night he asked them, 'Why don't ye close that door? There's an awful draught going through the house.'

'You can close it if ye like,' Watty replied, 'but it won't stay closed.'

'What are ye talking about?' Thomas replied, laughing. 'Of course it will.'

He got up, closed the door and sat around the fire again in conversation with his friends. After a while, the door swung open. Thomas looked at the other men incredulously. Examining the latch and finding it in good working order, he shut it again, and again it opened wide of its own accord. Thomas left the door alone after that and offered no explanation to me other than to wonder if the door might have been in the path of the old caretaker doing his nightly rounds.

Irish ghosts seemed for the most part to mind their own

business. They were not hostile. Yet the very thought of someone, whether friend or foe, coming back from the dead instilled an anxious dread. There was no reason for fear – but it was there. 'It's the livin' ghost ye have to be afraid of!' people said loudly, as if trying to convince themselves, and they'd know there was truth in it – but deep down in their trembling hearts the fear clung.

Ghosts, like people, had their favourites and their idiosyncrasies. They took to some people better than others. The record for the friendliest ghost must surely go to a place called Grange near Boyle in County Roscommon. Tubercurry man Pat James Duffy got the story from his aunt who lived there.

Her neighbour, Michael John, had lived in England for years. He didn't much like it there, so when he had saved enough money he returned home, in about 1955, and bought a two-storey house in Grange that belonged to the landed gentry at one time. Michael didn't know it was reputed to be haunted. No one else would buy it. Several other families had come to live there and had had to leave because of interference. Furniture was thrown all over the place, footsteps were heard on the stairs, beds were lifted in the air. It had lain empty for years, an auctioneer's nightmare, until Michael came along – an auctioneer's dream. He was delighted with his bargain.

Pat's aunt was appalled when she heard the news. 'Michael John,' she said, 'What in the name of God did you buy that house for?'

'What's wrong?' he replied. 'Isn't it a great bargain at eighty quid?'

'Didn't the people lived there before you have to leave because of all the noises and disturbances in the place?'

'I'm not worried about that,' he said. 'They'll do me no harm!'

'Do you hear anything at night?'

'Of course I do,' he replied, 'but so long as they're not bothering me, I don't give a damn.'

Some years later, when electricity came, he bragged to Pat's aunt that the ghost switched the light on for him when he returned home. She thought this was a very funny joke until one night he told her to come and see for herself. Sure enough, when they came within about a half mile of the house the lights came on. 'They must like me,' he said. 'They have nothing against me, anyway!'

At abandoned seats of old estates, ghostly riders, thought to be previous owners, continued travelling paths well known to them. No obstacle erected by mortals could stand in their way. Tommy Gillen was one of many who saw such a horseman, dressed in the old-fashioned style, gallop through a gateway at Derryloughan, County Leitrim. The old people said it was McVitie, a Scottish settler who once owned property there. Those who witnessed the spectacle heard no sound as he rushed headlong past them and continued on his mysterious journey into the darkness.

Passers-by recognised Young, once a landowner in Ardtrasna, County Sligo, and long dead, ride his horse through a gateway there at dead of night. The gate could never be shut. When it was closed in the evening, it was always found open again in the morning. Intolerant in death as in life, no mortal was allowed to hinder his midnight ride.[82]

In a neighbouring townland, riders were often seen emerging, on moonlit nights, from the ancient ruins of O'Harte's castle in Ballinfull. They could be heard 'goin' up Lissadell hill and round by the parson's.' Kathleen Leydon recalled her father telling her of a 'lovely bright starry night' when he went hunting rabbits down at O'Harte's. Finding nothing, they went over by the parson's and 'up the hill by Leydons', where a Protestant man by the name of Hall used to live.

Here they were amazed to hear the sound of galloping horses and the baying of dogs coming towards them across the valley. They had a clear view across the fields but could see nothing. Frightened out of their wits now, they took to their heels as fast as they could. The sound of a hunt in full flight followed their path through Lissadell and continued until they reached home. Later, when they told their story, no one was surprised. They were not the first to have experienced the midnight riders of O'Harte's castle.

Not so far away there is a spring known as 'Davy's Well' on the Gore-Booth estate. The road running near there is said to be haunted by the figure of a man on horseback. It is thought to be the shadow of a bailiff called Davy, much disliked by all around when he was alive. Once, when setting out with horse and hounds, his stable boy warned him that the animal he had chosen was a treacherous one. With characteristic arrogance, he replied that there was neither man nor horse that he couldn't handle and that he 'would ride him to hell' if he chose.

Shortly afterwards, going past the well, the horse bolted, throwing Davy and breaking his neck. Ever since, it has been called 'Davy's Well', we are told. Night after night, the reckless rider is doomed to spend eternity there, riding his horse to hell and back. There are many who will avoid passing there after dark for fear of what might befall them.

The air of Ireland was full of such people because of our wicked history, McIlhenny claimed in Seamus Deane's book *Reading in the Dark*: Lord Leitrim of Ramelton, who was shot dead because of his policy of harassment and evictions, continued to travel the road on which he was shot every night. The horse rider, silhouetted against the night sky, made no noise: 'It galloped along until it neared the spot in the hedge, and then, for a second or two, you could hear its hoofbeats drumming. As you heard these, the figure on the horse vanished for an instant; then when you looked up the road, there it was again, gliding away into the darkness in absolute silence.' Lord Leitrim and his kind, McIlhinney believed, would be like that until the day of judgement: never alive, never dead, just shadows in the air.

In 1836 an enterprising Mullaghmore man, Hugh Gilmartin, rented out accommodation and 'warm baths' to tourists on the seafront. Viscount Palmerston, the local landlord, appropriated the operation, expanded it and set up 'lodges' numbered one to eleven all along his newly built harbour. They became a mecca for the landed gentry of Sligo and the surrounding counties, who arrived there with their retinues of servants and horse-drawn carriages for the summer season.

Man's conceits are nothing more than a drop in an ever-changing ocean. Waning fortunes resulting from the political turmoil of a new century eroded lifestyles. Palmerston's lodges reverted to private ownership. All was changed and changed utterly: several buildings fell into the hands of the once-hunted priests and nuns. Lodge No. 2 became the presbytery of the Catholic curate. Buildings eight through eleven were acquired by the Sisters of Mercy, who established a convent and chapel there. Is it any wonder that the spirits of former occupants rested uneasily in such places where they once held sway?

The old fishermen, on the way to their boats, often observed a man dressed in a black topcoat and hard hat pacing on the front lawn of the convent in the pre-dawn dark. James McCannon felt there was something unearthly about his deportment. It unsettled him. The apparition never spoke. He bore an uncanny resemblance to one of the Wynnes of Hazelwood, a summer resident who had died long before. Others heard voices calling in upstairs rooms in the convent. A search revealed nothing. A young girl was seen, by nuns and workers alike, walking in the corridors. Some nuns feared to be left alone because of what they had experienced. The apparition was rumoured to be that of a servant girl made pregnant by her employer and 'smothered between two mattresses' to avoid a scandal in Lord Ashley's time.

Successive priests were bothered by strange noises in No. 2 Lodge, now the presbytery. Visiting relatives who stayed overnight were kept awake by footsteps pacing in the hallway for hours on end – but there was no one there! Father Doyle was reluctant to speak of his experiences when anyone enquired of him if the place was haunted. He would only admit that he was 'very much aware of a presence in the place'.

Strange powers were attributed to priests. Up to the 1950s they were regarded with awe and fear – and with very good reason. They ruled with an iron hand. Whether they were right or wrong, it was a brave man – or a foolhardy one – who crossed a man of the cloth. It may seem strange now, but many were convinced that clerics had the power to put horns on them, or worse, if they chose.

Father Devine was one of these strict disciplinarians whose very name instilled fear in others. He is best remembered for confronting John 'Taylor' Leonard on the hill road for his failure to attend Mass. John was on his way to the bog at the time in his ass and cart and was impatient with the delay. Locals recalled that, during an angry exchange, the priest struck John across the face with his whip, 'breaking the pipe in his mouth'. John was a rough man but a hard worker and a good neighbour too. The priest's action was resented, but fear and discretion dictated a sullen acquiescence. It was commonly held that 'If ye'd rise yer hand to a priest, ye'd lose the power of yer hand.' Men could be pointed out whose hands had withered away after raising them to threaten or strike a priest.

When death called, as it did at every house sooner or later, irrespective of disputes or disagreements, the priest was summoned to ease the soul's passage to the next world. Father Devine's strange power manifested itself on one such sick-call.

Max Boyce was a young boy when he was sent to the presbytery to bring the priest to his uncle, who was dying. It was a dark, windy night.

'How am I going to get up to the hill road without a light?' the priest demanded.

'I dunno,' Max replied. He had brought no light. The priest went into the house, lit a candle and handed it to Max, instructing him to lead the way.

Despite the wind, the candle remained lit on the journey to the sickhouse. The priest anointed the dying man and the pair returned along dark roads, their way lit by the candle. When they got to the presbytery, the priest handed the light to Max, saying it would show him the way home. When the door shut behind the priest, the candle went out and the young boy made his way home in the dark.

Surrounded by his family and friends, John Browne lay dying in the village of Durley in 1654. He was roused from his death coma when the lid of a large iron chest at the foot of the bed containing family papers unlocked itself and lifted of its own accord. With a tremendous effort, the dying man pulled himself into an upright position. Addressing the open trunk, he said, 'You say true, you say true, you say right. I'll be with you by and by.' Collapsing back onto the bed, he breathed his last as the lid of the chest closed and the locks snapped shut. No satisfactory explanation has ever been put forward for this manifestation of the supernatural observed by a roomful of credible witnesses.

A similar story lingers of a ghostly chest in the old abandoned post office on a lonely stretch of coast road overlooking the sea at Mullaghmore. A clever businessman had planned to acquire an old steamer trunk that had lain in an upstairs bedroom for generations. A dingy light glimmered through the cobwebbed window as he crept up the rickety staircase to claim his prize. Removing the contents – moth-eaten dresses from Victorian times, letters, old newspapers, assorted memorabilia and junk – he placed the empty trunk inside the front door for later collection.

Returning the next day to claim his prize, he was flabbergasted to discover that the chest had in some mysterious way returned to its place in the upstairs room. A tremulous check revealed that the clothes and other items which he had removed the day before were now restored to the trunk – and in their original order, known only to him! No one else could have entered the house, as he held the only key. A dread feeling welled within his chest; beads of perspiration stood out on his brow as he fled downstairs and out of the building. Did poltergeists now inhabit this lonely place? Was it the postmasters' old aunts, long dead, who, resenting the interference with their possessions, once treasured, had returned to reclaim their belongings? No! This story had a more earthly explanation when a local joker later demonstrated, to everyone's amusement, how he had gained access to the building and contrived to play a trick on the susceptible would-be trunk-owner.

Yes, indeed, it is true that some stories can be explained away by natural means. Do not, however, make the mistake of supposing they are all old wives' tales, mischievous concoctions or a product of fevered imaginations. Tomorrow's experience may make a believer of the most hardened sceptic. The spirit world runs in a parallel dimension to our own. It requires very little to cross over. Nor can we take comfort from the thought that these ghostly happenings are a thing of the past, that they couldn't occur today. On occasion, historical knowledge precedes tradition. Quite often, the reverse is the case and substance is given to unbelievable stories by subsequent archaeological investigations.

People listened incredulously when workers at the old courthouse in Sligo town told of hearing a buzz of noise and voices in the court at dead of night. Surprised that the court would sit at such a strange hour, they investigated and, on entering the room, were puzzled to find it empty and in complete darkness. Disturbed by the experience, they recalled an oppressive atmosphere and 'a cold clammy feeling' in the air. On numerous occasions, an ethereal, headless figure was seen travelling, not, as is usual, at night, but often in broad daylight from a point near the stairway along the corridor to a window where a 'hanging judge' once looked out on executions ordered by him in the courtyard below.

Images conjured by overwork or lack of sleep were blamed by scoffers who had not witnessed the apparition – until excavations carried out by Eoin Halpin of Archaeological Services, reported in the *Irish Times* of 20 May 2000, uncovered skeletons beneath the floor. One was found at the very spot where the ghost habitually commenced his restless wandering. The skeleton, like the uneasy phantom, was headless! Was this, then, the unsettled spirit of some tormented creature whose screams of innocence were choked off forever when his neck snapped at the end of the hanging judge's rope?

In recent times, visitors to a small village in the Gweedore area of County Donegal wondered at the unusual sight of a new bungalow there boarded up and abandoned. Neighbours were tight-lipped and reluctant to tell strangers what they knew of repeated attempts by families to live there, of how they were driven out each time by unexplained noises and violent disturbances, and of how the house lay vacant until an exorcism performed by the bishop brought an uneasy peace, which still holds. The disturbances were attributed to the house having been sited on an old fairy fort or graveyard. The name of the family or the village cannot be mentioned here in order to protect their privacy.

The *Irish Independent* recently reported the case of a family living in Corrib Park, Galway, who were forced to leave their home as a result of 'unexplained incidents'. A special Mass said in the house by the local priest proved ineffective. The paper stated that Jackie Fahy and his family were forced to vacate their home following a series of incidents ranging from 'furniture upturning and crashing to the floor, a child crying upstairs when there was nobody there, footsteps, lights and music going on automatically.' The incidents eventually abated, allowing peace to return again to the Fahy household.

According to a recent report in the *Irish Times*, the Catholic Church is introducing new rites for expelling demons. An exorcism is a ceremony of prayers in which a priest, with the approval of a bishop, casts out an evil spirit, calling on it aloud to leave a person or place. Speaking from Rome, Cardinal Jorge Arturo Estavez in a statement confirmed the modernisation, affirming in the *Irish Times* on 27 January 1999 'that demons are fallen angels as a result of their sin, and that they are spiritual beings with great intelligence and power.'

Father Malachi Brendan Martin, author and priest, stated in the *Irish Times* on 7 August 1999 that 'Exorcism can be extremely violent. I have seen objects hurled around rooms by the powers of evil. I have smelt the breath of Satan and heard the demons' voices – cold, scratchy, dead voices carrying messages of hatred.'

12

DOBHARCHÚ: HOUND OF THE DEEP

Do fearsome creatures inhabit the deep waters of our lakes and seas? Sightings of a water monster swimming in Loch Ness in north central Scotland were recorded as far back as the fifteenth century. Investigators today display photographic evidence to prove the claim while others maintain the pictures are fake. Sonar probes of the lake have proven inconclusive. Controversy raging around the claim generates a tourism windfall of £5 million a year for the Scottish treasury from hopefuls, binoculars and cameras in hand, wishful for a sighting.

In the great mysterious depths of the ocean, right now, creatures with eyes the size of dinner plates patiently await their next meal in the Stygian black, unseen by human eyes. They fear no creature. The flesh on their vast bullet-shaped bodies spasmodically changes colour, flushing in multicoloured pulses. Framing their beaklike jaws are eight muscular tentacles as thick as tree trunks; they are lined with powerful suckers ready to lash out and seize a victim. Here, the sun's light never penetrates and the water above presses down with a mass of several metric tons.

Seamen's stories that tell of such voracious monsters rising from the abyss to pluck humans from the decks are numerous. Ancient woodcuts show these giant squids, huge pulpy creatures with ten radiating arms, rising from the water to grasp a luckless ship, a screaming human held aloft by a curling tentacle. They are no figment of the imagination. The largest such creature on record, *Architeuthis Longimanus*, measuring fifty-seven feet in length, was disgorged from the deep and washed ashore in the Cook Strait in New Zealand in 1887. The largest specimen recorded in these islands measured an impressive twenty-five feet.

The stories are not just old wives' tales of long ago. A report in the *Irish Times* of 30 August 2000 related that workers filleting fish for market found a human head inside a 5.2-foot codfish in Queensland, Australia. Following the discovery, a search for a lost trawler fisherman, who had gone missing from his boat in unexplained circumstances, was called off. 'On preparing the fish, they observed the remains inside and contacted police,' Detective Sergeant David Miles told reporters.

Did water monsters large enough to threaten life exist at one time in Glenade Lake, County Leitrim? Do they still reside in its depths? The story of a horrific encounter that happened along the shores of the lake many years ago still puzzles and fascinates. Inspiring discussion and speculation, the question as to what really happened then or what secrets may still lie hidden under the placid waters of this Leitrim lake has never been fully answered. The story tells of a fierce struggle to the death between the McLoughlin brothers of Glenade and 'that fierce brute the whistling *Dobharchú*':

> *The rocks and dells rang with its yells, the eagles*
> *   screamed in dread;*
> *The ploughman left his horses alone, the fishes too*
> *   'tis said,*
> *Away from the mountain streams though far, went*
> *   rushing to the sea.*
> *Nature's laws did almost pause for death or victory.*

Sea and lake monsters have always inspired fear. One of the earliest and best known accounts, written between AD 700 and 1000, is the Anglo-Saxon tale of the Norse hero Beowulf's struggle with the lake monster Grendel. Seamus Heaney has recently published a modern translation of the epic.

Beowulf was a warrior and nephew of Hygelac, king of what is now southern Sweden. He was sent to the neighbouring kingdom of Denmark, where a blood-crazed monster was terrorising the countryside, butchering and gorging itself on King Hrothgar's subjects. The bodies he couldn't eat he kept in a pouch which he carried with him. Beowulf vanquished the brute, tearing off his arm and shoulder in the process. Victory celebrations were cut short when Grendel's equally monstrous mother arrived to wreak vengeance. It killed a royal counsellor and dragged his body, as well as the hewn-off limb of her son, to her underwater lair. Beowulf, a strong swimmer, pursued the creature, cut the head from the body and returned to Hrothgar's court in triumph.

There are many records of human encounters with beings of the deep, some benevolent, some evil. In the Rosses of Donegal, the *Dobharchú* killed and ate Sheila, the sister of Sean O'Donnell, at a place called Ros na mBallán. When Sean went there to meet her, all he found was a bag of bones. Vowing to kill the beast, he laid a trap by arranging a pile of stones and placing Sheila's red cloak on top. He waited in hiding nearby. The *Dobharchú* came in from the sea at nightfall and, seeing the cloak, made for it. Sean Ruadh, as he was known, waited until the brute was almost above him, took aim and killed the animal.

John Baxter's late-sixteenth-century map records the sighting by the armies of Clan O'Donnell of 'two water-horses of a huge bigness' near their encampment on the shores of Glencar Lake, County Sligo.

A creature resembling a 'big black boar' inhabited the depths of Urlaur Lake in the parish of Kilmovee in County Sligo. The prior in the nearby Dominican Abbey sprinkled it with holy water in the belief that it was the devil. When the monster retaliated by spitting out a litter of *banbhs* at them, they realised that this was a formidable beast and sent for the bishop. The bishop attempted to banish the fiend, which was now joined by a companion. The creature informed the cleric, to his astonishment, that he had once been his pet hound, fed on meat he refused to the poor people, 'who were weak with hunger'. The two unrepentant demons then set up a hideous screeching and kept at it until the friars went stone deaf.

The holy men were on the point of leaving the monastery for good when it was revealed to them in a dream that Donagh O' Grady, a piper from Tavraun, could help them. When, after a long search, they eventually found their saviour drunk in a shebeen, they must have thought the dream more of a nightmare than a revelation. O'Grady, equally unimpressed with the importance of his holy visitors or their dilemma, flatly refused to go anywhere until he had had another few drinks.

In his own good time, he made his way to Lake Urlaur. Tuning the pipes, he took up position on the shore and commenced to play. The wild notes that floated out across the water attracted the two monsters closer and closer. When they came close to the enchanted piper, a bolt of lightning from a clear sky struck them dead, thus bringing to an end their persecution of the priests – and the haunting of Urlaur lake.

Not all creatures that came from the water were so fearsome, but people encountering them needed to be wary. Thirteen miles on the Sligo side of Dromore West, there is a lake called Loch an Chroi. From ancient times, it had the reputation of being spellbound.

A farmer who had a sizeable tract of mountain and bog in that area fell into bad luck. Cattle died on him; when he replaced them, they too expired. Spring came around and he didn't have even a horse to plough the land. One evening as he walked his property deep in thought, wondering how things could go so wrong, he noticed a black mare grazing along the lakeshore. Knowing she didn't belong to any local farmer, he decided to stable her until an owner came along.

As he fed and looked after her, he became extremely fond of the mare, as she had a very gentle nature. Time went on and, as no one showed up to make a claim, he worked her with plough and cart. Gradually his luck improved, his stock of cattle increased and each year the mare had a foal, for which he got a good price. He had good reason to be satisfied with his newly found fortune and traced it all to the lucky day when he had found the strange horse. During all the years she was with him he was kind to her, never having cause to strike her a blow.

One day when riding her to the lake, preoccupied with his thoughts and impatient to get on with the day's work, he struck her with the bridle. She screamed and leaped in the air. Instantly all the foals she had ever reared came around her. The mare with the man on her back, followed by all the foals, dashed headlong into the lake. Next day the farmer's heart was seen floating on the surface of the water. From then on it was named Loch an Chroi ('the Lake of the Heart').

Few are aware of a similar incident in Glenaniff, County Leitrim, that took the life of a young man of the *Padraig Ruadh* branch of the Meguinney or McGuinness family. This happened in 1700. Patrick Tohall of Knappaghmore, Sligo, researched the incident in 1944. According to his findings, young Padraig went out on an early spring morning to the plateau overlooking the lake to bring down his own mare for the day's work. He found her grazing on the shores of the little lake on the boundaries of Gortenachurry and Carrowrevagh and was surprised to see a shining black stallion accompanying her. The strange horse was a powerful-looking animal, so on an instant's impulse Padraig decided to take the black steed instead of the white. His work finished for the day, he left home in the evening to return the animal to where he had found him.

Next morning when Padraig still had not returned from the lake, his neighbours went out to look for him. Searching all over the countryside, they eventually found his body, 'all gory and mangled lying in the waters of the Lochaun, called from that day Loch Phadraig Rua' Tohall said. The black horse that 'shone like a crow' was never seen again. Was the mysterious animal the *Dobharchú* in a different guise, or was Padraig set upon by another monster of the lake on his way home? Vague tales are told of a water-horse which gives its name to Loch an Chapaill ('the Lake of the Horse') on the same ridge. The details of the incident are unclear to this day and there has never been a logical explanation for the murder of Padraig Ruadh Meguinney.

The legend of the *Dobharchú* stems from the bestial murder of Gráinne Ní Conalaí at Glenade Lake on 24 September 1722. The details were well known at one time and the ballad sung at fairs on the streets of Kinlough. Some say she went to the lake to wash clothes; the ballad tells she went to bathe. It is no matter. When she failed to return, her husband Traolach Mac Lochlainn went to look for her. He was aghast when he found her body lying by the lake with, according to eyewitnesses, the 'beast lying asleep on her mangled breast'!

This and the chase that ensued would have little credibility today if it were not for the tombstone marking the grave of Grace Connolly. Although worn smooth now with the passage of human feet, it can still be seen at the old cemetery of Conwell near Kinlough. A carving on the stone clearly shows a strange beast being stabbed by a dagger. Tohall claims a similar monument existed at one time not so far away, in Kilroosk cemetery. Broken and lost around 1922, it may have been the inspiration for the Conwell memorial or indeed evidence of yet another monster!

According to Patrick Doherty of Glenade, local lore records that the chase, which started at Frank McSharry's, faltered at Caiseal Bán stone fort when Mac Lochlainn was forced to stop with the blacksmith there to replace a lost horseshoe. When the enraged monster caught up with them, the horses were hurriedly drawn across the entrance to form a barrier. Giving the terrified man a sword, the blacksmith advised him that 'When the creature charges the horse, he'll put his head right out through him. As soon as he does this, you be quick and cut his head off.'

Patrick insists the story's credibility is proven by the carved image of a hand and arm holding a sword engraved on Grace Conolly's tombstone. Cashelgarron stone fort, near where the chase ended and the *Dobharchú* met its gory end, still stands today, nestled on a height under the sheltering prow of bare Benbulben's head. Both monster and horse are said to lie buried nearby.

The words of the following poem reinforce Patrick's assertions. They form part of the legend surrounding an event which excites discussion and controversy to the present day. The words of the ballad, skilfully put together by a hedge schoolmaster of the time, brings the story vividly to life. The scribe's name is lost to us, as are the circumstances of his existence, but his voice speaks eloquently across the centuries, as clearly as if the words were penned yesterday. They are an articulate and enduring tribute to the event and to his genius:

By Glenade Lake tradition tells, two hundred years
    ago
A thrilling scene enacted was, to which, as years
    unflow,
Old men and women still relate, and while relating
    dread
Some demon of its kind may yet be found within its
    bed.

It happened one McGloughlan lived close by the
    neighbouring shore,
A lovely spot, where fairies oft in rivalry wandered
    o'er,
A beauteous dell where prince and chief oft met in
    revelry
With Frenchmen bold and warriors old to hunt the wild
    boar, free.

He and his wife, Grace Connolly, lived there unknown
    to fame,
There, years in peace, until one day from out the lakes
    there came
What brought a change in all their home and prospects
    too.
The water fiend, the enchanted being, the dreaded
    Dobharchú.

It was on a bright September morn, the sun scarce
    mountain-high,
No chill or damp was in the air, all nature seemed to
    vie

As if to render homage proud the cloudless sky above,
A day for mortals to discourse in luxury and love.

And whilst this gorgeous way of life in beauty did
abound,
From out the vastness of the lake stole forth the water
hound,
And seized for victim her who shared McGloughlan's
bed and board;
His loving wife, his more than life, whom almost he
adored.

She, having gone to bathe, it seems, within the water
clear,
And not having returned when she might, her husband,
fraught with fear,
Hasting to where he her might find, when oh, to his
surprise,
Her mangled form, still bleeding warm, lay stretched
before his eyes.

Upon her bosom, snow-white once, but now besmeared
with gore,
The Dobharchú reposing was, his surfeiting being
o'er.
Her bowels and entrails all around tinged with a
reddish hue:
'Oh God,' he cried, ''tis hard to bear but what am I
to do?"

He prayed for strength; the fiend lay still, he tottered
    like a child,
The blood of life within his veins surged rapidly and
    wild.
One long-lost glance at her he loved, then fast his
    footsteps turned
To home, while all his pent-up rage and passion
    fiercely burned.

He reached his house, he grasped his gun, which
    clenched with nerves of steel,
He backwards sped, upraising his arm and then one
    piercing, dying, squeal
Was heard upon the balmy air. But hark! What's that
    that came
One moment next from out of its depth as if revenge
    to claim!

The comrade of the dying fiend with whistles long and
    loud
Came nigh and nigher to the spot. McGloughlin,
    growing cowed
Rushed to his home. His neighbours called, their
    counsel asked, and flight
Was what they bade him do at once, and not to wait
    till night.

He and his brother, a sturdy pair, as brothers true
    when tried,
Their horses took, their homes forsook and westward
    fast did ride.

One dagger sharp and long each man had for protection
too
Fast pursued by that fierce brute, the whistling
Dobharchú.

The rocks and dells rang with its yells, the eagles
screamed in dread.
The ploughman left his horses alone, the fishes too, 'tis
said,
Away from the mountain streams, though far, went
rushing to the sea;
And nature's laws did almost pause, for death or
victory.

For twenty miles the gallant steeds the riders proudly
bore
With mighty strain o'er hill and dale that ne'er was
seen before.
The fiend, fast closing on their tracks, his dreaded cry
more shrill;
'Twas 'Brothers try, we'll do or die on Cashelgarron
Hill.'

Dismounting from their panting steeds they placed
them one by one
Across the path in lengthways formed within the
ancient dún,
And standing by the outermost horse awaiting for their
foe
Their daggers raised, their nerves they braced to strike
that fatal blow.

Not long to wait, for nose on trail the scenting hound
  arrived
And through the horses with a plunge to force himself
  he tried,
And just as through the outermost horse he plunged his
  head and foremost part,
McGloughlan's dagger to the hilt lay buried in his
  heart.

'Thank God, thank God,' the brothers cried in wildness
  and delight,
Our humble home by Glenade lake shall shelter us
  tonight.
Be any doubt to what I write, go visit old Conwell,
There see the grave where sleeps the brave whose
  epitaph can tell.

13

CHANGING TIMES

Mickey McGroarty, Maggie McGowan and their kind shared a rich lore with an admiring audience, but there are few now who will bide and listen. Will a future generation regret squandering the opportunity to experience an evening with the last of the *filí*?

For centuries, the old ways and the old world endured. It was embedded in the storytellers' souls. More than spectators, they were what they believed, they lived what they told. But their practices and customs collided with a rapidly evolving world. In a clash of traditions, they have lost. Or so it seems. Time will prove that the greater loss is ours. In a conflict as profound in its effect as when the Milesians drove the Tuatha dé Danann to their underground places, so too the new technology defeated the gentler ways. Mass communication and instant entertainment have obliterated customs and beliefs long held. They have vanished like snow, today glistening white, tomorrow silently and swiftly gone.

Robin Flower listened to and recorded the tales of the Blasket islanders in *The Western Isle:* 'It is only by a glint of colour here, a salient thread there, in the dulled material,' he wrote, 'that we who strive to reconstitute something of the intricate harmony wrought into the original fabric can imagine to ourselves the bright hues and gay lines of the forgotten past. The world has turned to another way of life, and no passion of regret can revive a dying memory.'

Mickey McGroarty, Maggie McGowan, Bernie Kelly: they and their stories and accounts will soon be history. The 'intricate harmony' is no more and the world a poorer place for its going! Understanding our origins through the fading fireside voices traces a path for us from an unbelieving age back through centuries to parents, grandparents and forebears whose survival was not allied to machines but reverence for nature and its eternal mysteries.

The twenty-first century demands to be heard. Its volume is deafening, its energy derived from an explosion of once-unimaginable scientific achievement: technological and engineering miracles of which previous generations could not even have dreamed. There is much to amaze and much to alarm. We have harnessed the fire, overpowered the wheel, turned it faster and faster. Will it hurl us into oblivion?

Our fear is not now of martyred saints but of corporate barons. We don't look for signs in the heavens; we don't kneel before a bloody heart. The Mecca is not Mount Tabor, Croagh Patrick or Lough Derg. It is the stock exchange, Brussels, the European Union. Slick promotion weaves a spell. Our beliefs, like our food, are produced and packaged. Swimming in a tidal wave of prosperity, we no longer look out on farms and fields, but on sites. Not saints but superheroes, industrial giants, answer prayers. Instead of pilgrimages to holy wells and sacred groves, we board the plane to Disneyworld, stand in long lines, ushered by talking ducks, to ride hurtling spaceships. Our rituals are high-voltage. We celebrate in discos under strobe lights, not starlight. Ecstasy derives from tablets. Miracles change but the demons remain!

The soft, welcoming light of candle or paraffin lamp was not efficient but it had its advantages. It forced a stop to work, gathering individuals around a single flickering source. Day and night could not be merged. Unlimited power leads to unlimited production – excess rather than sufficiency. At the point when comfort is assured because conveniences abound, we buy more and more, multiplying devices and gadgets beyond appreciation. Are they easing life or cluttering it? Is it an example of getting our wish and being devoured by it? Achieving the dream only to find it's not what we want at all – the unattainable always the objective?

We are organic beings, totally dependent on the earth, an integral part of it. Maggie McGowan ate simply but she knew every crumb that went into her mouth. She was on intimate terms with beast and plant. Exhibiting many of the unpleasant aspects of an affluent society, we must recognise the darker side of what we have become. Multiplying faster than the seeds of creation are the spoils of science: radioactive discharges poisoning life in water and on land, chemical weapons and phosphorous bombs leaking poisons on the ocean floor, holes in the ozone layer. Mad cows or mad scientists? Genetic foods, mangled genes, ingested pesticides, insecticides, defoliants, chemical growth-promoters, hormones, steroids: what are the dangers? They are many; we trust and we eat – by that we live, and by that we die.

Have we progressed, or does the progression that eases the body's burden rob the soul of its natural inheritance – earth, sky, fire and water? Are the flabby, pressure-driven, mortgage-burdened office workers on their exercise bikes, or the arm-swinging striders, recently released from pitchfork, turf-spade and washtub, really free, or victims of the illusory aspirations of a consumer society? Are we in danger of becoming the new aristocracy, as superficial and aimless as the last?

Wresting a living from the land breaks the back and strains

the will, but provides contact with the raw elements, the untamed forces that arrest and enthral the spirit. The essential riches providence bestows: air, water, trees, sunlight. They are the wellspring. Denied their teeming current, does the soul diminish? Are we sprung from a radiant inferno that, harnessed, loses its energy? Depression, fatigue, cynicism: infections of the spirit that sap the body. They are the ills of the present century. The city dweller aspires to the country idyll, builds his holiday home there and immediately fills it with noise, light and frenzy. Charged with artificial sound and substance, we lose sight of the stars! Where lies the balance, the harmony?

It is the plea of the soul.

GLOSSARY

Amadaun *(amadán)* a fool
Art (of wind)   direction
Back-band   length of chain stretched between shafts of cart
      which rested on the straddle, thereby transferring
      the weight onto the horse's back
Banbh   piglet
Beetle   pounder, masher
Besom   a tool for cleaning and sweeping made of heather
Borneoc   limpet
Brocket   a thick, reddish-brown network on the skin caused
      by overexposure to heat
Bruiteen   mashed-potato dish
Camaun *(camán)*   hurling stick
Carageen *(carraigín)* an edible seaweed
Ceilidhing   rambling, visiting the neighbours
Claddagh   stony beach
Clamp   small stack of turf, last stage in harvesting on turf
      bank before removal to road
Clocking (as in 'clocking' hen)
      broody
Coals   glowing turf embers
Couples   horizontal roof beams
Crannac   an edible seaweed
Crivening   rows of turf built around perimeter of cart-crib
Cutting   bad weather, particularly after frost
Druith   thirst
Dunkle   dunghill, usually at rear of cow byre
Elder: cow's udder   The words 'udder' and 'elder' are not related.
      'Elder' is derived from the Middle Dutch for 'a
      teate, maame or dugge'.
Famluc   bladderwrack
Farl   a cake of home-baked bread
Free   the outside vertical layer of a stack of turf
Glar *(glár)*   glue-like mud.
Griosach *(gríosach)*   hot ashes
Hams   part of ass or horse harness, secured to the collar,
      to which the draught chains were attached
Hate (as in 'not a hate wrong with me')
      a thing ('nothing wrong with me')
Keeper   scollop used to keep thatch and wire in place

Kitchen	meats or fish eaten with potatoes
Lok	a small amount
Overboard (as in 'to put overboard')	
	to prepare a corpse for waking
Pardog (*pardóg*)	a creel or pannier, particularly one with a hinged bottom
Pattern (as at holy wells)	
	festival day
Péacán	peak, crowstone – three-cornered stone at top of stone-built house
Pistroges (*piseoge*)	superstitions
Poheen	small potato
Ponger	flat-bottomed tin container made by tinkers (holds between a pint to a quart)
Pratie (*prátaí*)	potatoes
Rake (as in 'raking the fire')	
	to cover hot coals with ashes and surround with turf, thus preserving the fire overnight
Rowlt	colloquialism meaning 'rolled' (viciously)
Seanchaí	storyteller
Seisg	water-reed
Sí sidhe	fairies
Sink or 'group'	channel or drain in byre for cow faeces and urine
Slabhac	an edible seaweed
Scollop	twisted length of sally or hazel pointed at both ends (derived from Gaelic: reached Ireland with the Celts)
Scraw	sod of earth
Smur (*smúr*)	a light, misty rain – lighter than drizzle
Souple	part of flail used for removing grain
Traw-hook	rope-twister made from sally bush
Trawneen (*traithnín*)	
	dried grass stem, withered stalk of meadow grass
Treilya	division of land
Weans	wee ones, children

NOTES

1 W. G. Woodmartin, *Traces of the Elder Faiths*, Vol. 1, p 305
2 P. W. Joyce, *A Social History of Ancient Ireland*, Vol. II, p 511
3 Frazer CCCXXXII, p 234
4 Raftery, *Pagan Celtic Ireland*, p 199
5 'Archaeology Ireland', Vol. 7, No. 3, p 22
6 Ibid, Vol. 9, No. 4, p 13
7 Dr Healy, *Life and Writings of St Patrick*, p 72
8 Known as 'Ould Halloweve' because of the displacement of dates caused by the reform of the old Julian calendar to the Gregorian. Among the changes ordained by Pope Gregory XIII in 1582 was that ten days be dropped.
9 Sean Ó Suilleabhain, *Studies in Folklore*; edited by W. E. Richmond
10 W. B. Yeats, *The Celtic Twilight*, p 112; foreword by Kathleen Raine
11 Ó Suilleabhain, op. cit.
12 Jeanne Cooper Foster, *Ulster Folklore*
13 Kevin Danaher, *The Year in Ireland*, p 188
14 In 1808, at the age of twenty-two, Seathl became the chief of the Squamish American–Indian tribe. The chief's testament was an address given to the tribe when the white man was annexing Indian lands – mainly by exterminating the Red Man. It was a dilemma similar to that faced by the Irish chieftains in Tudor times when by a process of 'surrender and regrant' they were forced to give up their lands to the crown. The testament begins:

The Great Chief sends word
That he wishes to buy our land.
The Great Chief also sends words of friendship and goodwill.
That is kind of him since we know he has little need
of our friendship in return. But we will consider your offer.
For we know that if we do not sell,
The white man will come and take our land.
How can you buy or sell the sky,
The warmth of the land?
The idea is strange to us.
If we do not own
The freshness of the air
And the sparkle of the water,
How can you buy them?

15 'Garden' in this context is a colloquialism which means a walled-in area near the farmhouse and buildings where the hayricks were built and grain crops stacked. No vegetables were grown. Spearmint, comfrey and garlic often found growing wild there may have been survivors of earlier herb gardens.
16 E. Estyn Evans, *Irish Folk Ways*, p 162
17 Jeanne Cooper Foster, *Ulster Folklore*
18 Danaher, op. cit. p 194; from 'The Banks of the Boro', Patrick Kennedy, p 110-12
19 James Frazer, *The Illustrated Golden Bough*, edited by Mary Douglas

20 Ibid
21 The *Corran Herald,* issue No. 32, p 8
22 P. W. Joyce, *Joyce's History of Ancient Ireland,* Vol. 1, p 454
23 Old Irish law tracts mainly composed in the seventh and eighth centuries AD. Brehon Law was abolished at the beginning of the seventeenth century and replaced by English law.
24 Bernie Kelly, personal communication with
25 Martin Martin, *The Western Isles* (1703)
26 Evans, op. cit. p 122; C. Coote, *Cavan* (1802), p 251
27 Majella Flynn, *Harvest: A History of Grain Growing, Harvesting and Milling in Ireland,* p 81
28 See Joe McGowan, *In the Shadow of Benbulben,* ch. 8
29 Unpublished correspondence in Broadlands Archives at Hartley Library, University of Southampton
30 St Fechin's feast day is 29 January. He is best known for a church and mill he established at Fore in County Meath, the remains of which can still be seen near a well named after him. According to Cambrensus, women were not allowed to enter either the mill or the church. One of Hugh de Lacy's archers dragged a woman into the mill and 'lustfully violated her there. He was stricken in his member with hell-fire and immediately began to burn throughout his whole body. He died the same night.'
31 Wm Pollexfen's wife, Yeats's maternal grandmother, was a Middleton. It was from the Middletons that Yeats got his interest in the supernatural: 'and certainly the first faerie stories I heard were in the cottages about their houses.'
32 Canon John O'Rourke, *The Great Irish Famine,* ch. 1, and Alexander Somerville, *Letters from Ireland during the Famine,* p 62. The batatas, or sweet potato, was a delicacy in Ireland some time before the introduction of the *solanum tuberosum,* or common potato, which we know today.
33 Alexander Somerville, *Letters from Ireland during the Famine of 1847,* edited by D. K. M. Snell.
34 P. W. Joyce, *A Social History of Ancient Ireland,* Vol. 2, p 142. The Brehon Laws refer to a 'cake of man-baking' as twice the size of a 'woman-baking'. Three cakes of man-baking are the equivalent of six cakes of woman-baking. The women's cake was two fists or ten inches in width and one fist or five inches thick.
35 James T. Mackey, *An Introduction to Celtic Christianity,* p. 3
36 Hera was the patron deity of Samos, an island in the Aegean Sea. She married Zeus, the chief of the Olympian gods, and they honeymooned on Samos. The Greek religion explained the band of incandescent light across the night sky as the milk of Hera, squirted from her breast across the heavens. This was perhaps recognition that the sky nurtures the earth. The band of light is still known as the Milky Way.
37 Aurora borealis: pulsing, rapidly shifting multicoloured sheets and columns of light caused when the solar wind is invaded by an influx of high-energy atomic particles which peaks during periods of intense sunspot activity.
39 The Irish Met Service was established in 1936. It took on responsibility for weather forecasts broadcast by Radio Éireann in 1948, which had previously been provided from London. By 1961 the Met Service was providing weather information for RTÉ.
40 Many still consider a wedding gift of a statue of the Child of Prague

as particularly auspicious. The practice of putting it out in the hedge or burying it in the garden as a solicitation for good weather is, even in this age of unbelief, widespread in areas as far apart as Cork and Dublin, as well as Leitrim. Some believe that 'it'll not bring you right luck till the head falls off it,' but the decapitation must happen by accident. Devotion to the child began in 1556 when Maria Manriquez de Lara brought the image, a family heirloom, to Czechoslovakia from Spain on her marriage to Vrasitlav of Pernstyn. It is now housed in the church of Our Lady of Victory in Prague and is an object of veneration in many other countries besides Ireland.

Devotion to the Sacred Heart can be traced back to St John Eudes and St Margaret Mary Alacoque. It received a new impetus following the French Revolution and became popular during the Restoration period in that country. The devotion was introduced to Ireland by Dr Moylan, Bishop of Cork from 1787 to 1815. These were Penal times, so the rapid spread of this practice caused great alarm to the British authorities – and commisioners of education. Fearing a Jesuit plot, they 'inquired long and searchingly' into its origins and popularity.

41 The September and October moons appear larger than usual. They are the brightest of the year and used to be known as the harvest, stubble or hunter's moon. It was the custom long ago for farmers to take advantage of the bright moonlit evenings to finish their crops.

42 Evidence for the use of moss as a toilet accessory is found as far back as Roman Britain, and it is known to have been used as a lining for babies' nappies by some American Indian tribes. A Gaelic chronicle of 1014 relates that the wounded in the Battle of Clontarf 'stuffed their wounds with moss'. Due to its great absorbency and antiseptic properties, moss was manufactured into dressings at special 'sphagnum dressings sub-depots' and supplied to British hospitals during World War I.

According to a report published by the Central Statistics Office in February 2000, in 1946 nearly half of Ireland's 660,000 households had no sanitary facilities. The number of houses with flush toilets grew from just over 255,000 in 1946 to 970,000 in 1991.

Up to the 1960s, the only tissue available, for those who could afford it, was an uncomfortable sulphite paper. Toilet paper now holds a 70 percent share of the Irish paper market, estimated at €85 million. Volume sales, at 146 million rolls, are increasing at a rate of 10 percent per year. Luxury brand KittenSoft leads with sales of €13 million. Their latest, 'Cushioned Soft KittenSoft', 'incorporates the latest technology to trap air bubbles in ultrasoft tissue, creating a unique cushioned softness, complemented by new-look packaging which communicates the key brand messages of "soft", "strong" and "Irish". The product is in distribution now and is available in five colour variants – Soft White, Soft Green, Soft Pink, Soft Ivory and Soft Peach.'

Not quite as soft as a summer breeze, but if the 'Celtic Tiger' is roaring these days it's not because of any discomfort to its behind!

43 *Superstitions and Legends of Animals and Birds*, p 10; W. G. Woodmartin, *Traces of the Elder Faiths of Ireland*, Vol. II, p 127
44 Patrick Smyth, *Osier Culture and Basket-making*, p 66
45 Evans, op. cit., p 54
46 Mac Culloch, *The Religion of the Ancient Celts*, p 170
47 McNeill, *The Festival of Lughnasa*, p 21
48 Personal communication: John Harrison, Cliffoney, Book 4 J. H. 8
49 Danaher, op. cit., p 201

50 Ibid, p 207; from 'Lageniensis', *Irish Folklore* (1870), p 219
51 Oranges and other imported fruit were practically unknown then. To illustrate this, it is sufficient to quote from a report in the *Irish Independent* of 8 February 1946 on 'the latest shipment of Jaffa oranges into Dublin port'. Expressing a hope that the Minister's Order 'controlling the price of fruit would work out smoothly', the article stated 'fairly typical examples' of supply and price: 'Two cases of oranges costing 41/- in the market contained three dozen partially sound fruit; one case costing 16/- contained one sound orange. Two other cases purchased at 27/- were completely rotten.' (By comparison, 14 pounds of potatoes cost about 2/-.)
52 Danaher, op. cit., p 218
53 '*Irisleabhar na Gaeilge*', ii, p 370
54 Danaher, op. cit., p 216
55 Frazer, op. cit., p 221
56 A. J. Pollock, *Ulster Folklife*, p 224
57 Fergus Kelly, *Early Irish Farming*, p 300
58 Anthony Dent, *Donkey: The Story of the Ass from East to West*, p 55
59 Frazer, op. cit. Zoroastrianism, another great Eastern religion, also predated Christianity by at least several hundred years. Their God was Ahura Mazda, creator of heaven and earth, their devil Angro Mainyush. Their beliefs in heaven and hell, death and resurrection, the Last Judgement, a future saviour born of a virgin, and guardian angels, had a profound influence not alone on Christianity but on Judaism and Islam as well. Their founder, Zoroaster or Zarathustra (popularised by the German philosopher Nietzsche), took issue with perceived falsehoods in the Mithraic religion in much the same way as Luther did with Catholicism two millennia later.
60 Red Hugh O'Donnell (Aodh Ruadh O'Donnell) (1572–1602) reigned as lord of Tirconnell from his escape and successful return to Donegal in 1592. Prior to his imprisonment, he saw his first military action at the age of twelve. During the Nine Years War (1593–1603), he held Sligo Castle and exercised overlordship in north Connacht. When Spanish forces landed at Kinsale in 1601, he marched his army to Munster to join with them in the overthrow of English rule in Ireland. Following the Irish defeat at the Battle of Kinsale, he escaped and went to Spain to seek further help but was poisoned by British agents at Simancas. His death marked the demise of one of the last great chieftains of Gaelic Ireland.
61 Diarmuid Ó Muirithe, *The Wexford Carols*
62 Ó Muirithe, *A Seat Behind the Coachman*
63 In 1949 there were only 14,000 private phones in Ireland. In 1997 there were 1,427,000, excluding mobile phones. There were 23 calls made per capita in 1949; this figure had increased to 2,100 in 1996, excluding calls made from mobile phones. (from 'That Was Then, This Is Now', Central Statistics Office)
64 Mason, *Parochial Survey*, quoted in Danaher, *The Year in Ireland*
65 'Irish Independent', 5 April 1999
66 Extracted from *In Sligo Long Ago* by John McTernan, p 109
67 McGowan, *In the Shadow of Benbulben*, p 54
68 Danaher, *The Year in Ireland*, p258
69 Frazer, *The Illustrated Golden Bough*, p 193
70 *Bealoideas*, Vol. 23, 1965, p 113, Caoimhín Ó Danachair

71 See McGowan, op. cit., p 55. Local legend has it that the spirits of the banished return every year, in the form of barnacle geese, to their former homes and lands in Lissadell and the Seven Cartrons. These flocks were unknown there before the evictions.
72 Alan Gailey, *Irish Folk Drama*, p 60
73 Ibid, p 74
74 Ibid, p 257
75 Danaher, op. cit., p 246; 'Journals of the Kildare Archaeological Society', V, 452
76 McGowan, op. cit., p 79
77 The power of iron may be an ancestral memory of the overthrow of the Bronze Age people by the Iron Age Celts.
78 John J. Dunne, *Haunted Ireland*, p 64
79 Bob Curran in 'History Ireland', Vol. 8, No. 2
80 'Department of Irish Folklore', Vol. 8, p 53
81 Yeats, *Mythologies*, p106
82 M. Nicholson, personal communication
83 Ben O'Donnell, *The Story of the Rosses*, pp 18-22. Sean O'Donnell, or Seán Mac Mhanuis Óig Ó Donnell, as he was known, was married to a sister of Brian O'Rourke of Breffni. *The Annals of the Four Masters* record that he killed Manus O'Donnell, a cousin of Red Hugh O'Donnell's, in 1589.
84 Adapted from *Legends of Saints and Sinners* by Douglas Hyde, pp 127–35

BIBLIOGRAPHY

Bonner, Brian. *Our Inis Eoghan Heritage*. 1991.
Bulfin, William. *Rambles in Eirinn*. 1907.
Burke, Rev Willaim P. *Irish Priests in the Penal Times*. 1914.
Cahill, Thomas. *How the Irish Saved Civilisation*. 1995.
Carbery, Mary. *The Farm by Lough Gur*. 1937.
Craig, Patricia, ed. *The Oxford Book of Ireland*. 1998.
Danaher, Kevin. *The Pleasant Land of Ireland*. 1970.
———. *Irish Country People*. 1966.
———. *Folktales of the Irish Countryside*. 1967.
———. *In Ireland Long Ago*. 1964.
———. *The Year in Ireland*. 1972.
Deane, Seamus. *The Field Day Anthology of Irish Writing*. 1992.
———. *Reading in the Dark*. 1996.
De Paor, Maire and Liam. *Early Christian Ireland*. 1958.
Evans, E. Estyn. *Irish Heritage*. 1943.
———. *Irish Folk Ways*. 1957.
Fairley, J. S. *An Irish Beast Book*. 1975.
Flower, Robin. *The Western Isle*. 1944.
———. *The Irish Tradition*. 1947.
Flynn, Majella. *Harvest*. 1996.
Foster, Jeanne Cooper. *Ulster Folklore*. 1951.
Frazer, J. G. *The Golden Bough*. 1890–1915.
Gailey, Alan. *Irish Folk Drama*. 1969.
Gaughan, J. A. *Memoirs of Constable*.
Gerald of Wales. *The History and Topography of Ireland*. Written 1198, published 1861.
Gregory, Lady. *Gods and Fighting Men*. 1904.
———. *Cuchullain of Muirthemne*. 1902.
———. *Visions and Beliefs in the West of Ireland*. 1920.
Gunning, Paul. *Down Gallows Hill*. 1995.
Hazlitt, W. C. *Dictionary of Faiths and Folklore*. 1905.
Healy, Rev Dr. *The Life and Writings of St Patrick*. 1905.
Henri, Hubert. *The Rise of the Celts*. 1934.
———. *The Greatness and Decline of the Celts*. 1934.
Joyce, P. W. *Social History of Ancient Ireland*. 1913.
———. *Ancient Celtic Romances*. 1894.
Kelly, Fergus. *Early Irish Farming*. 1997.
Kilgannon, T. *Sligo and Its Surroundings*. 1926.
Kinealy, Christine. *This Great Calamity*. 1994.
Mac Neill, Maire. *The Festival of Lughnasa*. 1962.
MacGowan, Michael. *The Hard Road to Klondyke*. 1962.
Mahon, Bríd. *Land of Milk and Honey*. 1998.
Marreco, Anne. *The Rebel Countess*. 1967.
McGlinchey, Charles. *The Last of the Name*. 1986.

McGowan, Joe. *In the Shadow of Benbulben*. 1993.
McTernan, John. *In Sligo Long Ago*. 1998.
———. *Olde Sligoe*. 1995.
Ó Buachalla, Seamus. *The Literary Writings of Patrick Pearse*. 1979.
O'Crohan, Thomas. *The Islandman*. 1937.
O'Curry, Eugene. *Manners and Customs of the Ancient Irish*. 1873.
Ó hOgain, Daithí. *Myth, Legend and Romance*. 1990.
O'Muirithe, Diarmuid. *A Seat Behind the Coachman*. 1972.
O'Rourke, Canon John. *The Great Irish Famine*. 1874.
O'Rourke, T. *History of Sligo*. 2 Vols. 1898.
O'Suilleabhan, Amhlaoibh. *The Diary of an Irish Countryman*. 1970.
O'Sullivan, Maurice. *Twenty Years A-Growing*. 1933.
O'Sullivan, Patrick. *Irish Superstitions of Animals and Birds*. 1991.
O'Sullivan, Sean. *The Folklore of Ireland*. 1974.
Porter, Enid. *Folklore of East Anglia*. 1974.
Prendergast, John P. *The Cromwellian Settlement of Ireland*. 1865.
Raftery, Barry. *Pagan Celtic Ireland*. 1994.
Seymour, St John D. *Witchcraft and Demonology*.
Sharkey, Olive. *Old Days, Old Ways*. 1995.
Sharkey, P. A. *The Heart of Ireland*. 1927.
Somerville, Alexander. *Letters from Ireland During the Famine of 1847*. 1852.
Synge, J. M. *The Aran Islands*. 1907.
Twiss, Richard. *A Tour In Ireland*. 1775.
Yeats, W. B. *Autobiographies*. 1955.
———. *Mythologies*. 1934.
———. *Memoirs*. 1972.
———, ed. *Irish Fairy and Folk Tales*.
Young, Arthur. *A Tour in Ireland*. 1780.
Viney, Michael. *Another Life*. 1979.
Woodmartin W. G. *History of Sligo*. 3 Vols. 1882–93.
———. *Traces of the Elder Faiths of Ireland*. 2 Vols. 1902.

INDEX